girl

girl

my childhood and the second world war

alona frankel

Translated from the Hebrew by Sondra Silverston

INDIANA UNIVERSITY PRESS
Bloomington & Indianapolis

This book is a publication of

Indiana University Press
Office of Scholarly Publishing
Herman B Wells Library 350
1320 East 10th Street
Bloomington, Indiana 47405 USA

iupress.indiana.edu

Manufactured in the United States of America

Library of Congress Cataloging-in-Publication Data

Names: Frankel, Alona, author.
Title: Girl : my childhood and the Second World War / Alona Frankel ;
translated from the Hebrew by Sondra Silverston.
Other titles: Yaldah. English
Description: Bloomington and Indianapolis : Indiana University Press, [2016]
Identifiers: LCCN 2016003858| ISBN 9780253022288 (cl : alk. paper) | ISBN
9780253022356 (pb : alk. paper) | ISBN 9780253022417 (e-book)
Subjects: LCSH: Frankel, Alona. | Jews—Poland—Biography. | Jewish children
in the Holocaust—Poland—Biography. | Holocaust, Jewish
(1939-1945)—Poland—Personal narratives.
Classification: LCC DS134.72.F724 A313 2016 | DDC 940.53/18092—dc23 LC
record available at http://lccn.loc.gov/2016003858

1 2 3 4 5 21 20 19 18 17 16

to my mother, Gusta Goldman, née Gruber

to my father, Salomon Goldman

to my sons, Ari and Michael

girl

THEY WERE ALWAYS WITH ME. THE LICE, MY LICE.

I was familiar with two kinds of lice, head lice and clothes lice. Only later did I learn of the existence of another kind, pubic lice, from the four-volume *Encyclopedia of Sexual Knowledge* that survived from the Jewish gynecologist's library. The doctor himself, his mother, wife, two daughters, and baby son were murdered by the Germans. That was at the beginning of the war.

When Hania Seremet took me out of the village where I was hiding, pretending to be a Christian child, and dumped me at my parents' hiding place, I learned for the first time the difference between head lice and clothes lice—an important and meaningful difference.

When I was in the village, the lice never bothered me. They swarmed all over me, and of course I scratched constantly. I thought that's how it was in the world.

More than once, a careless louse would get caught under my nail. More than once one dropped out of my hair when I bent my head. What was the fate of such an adventurous louse that suddenly loses the head of its little Jewish girl? None of that worried me, everything was natural. Sleeping on straw in a coffin that was a bench by day and a bed by night.

The horse, the cow, the stupid geese that nipped my ankles. The carrots, the corn, the wheat, the flowers. The mice, the lice, the bugs. The boiling potato soup that burned my palms and congealed into grayish vomit when it cooled. The old man, the grandfather, who spit his lungs out until he died, but not before he pulled my tooth with rusty carpenter's pliers and rescued me from terrible pain.

It was my mother who was so very, very worried.

It was night when Hania Seremet dumped me at my parents' hiding place. The room my parents were hiding in had two doors, one of them from the stairs. We never used that door, and no one imagined it could be opened, not even the building's tenants. The room, a Jewish gynecologist's office before the war, was now disguised as the carpentry shop of Mr. Juzef Juzak, carpenter and alcoholic. The other door was from the Juzaks' apartment.

When the ghetto was about to be liquidated, the Juzaks were kind enough to hide my mother and father, but on one condition: that they come without the girl. Without me.

Softly, Hania Seremet knocked the agreed-upon knock on the staircase door. I sensed her anxiety and realized that fear has a smell. No one was allowed to see that door open. It would bring the Gestapo running, and that would be the end of all of us, including the Juzaks.

My mother, who must have been lying in wait for hours on the other side of the door, opened it instantly. Hania Seremet shoved me hard over the threshold. She tossed a bundle of papers and a bundle of rags, my clothes, after me. My green dress with the satin flowers, the one my mother made for me and sent to the village, the one I wore when my picture was taken with Hania Seremet in the photographer's studio so she could send it to my mother and father as proof that I was still alive—in addition to my drawings, which she sent from time to time—the green dress wasn't in the bundle of rags. Hania Seremet had obviously sold it.

Hania Seremet ran off quickly after finally getting rid of me. She must have breathed a sigh of relief, sure that we would all be dead before long. The smell of the sweat of her fear lingered.

Hania Seremet had wanted to get rid of me for a long time, but even so, she didn't throw me into the street like she did Daniel, the sweet boy she left at the ghetto gate after his parents were murdered in an *aktion* and there was no one to pay to keep him in the village. The ghetto had already been liquidated when Hania Seremet got rid of me, but even so, she didn't toss me into the street. Maybe she believed my mother's lies about her connection to the underground—the Polish underground, the AK, the "Home Army," whose members were not known as Jew lovers—and about their promise to kill her the minute they found out I was dead, and they'd do it even though I was Jewish.

The meeting had been set up in an exchange of letters that arrived in the Juzaks' name, written in a prearranged code.

The door closed behind me. The key scraped in the keyhole. The bolt fell into place.

I stood there. I thought that's how it was in the world.

I STOOD WITH MY BACK TO THE DOOR, MY PRECIOUS FORGED papers and the rags packed in a threadbare knapsack at my feet.

In front of me was a woman, my mother, thin and light-skinned, her lips sunken, her gold crowns pulled from her mouth in a series of exchanges—a gold crown for another week in the village, another week on the Aryan side, the side of life, the life of the child, Ilonka, my life. A man stood behind her, my father. I didn't remember them.

I didn't remember who they were.

My mother said, Ilonka, Ilusia.

My father struck a match stub and lit a lamp, or maybe a candle.

They looked at me, and looked and looked. My mother wept silently. My father covered his face with his hands and smoothed back his hair, leaving his hands on his forehead and eyes—a gesture that stayed with him till the day he died. His pale, high forehead invaded his dark, straight hair in two deep gulfs.

My mother picked me up, put me on the massive desk, undressed me and said, Ilonka, Ilusia, Ilitska. But I was Irenka. I knew that I was Irenka. I knew that I was Irena Seremet.

I saw and I was invisible.

In the light of the candle or the lamp—I recall a foul smell—the woman began inspecting me, checking every little part of my body.

My mother and father hadn't seen me for months, and despite all the proof, the photographs and the drawings that Hania Seremet sent them, they hadn't believed I was still alive. Every little part of my body astonished my mother profoundly. How healthy I was, how tanned. How many sores I had on my hands, how deep they were—my knuckles were scraped down to the bone from rubbing potatoes on the sharp, rusty grater. How shiny my cheeks were, so round and red. Like two apples, she said. How hard the skin on the bottom of my feet was—I'd run around barefoot in the village. How dirty I was.

And how I was teeming with lice.

She walked around me over and over again, and I wanted very much not to be there.

My father stood and watched, occasionally putting his palms back on his forehead and eyes.

My mother and father, who'd been in their hiding place for days on end, were pale, exhausted, and starved. My father had very large eyes, and my mother no longer had teeth. My father had pulled out all her gold crowns and bridges, the ones her brother Leibek, a dentist, had fitted her with after she'd come back ill from her pioneering escapade in Palestine.

My father had pulled out her bridges and crowns with his pocketknife.

My father's expensive, amazing, ultramodern pocketknife, the Swiss pocketknife he was so proud of, the first thing he'd bought for himself with his own money. My father had worked from the time he was a child, and others always needed the money he earned more than he did—his widowed mother Rachela Goldman, his younger brother Henryk Goldman, and his baby brother David.

That pocketknife was the height of sophistication. A remarkable tool that I found endlessly magical. The most wonderful in the world. Countless parts popped out of it.

Some of them had functions the world had never known.

From the time she was a child, my mother suffered from problems with her teeth, which got much worse when she was a pioneer in Palestine. She immigrated there with members of the Hashomer Hatsair youth movement. She paved roads and lived in Kibbutz Mishmar Haemek and Kibbutz Beit Alfa until she had to abandon the man she loved, Avreim'ele, along with her ideals and her girlfriends Clara and Ziga, because she had to go back to Poland to recover from a terrible fever she'd caught, and because her sensitive, almost transparent alabaster skin and her gorgeous Titian red hair could not survive the deathtrap of the Mediterranean climate.

Her good health was restored in Poland, but the teeth she'd lost in Palestine weren't, and her older brother, Leibek Gruber, who'd been to dental school in Berlin—or was it Vienna—made gold bridges and crowns for her. The Germans murdered Leibek.

In Krakow, after the war, a dentist who had gone to dental school with Leibek pulled out the miserable stumps left in my mother's mouth and made false teeth for her. That dentist was my worst nightmare, even worse than the Spanish Inquisition I'd read about in books—but that was after the war, before we immigrated to Palestine.

The gold of the crowns and bridges Uncle Leibek had made for my mother was given to Hania Seremet, and that gold bought me a few more weeks in the village, in the fresh air, the wide open spaces, the sunlight, on the side of life, the Aryan side. My good health, my tan, my apple-red cheeks, my bruised knuckles, the hard skin on the bottoms of my feet—all those disappeared in a flash in my parents' hiding place.

The lice remained.

I don't like all this digging up of the past.

I ABSOLUTELY DID NOT WANT TO BE THERE WITH MY MOTHER and father, two people I didn't remember, almost strangers, whom I didn't like at all.

My mother began asking me all sorts of questions; she asked, asked, and asked. I didn't understand her language. I'd forgotten. They didn't understand me. I'd come back speaking a dialect, a rural language in which every sentence ended with a mew of surprise: *ta-ee-ou!!!*

I wasn't much of a talker anyway, and I only answered questions when I had no choice.

My mother took a few small, damp rags and began wiping me all over, even inside my ears, even behind my ears, even between my toes. My cute little toes, my family. Fat father big toe, mother middle toe, and their three children: two slightly bigger children and a sweet baby—my little toe.

Those pink toes were like little birds. On the underside of each one was a small bump, like a tiny beak. Sometimes, when I had something to draw with, I drew little faces on my toenails. I liked to draw them on my palms too, and then distort them to give them funny expressions.

But when I saw the row of blue numbers on Uncle Isser Laufer's arm—he always wore a hat, and under it a kind of upside-down saucer made of soft velvet—I immediately stopped drawing on my body.

I saw.

I saw it, that row of numbers, when Uncle Isser Laufer rolled up his sleeve and wound a strip of black leather around his arm and attached a black box to his forehead, then wrapped a striped white shawl around his shoulders and swayed forward and back and sideways so strangely, not exactly a respectable way for a grown-up to behave, as he mumbled and made strange sounds.

Unlike the drawings I drew on my toenails and palms, the numbers drawn on Uncle Isser Laufer's arm couldn't be erased, even after he washed it. They were there forever. And from then on, I never drew anything on my skin or body again.

That was when there was no more war in the world and my mother and father and I lived in a room in an apartment with other people and my mother kept saying, saying, and saying that without her, we all would have been destroyed. She was right. All sorts of people began visiting us then. Uncle Isser Laufer also appeared suddenly and lived with us for a while. My mother said that before the war, he had a family, a wife and a child, but now it was just him. And the people who came, ugly, gray, tired, and sad, had those numbers. They would roll up their sleeves and show them to my mother and father.

I didn't look, but I saw. And they told us. They told us everything. Unbelievable stories that happened in the world. I didn't look, but I saw. I didn't listen, but I heard.

I hated all those ugly people. Uncle Isser Laufer was the only one I liked. I loved to breathe the smell that came from him, a sad, lovely smell, like the fragrance of lilacs.

My mother scrubbed and wiped my whole body with the damp rags. It wasn't very pleasant, being with those two people I didn't know, didn't remember, didn't understand, who were shocked and amazed by me, who were so excited to see me, who tried to wash and clean and fix me. I felt as if something was very wrong with me.

I didn't want to be there.

When the dirt that had accumulated on my body during all those months in the village—in the pigpen, in the straw-lined coffin I slept in—when all that dirt had been wiped away, the lice had their turn. And it was wonderful.

My mother spread a newspaper on a chair, bent my head so that my hair streamed downward, and began combing it with a fine-tooth comb. It hurt at first. My hair was full of knots. But at some point, the lice started to fall out. A shower of lice fell onto the newspaper, thousands of lice, millions, and every time a louse fell onto the newspaper it made a gentle tapping sound. A shower of taps. After a while, the shower thinned out—the time between taps grew longer and longer—until the tapping stopped altogether. And no more lice fell out. I watched the entire time, entranced by the creatures that rustled on the newspaper right under my nose and eyes.

When the shower of lice died away, my mother folded the newspaper that was teeming with life and went inside the apartment to the part where the Juzaks lived—of course, only after checking that the coast was clear—and threw the folded newspaper with millions of my lice into the opening of the oven under the gas range in Mrs. Rozalia Juzakowa's kitchen.

The lice burned silently.

Having my hair combed with a fine-tooth comb became a daily ritual. I enjoyed it very much.

I liked the closeness to my mother, who under different circumstances had not volunteered hugs, kisses, and stroking, and I liked the temporary and surprising relief from my itching head, but mainly I liked the reading.

I'VE ALWAYS KNOWN HOW TO READ. I KNOW HOW TO READ because of the lice.

While my mother spread the newspaper and combed the hair on my bent head, I looked at the black marks on the paper. I quickly learned to distinguish the ones that moved, running every which way, from the ones that remained quiet and orderly in their places.

Those weren't the lice, they were letters.

There were pictures too. To see them properly, I sometimes had to turn the paper around. That's how I realized that the letters—like the pictures—had a direction. They didn't stand on their heads or lie on their sides or decide suddenly to turn over and walk away. The lice, on the other hand, used to dart back and forth in total chaos.

I assume that my mother and father helped me distinguish between the scurrying lice and the inanimate shapes, and taught me how to decipher their meanings. They must have, because I knew how to read. I've always known how to read, and reading kept me sane.

The Red Army and Batiushka Tovarish Stalin saved my life, and books saved me from life.

I've always read, everything, every word: captions in the newspaper, headlines, articles, advertisements. I even read the four-volume *Encyclopedia of Sexual Knowledge* that survived from the Jewish gynecologist's library. Later, when we were liberated and we could come out of our hiding place and walk on the side of life, the Aryan side, I found that while my legs had forgotten how to walk, and I could talk only sparingly and in a thin whisper, I had no problem reading—reading signs, placards, graffiti, reading everything: what was written on bus tickets, on matchboxes, on cigarette packs, on labels, in books.

Books, those wonderful books. Those colossal heroes—Victor Hugo, Charles Dickens, Romain Rolland, Chekhov, Dostoyevsky, Kipling. . . . A terrible fear crept into my heart: Would there be enough books?

But there were, and there continued to be. They didn't stop.

Later on, they waited for me in libraries. Bound and rebound, again and again. Sometimes a careless bookbinder would distractedly slice off the edges of the pages, lopping off a bit of the body of the text. Then I had to guess at the beginnings or ends of the words that were missing.

And the smell. The smell of the books. The yellowing, crumbling pages spotted with oddly shaped stains, their corners folded into donkey's ears. Signposts left by those who had read them before me.

I loved them too, my brothers in reading, my brothers in spirit.

They were here before me.

Here's a note between the lines written in an educated handwriting. Here's a stain. Coffee? Or maybe fine, expensive cognac? Or maybe absinthe, a greenish poison the color of celadon, the color of the dress with the satin flowers my mother embroidered and sent me when I was in the village, the color of my reading robe, the color of the expensive varnish of our new furniture in Krakow, the color of my father's Skoda after the war. Like the green in Picasso's paintings. Our Picasso. He loved Tovarish Stalin too, and he even painted him—a strange painting.

Cosette of *Les Misérables*, the gracious Little Lord, Tom Sawyer, Tom Thumb, Emil and all the detectives, Mowgli and Bagheera the black panther, Jean-Christophe, David Copperfield, d'Artagnan, David of *The House of Thibault* and Sergei from Ilya Ehrenburg's *The Storm*, Levin and Pierre, blue-eyed Prince Myshkin, and the brave Oliver Twist.

Thank you all, my heroes.

You are the teachers I never had.

What a terrible shame that I didn't have a teacher.

Thank you all for the worlds you created for me, that opened up for me when I needed them so badly. Those were my real worlds. That was my chosen reality. I would not have survived if they hadn't been my parallel existence.

THE HEAD LICE, THE ONES THAT DARTED BACK AND FORTH and the ones that didn't move, weren't the most dangerous lice.

The other kind was the most dangerous, the kind that frightened my mother—the clothes lice. The lice that caused typhus. They were much harder to get rid of. They hide in the seams, and my mother and father spent long hours running their fingers along the seams of the rags that were our clothes. When they found a louse, its fate was sealed—to be crushed between two fingernails.

Along with the crushing came a soft popping sound that brought an expression of deep satisfaction to my parents' faces. Hunting for clothes lice also became a ritual, and like the hunt for head lice, a Sisyphean ritual.

My father and mother carried out that never-ending ritual of hunting for clothes lice with an air of quiet, almost idyllic calm.

It was always quiet; after all, we couldn't let anyone on the other side, the Aryan side, the side of life, know that Jews were hiding there.

For us, the side of life was the side of death.

I thought that's how it was in the world.

Sometimes, while the hunt for clothes lice was going on, my father would tell me stories. And so, to the soft popping sound of lice being crushed between fingernails, I heard for the first time about the heavens and the earth, the void, the sun, the moon and the stars, the plants and the animals. I knew all about the plants and animals from my time in the village. And I heard about the snake and about Adam and Eve, the confusion of Babel, and the man who gathered all the animals and put them into an ark right before the enormous rains fell from the sky and flooded the whole world.

That ark was their hiding place because outside of it was the side of death, just as it was with us. But that man had prepared a great deal of food. Each animal had the kind of food it liked, and there was enough for all of them. They weren't hungry, and the horses could neigh, the cows could moo, the birds could sing and chirp. We couldn't. If someone outside heard us neighing or chirping, that would be the end of us and of the Juzaks too. We had to whisper, to whisper very, very quietly.

I could smell the fresh fragrance of wood in the ark that man, Noah, built. Juzef Juzak was a carpenter too, and our hiding place, which was disguised as his carpentry shop, had the same pleasant smell of wood splinters, not like the rotting wood smell of the coffin I slept in back in the village, not like the varnish smell of the closet I hid in with my father when the Gestapo searched our hiding place.

Then, in my father's story, the rain stopped and the rainbow appeared.

The rainbow, my rainbow.

The man with the ark and all the animals were saved, they remained alive, and we too were alive in our ark.

By we, I mean my mother, my father, and I, my two beloved mice, Mysia and Tysia—who hadn't yet run away because the Red Army still hadn't begun its heavy bombing—and the millions of head and clothes lice.

The most wonderful stories of all were the ones about the children of light.

We never spoke the word "Jew." The word "Jew" was equivalent to the word "death."

There were stories mocking the evil pharaoh of Egypt—how much I loved reading, after the war, Mika Waltari's *Sinuhe the Egyptian* and Bolesław Prus's novel, *Pharaoh*. There was the story about the sea splitting apart. And then there was the most marvelous story of all—the story about manna falling from the heavens.

Father told me in a whisper—after all, we couldn't let anyone from outside know that the children of light were hiding here—that manna is a kind of cotton that you put in your mouth and eat, and it tastes exactly like the food you love the most, even cherries, for example.

My father also told me about the good soldier Schweik. My father loved that good soldier all his life. He always kept the book, with Lada's beautiful illustrations, next to his bed before the war and after it, but he didn't have it in the hiding place. He recited whole chapters to me that he knew by heart.

Sometimes my mother told me stories too. About elves in pointed red hats who lived in the forest, drank nectar from bellflowers, and helped Marisia, the little orphan. Sometimes the elves were mischievous and played pranks on people. They lived in lovely white-spotted red mushrooms.

And there were stories about fairies, good fairies and naughty fairies —nymphs who combed their golden hair and seduced sailors. That story was in rhyme. And I'd dictate stories to my father about fairies, flowers, princes, and elves.

My mother never told me stories about witches.

In my parents' hiding place, where I was hiding too, I wasn't hiding from the Germans at first, but from Rozalia Juzakowa and Juzef Juzak, who had agreed to hide my mother and father, but on one condition: that they come without the girl. Without me. No elves lived there. No fairies lived there. Just the smell of sawdust that was like the smell of the ark, but there was no manna.

My two gray mice, which my father and I trained, were there.

I believe in elves and mice.

Rozalia Juzakowa, a devout Russian Orthodox Ukrainian, believed that lice came from troubles.

Living people have troubles. The lice only lived on living people. If someone had lice, that was a sign that he was alive, a sign that he had troubles.

For the time being, we were alive. Dead people had no troubles and no lice.

We managed not to get typhus. But the Koch bacillus, the lethal tuberculosis bacillus, settled in my mother's lungs and gnawed a damp hole in them the size of a large plum.

A hole that almost sucked her into death.

MANY ANIMALS PLAYED A PART IN MY LIFE. THE FIRST WAS A white rabbit as soft as a Parisian courtesan's powder puff. An illiterate farmer from the area brought it to my father as a thank-you gift after my father wrote a letter to the city offices for him.

My father was flooded with requests from good people who were poor and illiterate. He never refused anyone. They would come after working hours, work-weary people, exhausted and smelly, who sat on the bench in front of my father's office, abashed, rubbing their palms around their hats, which they held between their knees.

Sometimes they didn't have shoes and were barefoot. The bottoms of their feet were tough—black, thick, and cracked. When they did have shoes, they would leave muddy prints that dried and crumbled on the shiny, polished parquet. Even the ones who had shoes would tie the shoelaces together and hang the shoes on their shoulder when they went out. Those were people who were born barefoot and walked barefoot.

That's what my mother told me, told me, and told me.

My mother thought they were disgusting. She was always angry that they stole time from my father, the time he devoted to all those bewildered, downtrodden, and barefoot people, work-weary farmers and laborers.

My father was a Communist who believed the world could be changed for the better. My mother was a Communist too, but she was a salon Communist—although even she was once imprisoned for her beliefs.

When his workday was over, my father would read to the ignorant farmers and laborers the letters they had received from overseas, from relatives as poor and wretched as they were who had emigrated in search of a decent livelihood, and he would write the answers they dictated to him in simple words punctuated by tears and longing. My father also helped them when they got into trouble with the authorities and the law.

One of those people who my father helped was Juzef Juzak, the carpenter and alcoholic. The grateful Juzef Juzak thought my father was a saint. We owe our lives to him. It was Juzef Juzak who offered to hide my parents in his house when the Lvov Ghetto was due to be liquidated.

He offered to hide them because he remembered my father's generosity and he did so over the objections of his wife, Rozalia Juzakowa, the devout Russian Orthodox Ukrainian. Like us, he had followed her to Lvov, escaping with his daughter Ania and his sweet little boy, Edjo. Juzak hid my mother and father in a room disguised as a carpentry shop, but only on one condition: that they come without the girl.

I'm the girl.

In the end, I hid there too, and my life was also saved because of him.

At the end of the war, when Batiushka Tovarish Stalin and the Red Army saved us and captured Berlin, when Communism began to build a new world, a just, good, and beautiful world, when my father, as a loyal party member, was given an extremely important job and once again was in a position to help Juzef Juzak and his family, he brought them with us to Krakow and helped him find housing and work. The Juzak family was smaller then. Teenaged Ania had already died of tuberculosis in my mother's arms. My mother had caught the disease, and barely, miraculously, came back to life after the war.

The white rabbit that was as soft as a Parisian courtesan's powder puff suffered a black fate. My mother said that I almost suffocated it with love. I was a year and a half old. They had to pull it out of my little arms, which clutched it as tightly as they could, and return it to the grateful man, that illiterate farmer.

The farmer and his family made a pie out of the rabbit and ate it.

My mother was honored with a gift of one of the dead, devoured little powder-puff rabbit's soft, adorable white feet, for luck.

My mother threw the poor foot in the garbage.

The long-haired, soft white cat in the yard played with the rabbit's foot, and dashing around with the foot in its mouth it looked like a fantastical mythological creature with five feet, four regular ones and one that grew from its mouth instead of a tongue. Later, when the Germans invaded and shells were exploding and we ran away on a freight wagon harnessed to a workhorse that had enormous brown hindquarters with white spots, the gypsy woman's prediction came true—everything we left behind was lost.

Even the white rabbit's foot in the white cat's mouth.

That's what my mother told me, told me, and told me.

We traveled at night and hid in barns and stables during the day. I wasn't teeming with lice yet. Lice are animals too. The lice were with me all through the war and later too, when the war was no longer in the world. I used to bring them from orphanages, from schools and summer camps.

Except for the fact that we went there in the summer, those damn camps were just like the orphanages.

I also brought lice from the camp for Jewish children in Zakopane. They shot at us in Zakopane. The Poles shot at us, not the Germans, and that was after the war was no longer in the world. They attacked the villa at night and shot at us.

They weren't Germans. They were Poles who didn't like Jews. Not even young Jewish children. They were against the Jews.

Anti-Semitic means being against the Jews, that's what my father said. They want to kill the Jews that the Germans hadn't managed to kill. He wasn't worried, not then. He said it was only a matter of education. They'll learn, those Polish anti-Semites, and understand that there's no difference between people and everyone should work according to his ability and receive according to his needs. That's what my father, who was a Communist, believed. And those Poles, those anti-Semites, hated not only the Jews, but the Communists too. They hated the Russians, who liberated them from the Germans.

The Red Army, the Communists, saved our lives, but there were Poles who treated the Russian Communists as if they were invaders.

That's what my father, who believed that everything would be better, explained to me. And he continued to believe it until the Communists arrested his best friend and the anti-Semitic Poles threatened his life.

WHEN THE WAR BROKE OUT, I GOT TO KNOW MANY LIVING creatures that weren't people. The squat, plump rats in the ghetto, for example, that the skinny, stiff-haired cats bolted from in fear. Do I remember that?

Or maybe I remember the rats, like the powder-puff rabbit, only from stories?

When the war broke out, I also got to know many bugs and other small creatures. Spiders and the wonderful masterpieces they spun, their webs. Shiny beetles, clumsy and slow. Roaches that ran away when the light was turned on, each at a different speed. Fleas and bedbugs. And of course, lice. The fleas were very hard to see—tiny, jumping dots that bit. I thought the fleas were terribly smelly. But maybe it was the bedbugs that stank?

Those were the animals I knew in the ghetto. But when Hania Seremet smuggled me out of the ghetto and took me to the village of Marcinkowice, to her parents—or maybe they were her grandparents—I met new animals, much larger and more exciting.

The biggest of all was the horse. I'd already seen a horse—the clumsy horse that had big brown hindquarters with white spots that was harnessed to the wagon we rode on to escape from the Germans.

But the horse in the village was my horse.

Everything about my horse was beautiful.

A thick, strong, massive creature. He was gigantic. Later, I thought he resembled the grand piano that belonged to Madame Halina Czerny-Stefanska, winner of the Chopin Competition prize.

In Krakow, when war was no longer in the world, Madame Czerny-Stefanska determined my fate in three minutes by stating that I would never know how to play the piano, and it was doubtful that I would ever know anything at all. The grand piano was black and shiny. The horse was slightly less black, slightly more brown. He was a beast of burden. He stood on four legs that grew from the bottom part of his body, one pair in front, the other pair in back. I never saw the horse lie down. His legs, relative to his body, were thin. At the ends of them were hooves nailed on by the blacksmith, a sunken-chested man who died of tuberculosis a month before Grandfather Seret died.

The horse's enormous head was very high and grew out of a stiff, arched neck. A rather sparse mane also grew from the neck.

You had to climb a tree in order to see the horse's back. When he bent his huge head, you could get a peek at his damp, black eye. He had another eye on the other side. You could see his flaring, quivering nostrils and imagine their softness.

How soft and pleasant to the touch that horse's mouth was. Sometimes I saw his teeth. So huge, so yellow. Long scraggly hair grew out of his quivering nostrils. Once, when I reached out and touched his lips, the sensation at the tips of my fingers was just like I'd imagined it would be, just as I'd always hoped it would be. His pointed ears twitched abruptly every once in a while, alert to every sound.

At the back end of his body was a tail that swung and whipped and drove away the buzzing green flies. Sometimes the horse whinnied, a happy, funny sound. There were always some sores on one of his forelegs and on his gigantic round hindquarters. The humming green flies loved those moist, open sores and would gather on them.

I loved everything about that horse: his smell, the steam that came from his skin and nostrils, even the smell of the dung that dropped out of the hole under his tail.

The birds and beetles loved the dung too.

The little birds would hop around on it and peck at it, and the especially beautiful, shiny purple and yellow beetles would climb onto it. There was another small and roundish kind of beetle, bright red with black dots, that wasn't at all frightening. It was so lovely, so innocent. I used to put my finger close to the blade of grass it was walking on and it would climb onto my finger and keep walking, tickling it gently. I was cautious and watchful, and when the beetle approached the tip of my finger, I would immediately offer it an additional path to walk on in the form of another finger. If it didn't have a path like that, the little beetle would eject a pair of fluttery wings from under its wonderful armor, spread them, and fly off. That was a *biedronka*, a ladybug.

My horse didn't gallop, didn't trot, didn't skip, and didn't jump. Hitched to the plow, he plowed the field; hitched to the wagon, he transported the sky-high piles of hay. When he wasn't working, he grazed in the small pasture, his forelegs tied so he could only take small steps.

I was that horse's shepherd.

That was my job, to watch the horse and make sure it didn't get into the neighbor's vegetable garden or cabbage, carrot, or lettuce patches. It must have been summer.

During those bright days when I, Irena Seremet, a Polish Christian girl, shepherded my horse, I would lie on the grass searching the sky for clouds that looked like horses. And there were many horses in the clouds: they galloped, flew, skipped, and jumped. Those were good days.

I pulled carrots from the neighbors' fields, sweet, stolen, orange carrots for myself and my horse. I tasted the grass that the horse ate.

The bottom part of the blades of grass was light-colored, soft and sweet. And there were bad blades of grass, sharp as knives. The sweetest of all were the carrots, with their heads of wild, mischievous, leafy hair. And there was clover, with its modest sweet flowers, three small leaves on a slender stem. Would I find a four-leaf clover, for luck?

And there were flowers. Flowers and butterflies.

There were pimpernels, with their hundred pink-edged white petals. You could pull them off, one by one by one, yes-no-yes-no, and guess your future. And there were purple lupines and bellflowers that the fairies used for hats. And at the far end of the field, in the damp muddy earth, little blue flowers that winked with a thousand yellow eyes, pleading: forget-me-not. And there were stinging nettles, the nastiest of all the plants.

My mother told me how I described to her and my father how I pulled carrots from the neighbor's field, shook the dirt off them, and wolfed them down. The stories I told helped my parents understand why I looked so healthy, why my cheeks were as red and shiny "as two apples."

I also told them about the fascinating guests who occasionally came to visit.

The cheerful knife grinder who was always humming lively songs that ended with a thundering cry of "Hoo-hah!" He had a huge wheel connected by a strap to a lever, and he would hold the knife and press the lever with his foot to turn the wheel, and sparks would spew from under the knife to the rhythm of the songs—like the sparks that sprayed from between the wheels of the tram and the tracks it was speeding along on.

And there was a man who fixed pots, armed with spools of iron wire, who would put together the pieces of a broken clay pot with a skillfully made net and make it usable again, even more beautiful than a new one. They would hang the pot out to dry upside down on the fence posts and it looked to me like a person's head.

I told them about the croaking, leaping frog and the storks that would drive the frogs out of their hiding place, the storks that traipsed around on their long, thin, red legs in the muddy corner of the field where blue forget-me-nots with winking yellow eyes grew.

My dear, sweet pigs also loved that corner, the mud corner.

The storks lived in a giant nest they'd built in the top of the church tower. The nest was woven around a broken wagon wheel the farmers had put there for the storks years ago. The farmers loved the storks because they brought luck and babies.

They said that the storks came back to their nest in the top of the church tower every year. The chiming bells didn't seem to bother them. And that's where they grew their huge chicks. They would make tapping sounds with their long, sharp, red beaks whenever I came to church for one of the plates of thick, gray, boiling pea soup and potatoes they gave out to the poor in the soup kitchen next door to the priest's kitchen.

They would spoon out the soup with an enormous ladle covered with congealed soup drippings, and so, with the help of the ladle, the soup passed from the steaming vat to my pot with the broken handle. More than once, the soup splashed onto my hand and burned me.

And on the way to Grandfather and Grandmother Seremet's house, no matter how careful I was, the sticky, boiling soup would spill and scorch my hands, adding burns to the sores on my knuckles—the sores from the sharp, rusty grater I grated potatoes on.

When the soup cooled, it turned into viscous, greenish-gray glue. And it had quite enough time to cool, because it wasn't a short walk. I went along paths that crossed wheat fields, and the spikes were taller than I was. Flowers grew there too, red poppies and blazing blue cornflowers.

It must all have happened in summer.

Of all the animals in the village of Marcinkowice, the geese were the stupidest.

It wasn't a large flock, and I was their shepherd. I was the horse's shepherd too, but the two jobs were totally unalike. The geese followed each other, waddling along heavily, shifting the weight of their round, plump, white-feathered bodies, from one short orange leg to the other, jerking their long, narrow necks forward, back, forward, and jiggling their rear ends right, left, right. Ridiculous.

When one of the geese—usually an enormous goose, their king—opened its flat orange beak and started honking, they would all go on a terrible, never-ending quacking spree. Later on, when I was twelve and a half, I met the wise Martin, Nils Holgersson's goose. He wasn't anything

like my geese, which were stupid, malicious birds. I learned about Nils
Holgersson and Martin the goose from Selma Lagerlöf in the beautiful,
thick book illustrated by Jan Marcin Szancer. My mother gave me the
book as a gift on the eve of our emigration from Poland to Palestine,
with this dedication:

To My Daughter Ilonka

*I give you this book along with a request and a demand that in this new stage
of our lives, you become more disciplined and more serious in your attitude
toward being independent.*

Mother 12.12.1949

What did she want from my life?

And I was such a good girl. I always ironed all the laundry, even my
father's handkerchiefs.

More than once, the leader of the geese, the enormous gander, would
chase me and manage to nip my ankles painfully. Bad, stupid animals.

I liked shepherding my dear horse better. He was such a noble horse.

Ewunia Lipska, a small girl my age, bouncy and full of happy energy,
who had been hidden in the village as a Christian child, like me—she
looked the part better because she was blond—once told me how they
made her work at force-feeding geese. Long hours. Day after long day.
She told me that geese had a very hard bump in their beaks that bruised
your hand when you force-fed them and made it bleed. And the bruise
on her hand, which never had time to heal, left a scar.

We only talked about that once, and she showed me the scar.

That was in camp, the summer camp for Jewish children, not in the
mountains, not in Zakopane, where the Poles shot at us, but on the shore
of the gray Baltic Sea. There were four of us there, all twelve-year-old
girls—Clara, Celinka, Ewunia, and me.

One morning, Celinka's bed and her nightgown were covered in
blood. Celinka went into shock. We were all shocked. The blood was
coming from her body. From between her legs. I knew that there was
such a thing in the world. Would blood come from between my legs too?

It did. On a gray day, December 31, 1949, on the deck, slippery with
vomit, of the disgusting immigrants' ship, *Galila*.

I'm still a girl. And I see and I am invisible.

I see a dark mountain taking shape in the fog, a golden dome in its center. But Flavius Josephus wrote that the Romans had burned down the Jews' Temple in Palestine.

I am surrounded by drab, tired, and smelly people.

We're here.

I want to go back.

THERE WERE ALSO OTHER KINDS OF BIRDS IN THE VILLAGE of Marcinkowice. Chickens, for instance, which weren't much smarter than the geese. They wandered around everywhere, in the yard, in the house, trying to take off and fly, landing heavily—on the table, on the bed, on the shelf under the holy picture: sweet pink Jezusik, Jesus, his face encircled by a wavy blond beard, his eyes looking skyward, a crown of thorns on his head. Beautiful red beads of blood dripped from where the thorns pierced his forehead.

With his delicate hands, he held open his shirt and the flesh of his chest, and his bright crimson heart glowed and beat inside his body. Yellow flames spouted from it.

The chickens ran around outside in the yard too, foraging, cackling, and pecking.

One even swallowed the most beautiful stone in my collection right in front of me. They would pull up long, pink earthworms, tear them into a few writhing pieces, and eat them. And they pecked everything, all the time, pecked and ate even the snippets of lung Grandpa Seremet spit up after every coughing fit, until he died of tuberculosis.

They had red combs and shiny feathers that were brown, yellow, green, and purple, like the colors of the beetles.

The rooster had a huge comb, a gorgeous tail, and yellow feet with very sharp nails. The rooster walked slowly, pecking the sand aristocratically, proudly, arrogantly.

The chickens had a blank look.

The goats had an even blanker look. A yellow eye with a black rectangle. I didn't like the goats. I loved the pigs. Pink, plump, round. Sometimes their stubbly skin had strangely shaped dark spots painted on it. Then, I wasn't yet familiar with the pungent odor of a pig's skin after it's killed or it dies and they make a schoolbag out of it or a suitcase you take with you on a stormy sea voyage to Palestine.

Their sweet little faces, with their flat pug noses and round, wide nostrils that looked at me like a pair of eyes that always seemed to express amused understanding. Their curly tails were especially merry. I didn't like their ears. They were flawed. All sorts of shapes had been cut out of them. The pigs were my best friends. They would make snorting sounds, and I'd answer them. We talked.

The pigs lived in a pen. The pen had a low door, and only a little girl like me, about six years old, could crawl inside. I spent many happy hours in that pigpen, on the straw that was sometimes fresh but usually damp, packed tightly and probably smelly. I loved straw. The coffin I slept in was lined with straw too. The pigpen was my hiding place, my most private place, and the pigs were my best friends. I thought that's how it was in the world.

I used to crawl inside and sit down in a corner. It was a small place, just a corner in the dark illuminated only by the dim light that came from outside. The darkness was pleasant. The pigs came and went around me, and I played with my doll.

A doll I made myself.

A stick that I found, not too long and not too thin, was the doll's body. An apple I stuck the tip of the stick into was the head. The little face was made up of dark pea eyes I pressed onto the skin of the apple, a white pea nose, and a piece of carrot or a petal from a red flower was the mouth. Later, when I was already in my parents' hiding place, after Hania Seremet threw me out of the village because my parents didn't have any more money to pay for me, I pasted some red flower petals on myself too, from the flowers my mother brought when she went out hunting for bread.

We were very hungry, we had no manna. My mother went out to the Aryan side, the side of life, the side of death. The red flower in the pot was her disguise. Walking around with the flowerpot in her hand, she wasn't a hungry Jew coming out of hiding to feed her beloved husband and her hungry child, but just another woman who'd bought a red flower in a flowerpot and was walking innocently down the street.

My mother brought the red flower with the bread.

I wrapped a rag around the stick, which was the doll's body, and my doll had a dress. She had hair too. Sometimes it was bits of yellow straw that I stuck into the apple skull, and sometimes it was marvelous corn silk—long, soft, shiny greenish hair like the hair of the water nymphs my mother told me about when were in the hiding place, the nymph sitting on a rock, combing her hair and seducing sailors. My doll was so wonderful—my dolls, actually, since I had many, because of the pigs.

That was the only conflict I had with my friends the pigs. When I had to leave the pigpen, I hid the doll deep down under the straw in the corner and the nosy pigs would always find it and gobble up the apple head. And again I had to put a new head on my doll. But that wasn't so bad; there were always enough apples, peas, and straw. My friendship with the pigs was more important. It was their nature to be likable, voracious gluttons.

No friendship developed between me and the cow. The cow was skinny and brown, and she might have had tuberculosis. Maybe Grandpa Seremet, who spit up his lungs, had caught it from her. And maybe I caught it then too, but instead of getting sick and dying quietly, I developed an immunity that later saved my life when I was in the hiding place with my mother and father.

The cow and I were neighbors.

The *szlufan*, the piece of furniture that was a bench by day and a bed by night, a kind of coffin, was lined with the same straw that lined the cowshed, and the same mice scurried between the cow's legs and over my body. Then, in the village, I didn't yet know what wonderful animals mice were. I trained my gray mice, Mysia and Tysia, later on, when I was in the hiding place with my mother and father—until they left us when the Red Army, which saved our lives, began its heavy bombing and volleys of *katyushas*.

But already then, in the village, I liked the mice. They were my nocturnal friends.

The village mice scurried around in the cow's straw and in the straw of my coffin. The cow and I had the same smell.

When Grandma Seremet milked the cow, sitting bent over more than usual on a round stool with three fat legs and pulling on the pink udders, the stream of milk would strike the sides of the tin pail and the smell was white, warm, and pure. It spread, filling the air and overcoming all the other smells—the smell of the fleas, the smell of the mice, the stench of urine, excrement, and dung. The smell of the milk blended with other, more pleasant smells, like the aroma of the straw, the green fragrance of clover, or the smell of sawdust. It wasn't a sad smell like the scent of lilac would be in the future.

Luckily, the hiding place Hania Seremet dumped me into, my parents' hiding place, had a nice smell, the smell of sawdust. After all, the room was disguised as Juzef Juzak's carpentry shop.

When Grandma Seremet sat on the stool and milked the cow, unruly hairpins from her sparse bun of hair would drop into the pail, and she would fly into a rage. But when the hairpins didn't fall out, and she was in a good mood, Grandma Seremet would pour some of the foamy, steaming milk into a small wooden bowl and hand it to me.

The aroma, the taste, the warmth.

Even the ice cream my father bought me from the man with the wagon didn't taste as wonderful as that milk. That was the first ice cream in my life. It was after Tovarish Stalin and the Red Army liberated us and saved our lives, and my father had to take me from the villa that belonged to the evil, cruel Fishmans because I bothered them. I couldn't stop crying, and crying was permitted then because they hadn't killed us and Batiushka Stalin had liberated us. My father took me from the Fishmans' villa to the orphanage on his way to sell newspapers, while my mother was dying of tuberculosis in the hospital.

I thought that's how it was in the world.

EVERY NOW AND THEN, HANIA SEREMET CAME TO THE VILLAGE, the strange woman with the white face and the clenched jaw who took me out of the ghetto one damp night when I was walking between my mother and father as plump, squat rats scampered along the walls in the opposite direction.

Hania Seremet would order me to draw on the pieces of paper she brought me. After only drawing in the sand with a stick or on the walls of the pigpen with a lump of coal, I enjoyed drawing on paper with colored pencils.

Once, Hania Seremet brought me a magnificent satin dress in sweet, light pastel colors, washed me, and combed my hair—the lice were hiding close to the roots—and we went to the photography studio in the nearby town. The studio had an unfamiliar smell and it was dark, like the office of the handsome, sad eye doctor would be in the future.

The photographer stood Hania Seremet and me close together. He touched me and arranged my hands in the pose he wanted.

Hania Seremet was wearing a sweater embroidered with tiny flowers. My mother had embroidered those flowers too, just as she had made my magnificent satin dress. She would sew and embroider in the hiding place and Hania Seremet and Rozalia Juzakowa would sell her work in the market so there'd be a little more money to pay them.

The photographer also took pictures of me alone. He told me to sit this way or that and look here or there.

I never saw the dress again. The pictures exist. Like my drawings, they were proof that I was still alive. Hania Seremet gave the proof to my mother and my father, and they gave Hania Seremet money for hiding me in the village. When the money ran out, they sold the gold bridges and crowns that my father so skillfully pulled out of my mother's mouth with his magical Swiss pocketknife. When there was no more gold left in my mother's mouth and the search for the treasure left in my father's villa failed to uncover anything, Hania Seremet dumped me into my parents' hiding place, even though Juzef Juzak and his wife Rozalia had not agreed to hide them with their daughter, that is, with me.

And so I continued to hide in the hiding place for a long time.

And just as she threw me out, Hania threw out the beautiful little boy, Daniel.

She dumped me at the hiding place. The beautiful little boy, Daniel, she threw out to die.

Daniel, the beautiful Jewish boy Hania Seremet took out of the ghetto, was my age. His favorite animal was the cow, and he always tried to be there at milking time. When Grandma Seremet wasn't looking, he'd dip his fingers into the tin pail of steaming milk and lick them. The beautiful boy Daniel stayed in the village with me for a very short time. His parents gave Hania Seremet a great deal of money, jewelry, diamonds, and gold to take him out of the ghetto and hide him in the

village. They promised to keep on paying her. They even registered their
house in Lvov in her name—just as my father registered the villa in
Bochnia in her name—so that if the Germans murdered them and Daniel remained alive, he would have someone. The beautiful boy Daniel's
parents were murdered and Daniel was an orphan. There was no one to
keep paying for his life. Hania Seremet took him to the ghetto and left
him at the entrance gate, and the Germans murdered him there. Daniel,
a beautiful little Jewish boy, had curls and translucent white hands. A
long time later, when the war was no longer in the world, I saw Daniel
in a painting by Maurycy Gottlieb, who painted many pictures of Jews
with shawls on their shoulders and head coverings like the one Uncle
Isser Laufer had.

That wasn't the first or the last time that Hania Seremet, the pretty
woman with the white face and clenched jaw, took money from persecuted Jews, then turned them in or left them to die. My mother called
her "the murderess." My parents knew about what she did and about the
deals she made with the Jews in the ghetto. They knew she had a lover in
the ss who shared her profits.

Hania Seremet threw me out too, but not at the gates of the ghetto.
Maybe because there was no more ghetto. The ghetto had already been
liquidated. But still, she didn't throw me into the streets, to sure death.
Maybe girls who sleep in coffins don't die so quickly.

Hania Seremet dumped me into my parents' hiding place.

My mother said that when she heard about the murder of Daniel's
parents, she wanted to adopt that beautiful boy—if the war ended, of
course, and if he remained alive, of course. But there was no more money
to pay Hania Seremet. There was no more money to pay for me, either.
And the beautiful boy Daniel was murdered like hundreds of thousands
of other Jewish children.

I was alive.

I FIRST BECAME ACQUAINTED WITH MY TWO LITTLE GRAY MICE
—Mysia and Tysia—in our hiding place at the Juzaks' house on Panienska Street, in the room disguised as a carpentry shop.

Mysia and Tysia lived in an old black cast-iron stove. The stove was
round and had a small door that closed with a hook. The door might have

been transparent. Its legs were curved like a lion's or a tiger's, or maybe a small dragon's.

The stove wasn't in use.

Once, in the past, before I was taken out of the village of Marcinko-wice, they used to heat the house by burning books in that stove. The books were taken from the large library that had belonged to the man who owned the apartment before the war—the Jewish gynecologist. A few books from that library survived. They're in my house. The doctor himself, his mother, wife, two daughters, and baby son were murdered by the Germans. That was at the beginning of the war.

Living in the apartment now were Mrs. Rozalia Juzakowa, Mr. Juzef Juzak, and their son Edward, Edjo, who was my age. Their daughter, Ania, was already dead.

They agreed to hide my father and mother, and later, against their will, me too.

Their daughter Ania died of open tuberculosis in my mother's arms when she was sixteen, and my mother must have caught it from her. After the Red Army led by Stalin liberated us and saved our lives, my mother was admitted to a tuberculosis hospital in Lvov and almost died because her left lung, or maybe it was the right one, had a damp hole in it the size of a large plum. Professor Ordung saved her life. The hole had been gnawed by the tuberculosis bacillus, the Koch bacillus.

I was the first to hear the rustling of my little gray mice.

I still didn't know they were mice.

I still didn't know what color they were.

They still didn't have names.

And they still weren't mine.

I don't know whether I first heard the rustling during the day or at night. Most of the time, both day and night, my mother, my father, and I, and our millions of head lice and clothes lice, lay on the makeshift bed in the right-hand corner of the room among the blankets and pillows and the torn, tattered, threadbare rags.

We had to be very quiet in that hiding place.

We couldn't walk.

We couldn't talk.

We couldn't laugh.

And I didn't cry.

No one, not a single living soul, could know that we were there. They would report us to the Gestapo and that would be the end of us, and maybe of the Juzak family too, Rozalia, Juzef, and little Edjo. The Germans also killed the people who hid Jews.

We hid in that little room disguised as the carpentry shop where Mr. Juzef Juzak, carpenter and alcoholic, supposedly worked when he came home from his job at the factory.

Since there was no vodka, Juzef drank wood alcohol, suffered from delirium tremens, and had hallucinations filled with hideous white creatures.

My mother was the only one who knew how to calm him down when those horrors attacked him. From inside the apartment, we'd hear screams, curses, the sound of objects smashing and shattering. Rozalia Juzakowa would burst into our hiding place, disheveled, pitiful, weeping and agitated. She'd wring her hands and beg my mother—Pani Goldmanowa, Pani Goldmanowa, please, I beg you. Juzef is having an attack. He'll kill himself, he'll kill all of us. Come, please, come right away. You're the only one who knows how to cure him, to "cool him down," to restrain him, to soothe him.

And my mother would go.

After a while, the voices would die down and there would be silence. My mother would come back to our bed in the corner, her clothes and hair reeking of *machorka*, vomit, sour sweat, and vile alcohol.

Juzef Juzak was a good man.

After all, he had agreed to hide my mother and father before the ghetto was liquidated. Without the daughter, of course. I could see why. He didn't know me. He'd worked in my father's storehouses in Bochnia before the war. And he hid us for money, of course. He didn't know we had a lot less money than he thought, but after the war, after we survived, my father took care of the Juzak family. Even after we moved to Palestine, we sent them money. Even during the very hard times in a new and violent country.

Mr. Juzak loved and respected my father. Like us, he'd fled to the east when the Germans took over. His wife, Rozalia, was Ukrainian and had relatives in Lvov. He found work again in Lvov, in the slaughterhouse and tanning factory where my father was chief accountant. That was when the Russians still had control of Lvov following the Ribbentrop-Molotov Pact. Juzef Juzak and my father continued working there even under German occupation, after Operation Barbarossa, when the Germans attacked Russia and pushed the Red Army further and further back, winning victory after victory, until Stalingrad.

MY FATHER'S MANAGER DURING THE GERMAN OCCUPATION was a good German. He even let my father bring me and my mother to live in a tiny room next to the slaughterhouse. It was a dream, a paradise compared to where we lived in the ghetto. And food was plentiful too— the entrails and blood of the animals. Herr Knaup—that was the name of the good German manager who helped save our lives by allowing my father to live in that tiny room next to the slaughterhouse.

My father helped save many Jews from hunger by hiding entrails and keeping pails of blood from the slaughterhouse for them. They drank the blood on the spot. The entrails they wrapped around their bodies and smuggled into the ghetto in the hope that the Germans wouldn't catch them. They were the Jewish workers who left the ghetto in the morning to work in the slaughterhouse and tanning factory and returned to the ghetto at night, bone-weary and crushed, but alive.

One of the Jews who came from the ghetto every day in well-guarded groups to work in the slaughterhouse snuck into our tiny room and begged my mother, even kissed her hands, to keep a plain, not very large wooden box for him "for only a few days." The box was locked with a key, and it had a flower carved on its cover.

That was very dangerous. My mother didn't like it. But even so, she did what the man asked. "If I'm not back within a month, the box and what's in it are yours, Pani Goldmanowa," he said as he handed it to her.

That's what my mother told me.

It was already evening. A key hung on a thin string around his neck. He took it off and opened the box.

Light streamed from it.

It was like "open sesame" from the Arabian Nights, my mother said. Jewels, precious stones, diamonds, pearls, gold chains, treasures.

To show how much he trusted my mother, the man left the box open and didn't relock it with the key.

The man came back two weeks later.

"Pani Goldmanowa, in return for your generosity, please choose what you like best and take it," the man said. My mother, former member of the Hashomer Hatsair youth movement and pure, modest salon Communist that she was, picked out a small, unpretentious pin: a line of white gold set with a small diamond.

Perhaps if she'd chosen something else, something more valuable, there might have been a little more money to keep me in the village among the living. But that's how it was.

The man swept the contents of the box into a bag that tied with a string, hung it around his neck, pushed it under his armpit, and left.

He didn't go back to the ghetto. We'll never know if he survived or was killed. Maybe they picked him up in an *aktion* and sent him to the Janowska camp, the way they once caught my father in the street and ran him to the camp where they tortured him on the parade grounds for two days, along with other prisoners, other Jews.

That's what my mother told me, told me, and told me.

She told me how much she worried, and how she ran out to look for my father and how he finally came back half-dead, filthy and crushed.

That's how it was.

But my father remained alive, and no one knows what became of that man with the box.

My father promised to pay Juzef Juzak a fortune for hiding him and my mother. There was no fortune. A few weeks before the German invasion, when I was two years old, my father had invested all his money in purchasing a huge quantity—a trainload full—of building materials.

My father had a wholesale building materials business. That was in Bochnia.

The war started, the train loaded with building materials arrived and stopped on the private track leading to my father's storerooms. The old gypsy woman's prophecy had come true. My mother, my father, and I, along with Dr. Fishler, a family friend who had performed an abortion on my mother a month earlier, escaped in a wagon harnessed to an enormous workhorse. My mother, as befitted a salon Communist intellectual, condemned uncontrolled reproduction, and like many of her milieu, preferred to have only one child.

She had been carrying twins.

And if they had been born?

EVEN IN THE SILENCE OF THE HIDING PLACE, THE NEW RUST-lings were quiet. I realized very quickly that they were coming from the old iron stove.

It happened when I found my wonderful little figurines nibbled away, the ones I molded from breadcrumbs I'd managed to save from the bread my mother heroically, miraculously brought us from the soda factory manager's wife. They lived in the neighboring house, on the Aryan side, the side of life, the side of death.

It happened when we'd had nothing to eat for a long time, when the Juzaks went on a trip and left us in the house without food. My mother said that Juzakowa—Juzak, almost always drunk to the point of unconsciousness, was never much of a thinker or planner—wanted to starve us to death so she could finally be rid of us, of that terrible curse, the Jews, who endangered her life and the lives of her husband and little boy, Edjo.

When the war was no longer in the world, Juzakowa told us that Hania Seremet had offered her poison to kill us with.

Only some breadcrumbs were left. I used to mix them with saliva, knead them for hours until the mixture was uniform and smooth, not too moist and not too dry, not too soft and not too hard, but just the right consistency.

My fingers would seek the same consistency from the clay I molded into fancy ballerinas when the war was no longer in the world but I was, and we lived in beautiful Krakow.

In the hiding place, I molded tiny birds.

In the shape of my toes.

I had a marvelous flock of birds.

I hadn't seen a bird for a long time.

In our hiding place, we weren't allowed to go near the window, but I remembered the birds from my time in the village. I remembered clearly their shape, the beating of their wings, their chirping and singing.

I arranged the flock of wonderful birds in a splendid row to dry.

I looked at them proudly for hours.

In the morning, the row was in ruins.

The birds were nibbled away. A strange sort of nibbling. One was missing its wings, another its tail. One had lost a wing, another its beak. The bodies of some of the birds had almost completely crumbled, and others had simply vanished.

Scattered among the crumbs of my wonderful, tiny bread birds were small black droppings.

Mice, my mother said.

I was so glad.

I'd known many mice in the village. For whole nights, they scurried around the coffin I slept in, even inside it right on my body. I liked the mice. I liked the horse and the pigs better, but still, I was fond of the mice. They were my nocturnal friends, like the moths, the fireflies, and the owl that lived above the cow, a small owl I didn't see very much, but I heard his faint voice every night. He flew silently. Hoo . . . hoo . . . hoo . . . that little owl would hoot.

When we trained my dear gray mice, my father told me that owls like to eat mice. How lucky for me that I'd never seen my owl eat any of my mice.

My father told me there was an old proverb that said church mice were extremely poor. Mice hiding with Jews were even poorer, he said.

Until then, I'd never heard the word "Jew," *Zyd* in Polish. We never spoke that word. Maybe my father was sorry he'd said it. My mother, who was painstakingly searching the seams of a patched shirt for lice—the dangerous lice, the typhus lice—gave him a piercing stare.

We decided to train the mice, already mine though I still hadn't seen them. I didn't even know how many there were, whether there was only one or two or more.

There were two.

We saw them for the first time after lying in wait for days.

We sat very, very quietly. That wasn't actually very hard to do. We always sat quietly. We waited for them to come out and partake of the wonderful meal I'd prepared especially for them. They didn't need manna from heaven. They had me.

They were so dear to me that I continued to save precious breadcrumbs for them, mix them with saliva, and knead the mixture for hours. Only when it was uniform and smooth, not too moist and not too dry, not too soft and not too hard, just the perfect consistency, did I mold it into little baskets filled to the brim with Lilliputian treats: miniature apples, tiny rolls, miniscule pears, diminutive wine bottles, and even minute slivers of cheese.

I put those marvelous refreshments at the foot of the old black iron stove, right next to the rounded lion's feet—or the tiger's feet, or maybe the baby dragon's feet—under the slightly open door.

And then it happened, the wonderful thing I'd dreamed of for so long. From the crack of the open door emerged the tip of a sharp little quivering pink nose, twitching gray whiskers, an elongated head that looked at me with shiny black beads, pinkish, transparent ears, tiny legs with long toes, each with a white nail at its tip, and between them, a tiny body rounded into a backside that ended in a glorious tail! A long, narrowing, hairless tail, a flexible, magnificent tail.

It was a mouse.

I immediately gave it the name Mysia. From behind it—how wonderful!—another mouse emerged. I could see right away that the second one had a shorter tail. I called it Tysia.

With endless patience, my father and I trained the little mice.

There were successes and setbacks. We were patient. Time was something we had plenty of. What we didn't have was food. But I kept on saving crumbs and molding them into treats.

My father and I, with the baskets I'd molded from the breadcrumb mixture, sat very, very quietly, lying in wait for long hours until the little mice appeared at the door of their house—the old black iron stove. At first they would snatch the baskets and scurry off, but they grew more confident with time and would stay longer, move a bit closer, to my father's shoe, onto his shoe, and finally—how wonderful it was, how exciting!—they'd climb up my father's leg to his knee. Hooray! The gray mice were mine, they were trained.

We lived in conditions that were perfect for training mice.

After a while, I saw that Mysia was getting rounder and rounder, fatter and fatter.

I wasn't surprised. After all, she was the one who always came out first and grabbed the food first. She was also the first to be trained. Mysia the glutton.

ONE NIGHT—WHEN THE NIGHTS WERE STILL VERY QUIET,
before the Red Army Air Force began its heavy bombing, before the volleys of *katyushas* began ringing in our ears like the sounds of paradise,
the sounds of fierce pride, of joy—I was listening, as I usually did, to the
rustling and whispering of my two little mice, when I suddenly seemed
to be hearing other, unfamiliar sounds, very soft sounds, a sort of quiet
chirping, a subdued murmuring.

Mysia, as usual, the first to come out, was no longer plump. She sat
on her hind legs, holding some crumbs from the miniature basket, and I
could see tiny, erect, pink nipples on her red stomach.

I knew immediately what had happened.

After all, my pig in the village had given birth too. And she'd had
beautiful piglets, soft and pink, with cheery little tails. She had lain on her
side, exposing her fat, whitish stomach, and all her many babies pressed
up against her, shoving and kicking each other, hitting and butting to get
close to one of the nipples and stay there forever.

Mysia had become a mother too, and Tysia a father—and I'd given
them both girls' names! Tysia was actually a boy.

How wonderful. What a marvelous surprise!

Another family was hiding with us.

I wanted so much to know how many mice had been born.

My pig in the village had given birth to a lot of piglets. I didn't know
how to count, but I could see that after a while, fewer babies were left,
and I didn't try to find out how many and why.

My father peered into the nest of my wonderful gray mice and managed to count fifteen tiny babies. My father knew arithmetic. Later, I
looked inside too. I could barely see anything. The inside of the stove
was dark, the nest was lined with straw probably taken from our mattress,
feathers from our tattered pillows, and wool threads from our unraveling blankets. A red thread was interwoven with them, a thread I knew
very well, my thread, which had come undone from one of the flowers
my mother had embroidered on the beautiful pink vest she'd sent to me
with Hania Seremet when I was in the village, and the one who gave me
that vest was the one who took it from me and obviously sold it, just as
she had sold the green satin dress I'd worn only once, when I had my
picture taken, proof that I was alive.

I loved that red thread. It was one of my treasures, along with some beautiful stones, a little red rag with white polka dots, and a pine cone that gave off the scent of resin. I used to wind the string around my finger, a different one every time, or tie several fingers together with it, carefully, not too tightly. Grandpa Seremet warned me not to cut off my circulation. He spit up and vomited his own blood all the time.

I loved seeing my fingers with the string around them turning red, then pale.

I'd brought the thread with me from the village, and it continued to be an important item in my treasure, along with the picture of a girl with a ribbon—a picture torn from a newspaper that I'd rescued from the latrine in the hiding place. Until one day, the thread disappeared. I was sad about losing it, and puzzled. How could it have vanished from the hiding place that no one ever went in or out of? My mother said that maybe elves took it. Everyone knows that elves are partial to the color red.

My mother was almost right. The thread *had* been stolen, but it was my wonderful little gray mice that had taken it. I forgave them instantly. I wasn't angry. In my heart, I gave them the thread as a gift.

The nest inside the stove had a special smell, the smell of rusty iron, vestiges of the smell of burning pages from the Jewish gynecologist's library, the smell of frayed cloth the mice used to line their nest, and the smell of damp warmth. I wanted so much to touch Mysia and her sweet babies, but I was afraid that mother and babies wouldn't like that closeness imposed on them, so I controlled myself and pulled my hand back. As it was, I thought it was almost a miracle that the little gray mice let us peek in at their warm family nest.

A few days later, my father looked in at the nest again. He turned around abruptly, and in a characteristic gesture ran his hands over his head, his forehead and eyes, and with unexpected, unfamiliar firmness forbade me to look inside.

I didn't try to find out how many babies there were this time either, but I didn't mold any more wonderful baskets brimming with treats from the breadcrumbs I saved. I just left them on the floor at the door to the black iron stove. Something in my heart had changed.

The heavy bombing started. After the first explosion, we no longer heard the rustling and chirping of the mice.

There were no more mice.

Maybe they'd gone down to the shelter when the first siren sounded, the way everyone else did?

We, of course, didn't go. We were Jews. No one was allowed to know that we existed. If someone found out and informed the Gestapo, that would be the end of us, and before some Communist bomb managed to blow us up, the Germans would murder us. We stayed in our hiding place.

But the small mouse family didn't stay with us. Apparently they weren't Jews. Maybe they were Aryans.

We remained alive, we survived the heavy bombing. My mother, my father, and I, and all of our millions of lice. The Red Army came, Tovarish Stalin sent it, liberated us and saved our lives.

And as Batiushka Stalin said in Russian: We shall celebrate in our streets too.

It was summer.

It had finally happened, but it had taken a very long time.

After the heavy bombing that had driven my non-Jewish mice away but not the lice, the mighty German army began to retreat. That was after Stalingrad, of course, and after the Allies finally opened a second front— those imperialists who waited to see whether the Red Army would win or be defeated, until it was victorious at Stalingrad and showed them just who Stalin and the Red Army were.

The Red Army, with the momentum of their great victory at Stalingrad, could have conquered all of Europe, defeated the Germans everywhere, taken Berlin by itself and turned all of Europe into a just place that had no poor, exploited people, a place where everyone worked according to his ability and received according to his needs.

And what if the Red Army had gone on to capture the whole world? Why shouldn't there be justice in England? In America? In capitalist America that had no justice?

But they were alarmed then, all those capitalists who sucked the blood of the proletariat, and they opened a second front because they were afraid that lofty Communism would sweep them away too and divest them of all their money.

That's what I thought.

THE GERMANS RETREATED. A DEFEATED, EXHAUSTED, BROKEN army. Soldiers who were thin, tired, and thirsty. Rozalia Juzakowa told us. She saw them. So young, and sometimes so handsome.

She'd bring them water from the house and give it to them when they were lying down for a short rest, leaning against the walls of the buildings. They also leaned against the wall of the house we were hiding in, the house on Panienska Street. Then too, if we had come out of our hiding place, they would have murdered us, even though they were exhausted and drained. You don't need much strength to murder a sick, almost dying woman, a starving man barely able to walk, and a not-very-big girl.

The German soldiers, members of the superior race. Lying against the wall of the house we were hiding in, their blue eyes were closed, their blond hair messy and scraggly. How many of them were murderers? How many of them were Nazis who followed Hitler happily, as he wrote in *Mein Kampf*? *Mein Kampf* was one of the books left from the Jewish gynecologist's library, and it survived the war with us. Hitler's eyes in the cover picture have holes in them. Maybe I did that.

Another great war awaited those soldiers. The road to Berlin would be a long one. They left, they were gone.

The German occupation was over.

Silence.

It was over.

We were saved.

Some of the Jews who survived crawled out of their hiding places, out of the burrows and the pits, into the air of the world, and when they did, they were murdered by the Ukrainians and the Poles. They'd survived the entire German occupation and now, right after the liberation, they were murdered.

There were people like that there too. Murderers. And they weren't even Germans. They were Ukrainians, they were Poles. They really did hate the Jews. They even hated Jewish children.

Or maybe they were afraid that now, after the liberation, those Jews who'd managed not to be murdered would ask the Ukrainians and the Poles to return their businesses, homes, property, everything that had been stolen from them?

As Juzakowa talked and talked and talked, my mother and father listened and were wise enough to wait in the hiding place seven more days. Like the number of days it took to create the world. Only then did they go out into the world that had been newly created for us.

We didn't know how to walk in the new world. We continued to whisper in the new world. My mother was dying of tuberculosis in the new world. And they dumped me in an orphanage in the new world.

For eighteen months, my mother and father had been in their hiding place in the home of Juzef Juzak, carpenter and alcoholic, and Rozalia Juzakowa, the devout Russian Orthodox, anti-Semitic Ukrainian who was full of superstitions.

I'd been with them too. They saved our lives.

We went out into the street. The sunlight dazzled me, almost blinded me. My legs didn't carry me. I didn't know how to walk. I stumbled and sat down on the sidewalk. My mother, who was very sick, sat down too, and so did my father. We couldn't speak, only whisper. The light and the noise stunned us. We hurried back into the hiding place. But we managed to see the army that liberated us, soldiers of the Red Army, those dear, beloved heroes.

Hooray! Hooray!! Hooray!!!

We owe them our lives.

It was good that they came to liberate us.

It took them a very long time.

They probably never imagined that there was a little Jewish girl who no longer had food, who'd forgotten how to walk and forgotten how to talk, whose beloved mice had run away and abandoned her during the first bombing, who could only whisper very very very quietly so they wouldn't hear her outside, on the Aryan side, because all those Germans outside wanted to hunt her down and murder her.

A little girl who never cries.

FREEDOM.

Three years had passed since my father came home and told my mother that a flag with a swastika on it was flying on top of the city hall tower. Now it was replaced by the red flag, the flag with the golden hammer and sickle, the flag of the good people.

That was it, it was over. For us, the war was over.

It had happened. Absolute good had defeated absolute evil. I was seven. From now on, everything would be better.

The world would improve.

There would be no more wars.

No one would exploit anyone else.

People would not be discriminated against, and everyone would be able to take care of their children, healthy children who would have books and never be hungry.

We were liberated, but my mother was invaded. The tuberculosis bacillus had invaded her, and she almost died.

Thin, too weak to get out of bed and walk, her emaciated body was wracked with coughing and she spit up blood that often had lumps in it, maybe pieces of her lungs, like Grandpa Seremet in the village before he died. At least there were no chickens pecking at what she spit up. The rag she covered her mouth with when she coughed was always filthy with bloodstains.

My father took my mother to the tuberculosis hospital, and he took me to the luxurious home of Mr. Fishman and his wife, Hela Fishman, who had hidden in a bunker behind their photography shop. Their son, who had been my age, died in the bunker a few weeks before the liberation. He choked to death. He had diphtheria. Many children choked to death from that terrible disease, even when there was no war in the world.

The Fishmans were born in Lvov and had always lived there. At the time of their birth, the city was part of the Austro-Hungarian Empire, and they continued to live there during the time Poland was free between the two world wars, then when the Russians ruled after they invaded following the Ribbentrop-Molotov Pact, and during the German occupation, after Operation Barbarossa. And now the Russians, the Communists, were back; the Red Army had come back and liberated them.

The Fishmans weren't Communists, not even salon Communists. They were wealthy businesspeople, very wealthy. They had a thriving camera shop and photography studio in the center of the city.

The man who saved them, who hid them, who managed the shop while they were gone and looked after their luxurious villa, was a good, decent man who'd worked for Mr. Fishman before the war. He was probably the only man who ever liked Mr. Fishman and his wife, Mrs. Hela Fishman—liked them so much that he was willing to endanger his life for them, to save them and even look after their property.

When the liberation came, Mr. Fishman and Mrs. Hela Fishman came out of their hiding place behind the darkroom of their photography shop and went back to the luxurious villa they had lived in until the war. They spent the first night of liberation in the bedroom they'd slept in before the war. That was a special story, a very rare one. But the boy was dead.

My father took my mother to the tuberculosis hospital and had to find a job right away. We didn't have a penny. The only job he could find was selling newspapers in the street. And so my father, educated and proud, sold *Czerwony Shtandar* (The Red Flag) in the streets of newly liberated Lvov where confusion and want still reigned because the war was still going on, Berlin had not yet fallen. And since my father was not used to walking and was hungry and weak, he fell and broke his hand. He walked around the streets and sold newspapers with only one hand, and it was hard for him to take care of me. That problem was always there—what to do with the girl. He went to the Fishmans, whom he'd known before the war, and asked them to let me stay with them in their villa.

My father also hoped they'd find clothes there for me because I was wearing disintegrating rags swarming with lice, and over them the scratchy wool jacket that had belonged to the manager of the soda factory. My mother had brought it back when she went out to look for bread for us because we were hungry. The jacket was tied with a rope, and since the sleeves were longer than my arms, they were rolled up thickly and weighed heavily on my wrists. They weigh heavily on me to this very day. The rags I wore were patched, patch over patch of various fabrics with various patterns. My mother, who knew how to embroider so beautifully, was constantly busy patching. Delousing and patching, patching and delousing the patches again. It was all falling apart. Your clothes look like a political atlas of an unknown continent, my mother said, and told me about an atlas and its heavy freight. This whole big world in the colors of my patched underpants.

My father and I went to the Fishmans' villa.

I was seven.

I thought that's how it was in the world.

IT WAS A LONG, EXHAUSTING TRIP. WE HAD TO CLIMB LONG, steep streets, and we were very weak. We walked slowly, my hand in my father's—like in the closet, when the Gestapo searched our hiding place. I expected his grasp to tighten around my hand when we crossed the street, but the opposite happened, it loosened and he walked so much more quickly that I could hardly keep up with him. I was a little girl.

We arrived.

The house stunned me. It was the first time I'd ever seen a place like that. Gleaming parquet floors, huge French windows, chiffon drapes, carved furniture covered with velvet fabrics, the so-familiar smell of varnish, and a piano, a gigantic piano, like my horse in the village, maybe even larger, as large as the piano of the Chopin Competition prize winner, Madame Czerny-Stefanska, who determined my fate by stating that I would never know how to play the piano.

But most miraculous of all were the bathroom and the toilet. It wasn't the smelly alcove of the ghetto or the small, crumbling wooden shack in the backyard in the village. It wasn't the tiny, peeling room in the hiding place at the Juzaks', whose slippery floor was always covered with damp, stinking, chewed-up *machorka* cigarette butts.

It was a fairy-tale castle. The little mermaid's palace. Green porcelain tiles, polished faucets, thick furry towels that looked like colorful animals.

In a glittering box on the sink was a piece of soap. Real soap. Round, pink, lilac-scented soap. Wonderful magic: the scent of lilacs instead of the stench that burned your eyes and made them tear.

My father said that, for the time being, I had to stay there.

My mother was dying from the hole that the tuberculosis bacillus had gnawed in her lung.

My father left and I started to cry.

There were no more Germans and I was on the Aryan side. I started to cry.

I started my crying.

I sat down at one of the French windows and cried.

I cried and cried and cried.

Sitting on the living room couch was a clown whose clothes were made of shiny yellow satin. It had a white porcelain face, black hair, sad eyes with a tear falling from one of them. A beautiful, heavy blue tear, not like my tears, which were just wet and salty.

It was remarkably beautiful. I touched it. The satin was smooth and pleasant. That clown was nothing at all like the clumsy dolls I used to make for myself out of sticks, rags, and apples, the dolls whose heads my friends, the pigs, gobbled up. That sad clown was the most beautiful thing I'd ever seen. I wanted it so much through my tears.

But the minute Mrs. Hela Fishman saw what I wanted, the clown disappeared from the couch. She must have hidden it far back in one of the closets. I didn't even get to see it anymore. I wanted so much, I yearned so much to hold it in my hands.

I didn't have the clown.

And my father didn't come.

I waited and waited and waited.

I cried and cried and cried.

I didn't eat, didn't drink, didn't sleep.

I didn't move from the window. I waited and cried, cried and waited. Hours, days, nights.

Until I saw my father trudging up the street, his right hand in a sling, a threadbare rag tied around his neck, very pale, very thin, limping.

I told him about the clown and he spoke on my behalf to Mrs. Hela Fishman, but his request was also denied.

I would never play with that clown.

My father asked them to give me some clothes, my rags had completely disintegrated, and they had so many clothes they didn't need, their dead son's clothes. But they absolutely refused. The clothes are a memento, Mrs. Hela Fishman said.

In the future, they'd find a sweet, blond orphan and adopt her. Those two mean people didn't deserve to have a sweet child like Kashya.

The rags continued to disintegrate on me, and the rolled-up sleeves of the soda factory manager's scratchy wool jacket continued to weigh heavily on my wrists.

They weigh heavily on me to this very day.

Mrs. Hela Fishman and Mr. Fishman told my father that I was intolerable.

That I sat at the window and cried all the time.

That it bothered them a great deal and disturbed the neighbors.

That the neighbors had come to complain.

That this was a very respectable community.

Respectable even before the war.

A quiet, elegant neighborhood.

Even the cat hid from my weeping, and they couldn't bear it any longer.

A seven-year-old girl in tattered rags, sitting at the elegant French window of the Fishmans' villa, crying, crying, crying, her tears wetting the chiffon curtains.

My father came and took me away from there.

Thin and pale, he plodded up the street and took me away from there.

The clown and the dead boy's clothes stayed in the closets.

They took down the chiffon curtains and gave them out to the laundress.

We walked slowly.

We walked, walked, and walked. We walked to the orphanage.

We arrived, and I was seven years old.

THE ORPHANAGE WAS A VERY LARGE HOUSE BUILT OF RED bricks. It had endlessly long, dark hallways. Hanging from the ceiling were light bulbs trapped in little wire baskets, their dim light only increasing the darkness. On either side of the hallway were doors painted in peeling, sickly, dark green oil paint. Through the open doors you could see rooms with narrow barred windows. The windows were tall. Someone the height of a child couldn't reach the sill to look outside.

Children of all sizes wandered through the hallways and the rooms. There were very small children, smaller than I was, and there were very big children the size of grown-ups. My father talked for a very long time, talked, talked, and talked, then pulled his unbroken hand out of mine and left.

He left and was gone.

I cried, cried, and cried.

I cried, cried, and cried.

I cried, cried, and cried.

In the orphanage, no one interrupted my crying.

That was very nice of all those children of every age and size. They just walked right past me and didn't interrupt my crying.

We won the war. True, we hadn't taken Berlin yet, but there were no more Germans. Crying was allowed.

And I sat in a corner of the hallway and cried.

That crying, this crying, hasn't stopped yet. It never will.

These are tears that have no end.

You can't stop crying them.

New children of every age, size, and shape were always coming to the orphanage built of red bricks the color of clotted blood. Some children were like little animals. One boy walked around on all fours. He didn't know how to stand. Another boy didn't speak, but only uttered strange barking, growling, and grunting noises. One little girl didn't have an arm. She had only an elbow.

One big, strong boy with muscles and a broad back had legs that were folded back and he couldn't straighten them out or stand on them. He dashed around at enormous speed on crutches and hit other children with them. For no reason.

And there was a boy who refused to get out of bed. He lay there, his head covered by the blanket, and was silent, didn't speak. He never ever said a single word.

Strange words were spoken there. Odd sounds. Many languages. We all understood each other.

There was a boy who only slept under the bed. One girl always held a cross in her hand.

Children of war. Little Jews, Poles, Gypsies, Russians, Ukrainians. And there were quick, mischievous children who laughed, played, and ran around.

They'd been found in hiding places, in forests, caves, holes, walls, pits, sewers, damp wells, cellars, attics, stables.

Abandoned orphans, survivors. But all of them were alive—not like the little naked girl Juzakowa found in the garbage pail in the yard, strangled, dead.

War isn't healthy for children.

And I cried, cried, and cried.

I didn't talk to any of the children.

I cried, cried, and cried.

They spooned out food from enormous blazing vats with a ladle decorated with congealed drippings, like they did in the soup kitchen next door to the church in the village where I was a Christian girl. Every child had a dish, and you could ask for more. The food was very good. And the bread was light and delicious. There was an abundance of light, delicious bread. As much as you wanted.

The toilets were horrible. Wooden benches with holes in them, always filthy and as smelly as the ones in the ghetto. There usually wasn't any paper. In the hiding place on Panienska Street, there were always newspapers speared on a crooked nail, and sometimes they had beautiful pictures on them, like the picture of the lovely girl with the curls and the ribbon.

Sometimes I had to go there at night, in the dark. On my way, in the long hallway, a dim bulb trapped in a wire basket dangled above me, spreading a gloomy light that made the darkness darker. But in the toilet cubicle itself, total darkness awaited me. Not even a single, faint beam of light filtered inside. How terrible it was to step into that darkness, barefoot on that slippery, filthy floor. I slipped once and fell, and the slime stuck to me.

That's how it was.

The children fought with each other all the time. They yelled in many languages, hit and punched, pushed and shoved, pinched, tore off ears, noses, braids. The boy with the folded legs who dashed around on his crutches hit the hardest. The children cried the most when he hit them. No one hit me.

One morning, we woke up to a loud commotion. A rumor spread that a boy had been hanged. They found him completely dead. He was hanging from a belt. They said that the belt was filled with dollars and his parents had wound it around his waist before they escaped from the ghetto. They sent him to a hiding place in a village, just as my parents had done with me, but *his* parents were murdered.

That boy had managed to survive until the liberation without being murdered. Now they'd hung him from a belt. He had a treasure in that belt. Like the treasure my father's little brother David had, the treasure that was buried in the basement of my parents' villa in Bochina.

And I cried and cried, cried and cried there, in the orphanage built of red bricks.

MY FATHER CAME TO SEE ME. HE STILL DRAGGED HIMSELF along, stooped, pale, and thin, while I was already walking quickly; I'd even learned to run. My father took me to visit my mother in the tuberculosis hospital. My mother was lying in the dying women's ward.

Inside, everything was painted in a peeling, shiny white oil paint, a leprous color that had a strange smell.

My mother lay in a high iron bed. The iron was painted white too. My mother was as white as the pillowcase, and two orange-red spots blossomed on her cheeks like a clown's makeup. She smiled at me with her hollow mouth that had only a few stumps of teeth in it because my father had so skillfully pulled all the crowns and bridges with his marvelous pocketknife, the red pocketknife with the white cross painted on it, the symbol of Switzerland, where there hadn't been a war because it was neutral.

I stood next to my mother's bed and she held my hand limply. My father dragged over a chair, sat down beside her, and stroked her hair with his unbroken hand. She always loved that so much. My mother's hair was golden, straight, and shiny, a source of pride for her. Once, before I was born, when she was working in a kindergarten, the children loved her because of her hair, that's what my mother told me.

In the huge, endless hall my mother was lying in, the hall of dying women, iron beds painted in peeling white paint were on her right, her left, all around her, and in all of them lay pale women with blazing clown cheeks. Some beds were surrounded by screens. Those women weren't dying, my mother said; they had already died. They died every night and every day there.

They died, died, and died.

For the time being, my mother was alive. The Koch bacillus, the tuberculosis bacillus, had still not completely gnawed away her lungs.

The damp hole still hadn't sucked her into it.

My mother asked me questions. What did I eat, what children had I met, where did I sleep, how was the bed, how many lice, bedbugs, and fleas were in the mattress. She was terribly sad when she heard about the filthy toilets and how I walked barefoot in them. Then her strength was gone. Her eyes, a yellow-green color she never liked, closed.

We left.

My father took me back to the orphanage made of red bricks and vanished. And I continued to cry.

When my father came to see me again, he brought a pair of wonderful slippers my mother had sewn and embroidered especially for me. Lying in her bed in that hospital where women died every night and every day, the tuberculosis hospital, she had made me a marvelous pair of slippers.

My mother, with her superb ingenuity and talent, had cut a piece of thick fabric from the hospital blanket, unraveled some threads from her robe, and even found a bit of red thread to embroider a tiny flower on each gray slipper.

That's the sort of person my mother was.

And I continued to cry.

The crying that will never ever stop, that will go on for all eternity.

The crying seeped into the depths, ancient lakes of tears, tears from the abyss burst forth.

They stole my slippers. But the slippers weren't very practical anyway. The filth of the toilets, the vomit, urine, and excrement were absorbed by their felt soles, and after a few days they stank terribly. I didn't tell my mother that my slippers had been stolen. They were so pretty, the only ones in the world. And the embroidered red flowers—if only I'd unraveled the flowers before they stole the slippers, I would have had a red thread like the one my wonderful gray mice took from me and wove into their nest.

My mother knew how to embroider so beautifully. While in the hiding place, there was no end to her inventiveness, the things she thought up and made and gave to Juzakowa to sell in the market. So there'd be a little more money to send to Hania Seremet to keep me in the village, on the side of life. So there'd be a little more money for bread. She made purses out of old sacks and embroidered gorgeous designs on them. She embroidered tiny flowers on cheap sweaters and turned them into unique, extraordinarily beautiful sweaters. Juzakowa would go to the market, stand among the haggling peddlers, and sell my mother's creations.

Juzakowa also sold the stones for cleaning cloth shoes that my father made using my Uncle Dov's formula.

The Germans murdered Uncle Dov, his gentle wife Minka—my mother's beloved older sister—and their two daughters, Rachel and Pnina.

Once, Hania Seremet came to the village with a dress made of shiny material the color of fine celadon, decorated with flowers made of the same material, but in pastel colors—pink, powder blue, yellow. Hania Seremet ordered me to wash, comb my hair, and wear the magnificent dress. I didn't know that my mother had made the dress. Hania Seremet didn't tell me. She took me to the neighboring town, to the photography studio, and tied a stiff ribbon on the top of my head. The photographer asked me to move closer to Hania Seremet, and he took a picture of us together.

When we went back to the village, I untied the stiff ribbon, took off the dress, and never saw it again. Only after Hania Seremet had dumped me at my parents' hiding place did I see the dress again, in the pictures taken the day she gave me the dress and stole it from me, pictures she'd sent to my parents as proof that I was still alive. They no longer believed it, and they'd never trusted Hania Seremet. They called her a murderess. And yet, they'd given me to her, to a murderess.

Such beautiful pictures. In one of them, Hania Seremet and I are together, and in the other, I am by myself. The photographer had painted them in lively pastel colors. But he had made a mistake. In the picture the dress is pink, but in reality it was green.

The touch of the photographer's hands as he moved my head, crowned with a stiff ribbon, until he thought the pose was right, the unpleasant closeness of Hania Seremet with her white face and clenched jaw. In the picture, Hania Seremet is wearing one of the sweaters my mother embroidered with tiny flowers. The sweater had most likely been given as part of the payment for my life. I remember the smell of damp, sweaty wool, a nauseating smell, and the slippery softness of the satin dress.

The photographer asked me to smile.

Sometimes, when she came to the village, Hania Seremet would bring me paper and colored pencils and tell me to draw. The drawings were also sent as proof that I was still alive, and Hania Seremet received money for them too. Then she received for them my father's will bequeathing her

my parents' villa in Bochnia to use for the expenses involved in continu-
ing to keep me alive, if I remained alive. Later, there were promises and
threats, and when nothing was left, Hania Seremet had had enough and
acted on her decision to get rid of me, that Jewish girl, and dump me at
their hiding place after sending a strange, surreal telegram: Come at once
and take your child!

Who would come? How? To the side of death, the Aryan side?

She wanted to get rid of me and my parents definitely did not want
her to bring me to them. After all, Juzef Juzak had agreed to hide them
on one condition: that they come without the girl.

Did I remember my mother and father when I was in the village, did
I miss them?

MY MOTHER TOLD ME ABOUT THE LIQUIDATION. SHE HEARD
everything and smelled everything. Panienska Street was right next to
the ghetto. She told me, told me, and told me.

They heard the shots, the explosions, the volleys, the orders, the
screams, the shouts, the pleas. They smelled the raging, roaring fire. A
scorched smell filled the world and the wind bore flakes of ash.

Juzakowa saw everything. She told us about a woman mad with terror who handed a small bundle with a baby in it to the Poles, Ukrainians, and Germans who lined both sides of the street watching the herd
of Jews on their way to be murdered—maybe one of them would take
it and save its life. The Germans used their bayonets to hurry the Jews
being led to death, and they had dogs. They were evil dogs, Juzakowa
said.

That baby was murdered in its mother's arms. No one took it.

One young boy ran away. He hid in the doorway of the house. Night
came, and the hunters, the Jew hunters, found him. My mother and father heard his pleas. They murdered him under the windows of the hiding place.

A shot.

My mother heard everything.

The young boy was murdered too, and after the war, my father gave
testimony about that murder and about the strangled girl tossed onto a
pile of garbage.

My mother told me how they found that Jewish girl, naked and strangled, in the garbage bin. It happened after the Gestapo had searched our hiding place, when I hid in the closet with my father and my mother hid under the massive desk. Juzakowa said that she had a long neck, that Jewish girl. She was redheaded. Juzakowa said she had freckles.

That girl was dead, and I was alive.

Abandoned in the orphanage made of red bricks, I cried and cried and cried. My father, the Communist, broke his hand, and with his other hand he sold the *Red Flag* for a living, and my mother the salon Communist was dying in the hospital.

With the pennies my father earned, he bought my mother carrots. Carrots were cheap and considered healthy. He'd bring her small bunches of carrots or tea leaves when he went to visit her, lying helpless in her white bed, her face the color of the pillowcase and her cheeks a blazing orange-red, the image of every dying tuberculosis patient. And she always had a fever. A constant, low fever. The fever that tuberculosis patients have.

I loved carrots very much. Carrots reminded me of my horse, the horse I shepherded in the village, in Marcinkowice, and those lovely days when I lay in the tall grass nibbling carrots, occasionally giving one to my horse and touching his soft, quivering nostrils, staring at the blue sky and letting the clouds take shape—dragons, ships, butterflies, and especially horses. Their whiteness darkened the blue of the sky.

My mother's hospital was full of men and women patients. There was a constant turnover of the dying. Many died, and new patients were admitted immediately in their place. There was no medicine, no food, and everyone was suffering—not just the patients, not just the Jews. We still hadn't taken Berlin and the war continued. Only the rich village girls who lay near my mother always got food from their families in the village, food too plentiful to be comprehended—lard, chickens, sugar, fruits and vegetables, bread and cake, and long salamis. They ate and ate and ate, shoved butter into all their orifices, that's what my mother told me, and it was disgusting because they kept getting thinner, shriveled up, faded away, and died.

All that rich food fed the bacilli that were gnawing them to death. The more they ate, the faster they died. On her right and on her left, in front of her and behind her. All around my mother. And my mother, who was so sick and starved, so thin that she was almost transparent, whose only food was the carrots my father brought her, began to get better, and her life was no longer in danger. My mother continued to live.

The special gas they injected into her lung kept decreasing the size of the damp hole the Koch bacillus, the tuberculosis bacillus, had gnawed, until only a scar was left.

My mother said that she defeated both Hitler and tuberculosis. It was a miracle. When the war was no longer in the world and we went back to Krakow, my mother found out that, in the meantime, a new drug had been discovered, penicillin, that ate the bacilli right away, and there was no longer any need for those painful injections of gas into the patient's lungs with a hollow, very long needle.

My mother was saved. Professor Ordung saved her life. To us, he was a saint.

THE WAR CONTINUED WESTWARD. MY MOTHER RECOVERED, managed not to die of tuberculosis, and left the hospital. My father's broken hand healed and he stopped selling newspapers in the street and went back to being the chief accountant in the same slaughterhouse and tanning factory he'd worked for until the ghetto was liquidated. They took me out of the orphanage built of red bricks that break and crumble into red dust and paint the puddles the color of blood like the blood in the pails my father would steal from the slaughterhouse and give to the starving Jewish workers from the ghetto.

We lived in a room in an apartment with other people, sharing the kitchen and bathroom with them. It was paradise, like the paradise Adam and Eve lived in that my father told me about when we were in the hiding place. We didn't have to hide anymore. Enough, we'd been liberated. We'd take Berlin too, and there'd be no more war in the world. We were together again, my mother, my father, and I. My crying didn't stop, but it no longer flowed from my eyes.

We lived in a large apartment house built around a square cobblestone courtyard. The kitchen balconies overlooked the courtyard on all sides. The building had four stories, attics and cellars, and you could walk from one kitchen balcony to another, round and round, on the same floor and from one floor to the other, because they were connected by metal stairs. The stairs and the balconies were very rickety, and they shook with every step you took on them—even my steps, and I wasn't even big or heavy.

My mother began cooking. Not from the recipes in the black cookbook my father bought her when they went to live in the luxurious villa he built for her in Bochnia—she always mentioned, jokingly or perhaps seriously, how disappointed she'd been that my father never sensed, never realized, that even though she was a Communist, albeit a salon Communist, she would have preferred a more romantic gift. Nor did she cook from the wonderful recipes in the detailed menus she'd dictated to my father when they were hungry together in the hiding place—a notebook of menus for all the seasons, for a whole year, in which no dish appeared twice. After all, it was inconceivable that after the war, the same dish would appear on the table twice in one year. That was a notebook of recipes for starving people, improvised on individual pieces of paper that I decorated with drawings I thought were absolutely beautiful when I was with my mother and father in the hiding place after Hania Seremet threw me out of the village.

No. My mother didn't cook from the recipes in the black book that survived the war with us, or from the menu notebook. She cooked other things. We were still thin and weak, but not hungry, and my mother cooked us all sorts of fattening dishes. Especially fattening was a yellow flour, not bright yellow like the satin of the splendid, unattainable clown at the evil Hela Fishman's villa, but a soft yellow. That flour was called *mamaliga*, and it was made of corn. I'd loved corn since the time I'd hidden as a Christian girl in the village—that wonderful corn enveloped in hair as soft and shiny as the hair of the enchanted nymphs.

My mother cooked numerous dishes from that flour, all of them delicious. She even baked cakes from it.

My mother always fed me and my father. My father called her "mother bird." A mother bird who brings food she puts in her chicks' mouths.

She always had something for me to eat when I was hungry. Everywhere, anytime, like she used to then, when the war was in the world and there was no food because Juzakowa and Juzak and their sweet little boy, Edjo, went away and left us in our hiding place without food. My mother said that Juzakowa wished we would finally die of hunger, or get so desperate that we'd leave, and outside there'd be people to make sure we didn't live.

And then, risking her life, my mother left the hiding place and came back with food, and we lived.

Mother bird, my father said.

IN THE APARTMENT BUILDING, AFTER THE WAR, I PLAYED with other children for the first time. I never got a chance to play with Daniel, the beautiful little boy Hania Seremet brought to the village for a short time and left to die at the gates of the ghetto after his parents were murdered. I actually did play with Edjo, Juzak and Juzakowa's son, quiet, wonderful games. But I'd never played with more than one child at a time until I lived in the apartment house built around the square courtyard.

Although there'd been a lot of children in the orphanage built of red bricks that crumbled and melted into the color of clotted blood, all I did there was cry, cry, and cry all the time, every day, every night.

The crying died down. I stopped crying even though the crying had not ended, and I started playing with the children who lived in the apartment building. There was an attic that had a strange smell and laundry lines, and we used to go up there to play. There were cellars too, with compartments for coal that smelled like ashes and burnt wood, a smell I knew very well from the stove in the ghetto that we used to crawl through to the bunker my father designed.

My mother claimed that she developed claustrophobia after we crawled into that bunker, and more than once after that, we had to get out of a railroad car or a bus on the way to some trip or vacation, and all our lovely plans were ruined.

I also went down to the cellar to play with the children, although I liked the attic better and the square courtyard best of all. But the courtyard did have failings because the grown-ups could see us from the balconies that overlooked it all around, on every floor. Naturally, we preferred playing where the grown-ups couldn't see us.

My mother made me a doll. An after-the-war doll. A wonderful doll. Nothing like the dolls whose heads my amiable friends, the pigs, used to eat, the dolls I made for myself in the village out of a stick, a rag, and an apple. This was a cloth doll stuffed with the cotton that stuck out of rips in our blanket. The doll's eyes were shiny black buttons and she had an embroidered nose and mouth. She had arms and legs and hair made of a piece of fur taken from an old, crumbling, moth-eaten collar, black fur with tiny curls. Later I learned that it was fur taken from lamb fetuses, and it was called Persian lamb. That made me very sad.

The doll wore a red dress with white dots—polka dots, they were called. She was my wonderful doll, the doll my mother made just for me with her nimble fingers.

The other children were jealous of me for having such a wonderful doll. I was afraid they'd take her away from me, the way the children had stolen my slippers in the orphanage. The children said that the doll was our baby, and in our games in the attic, the girls would lift their dresses and give birth to the doll or unbutton their blouses and nurse my doll with their tiny nipples. I did too. Those were very exciting, embarrassing games, games we couldn't play in the courtyard, attic games.

Later on, I stopped bringing the doll to our games in the attic. I'd lay her in my parents' bed and pull the blanket up to her chin. So she'd be protected and safe. So she wouldn't be embarrassed.

Sometimes the doll would unravel and the cotton stuffing would protrude. My mother always knew how to fix her. Not like back in the village when I had to take care of everything myself. And I'd been much smaller then.

My mother was looking better all the time. Her face wasn't as pale and her cheeks didn't blaze as much. And her low afternoon fever, the tuberculosis fever—37.3, 37.4 degrees Celsius—disappeared. We were all stronger. My mother cooked fattening foods all day. We continued not to be hungry.

How different life was. We'd come out of the room we were hiding in. We were free. We could walk, run, even speak out loud. I continued to speak quietly. Not in a whisper, but quietly. My father would go to work and come home from work, my mother talked with the neighbors, I played with the children, and all of it on the Aryan side, the side of life, which was no longer the side of death for us, the Jews.

My mother became particularly friendly with one of our neighbors, a woman who wasn't Jewish. Almost none of the tenants in the building were Jewish. Most of them had lived there before the war. That woman, Pani Mleko, lived on the third floor right across from us. She'd always lived there, before the war and during the war. She was an old woman.

That old woman had a dog, a lovely brown dachshund. His name was Bobi. He had soft, black, droopy ears and his cheery tail stood straight up and moved right and left in the funniest way, like the pendulum of the grandfather clock in the old woman's apartment that chimed every hour, serious chimes, a reminder of all the things that still hadn't been done.

The little goat in my favorite story hid in a clock similar to Pani Mleko's clock. That was the story about the little goat that hid in a clock while the bad wolf was eating up his six brothers. I was that goat.

Bobi, the cute dog, was chubby and squat, and he ran very slowly on his short bowlegs. All day, he ran along the third-floor kitchen balconies, round and round. He couldn't climb the stairs from floor to floor. His short bowlegs would get stuck between the steps. I loved Bobi and was glad that Pani Mleko let me come and play with her little dog. Poor children with rickets had bowlegs like Bobi's. Those were children whose parents were penniless, children born in dark cellars who didn't eat enough and were never exposed to the sun, which never shone on them from the windows that looked out on the feet of people walking on the street.

When Communism won, children would no longer be sick from hunger and a lack of sunlight. The sun would shine on everyone, my father said.

And Tovarish Stalin was, as everyone knew, the sun of the nations.

Meanwhile, they made me swallow a spoonful of cod liver oil every day, a slimy, yellow, smelly liquid. It was so sticky, so repulsive. And the taste! Its terrible smell stayed in my mouth for hours.

Ugh!

Cod liver oil would keep me from getting rickets. I wouldn't have bowlegs. All I'd have was flat feet, and lots of other things that would be treated in the future, and would also make my life miserable. They made me take cod liver oil for years. After I read *Moby Dick*, the taste got a thousand times more disgusting. But that was after we went back to beautiful Krakow and I was older.

Sometimes my mother would ask me to bring the old woman a sample of something she'd cooked. We had enough food, enough even to offer to others. I was happy to bring Pani Mleko the food. It gave me an opportunity to play with Bobi.

Once, my mother baked cookies that were different from any I'd ever seen or tasted, made from real flour, white flour. My mother used molds to shape the cookies into flowers, crescents, triangles, circles, stars. She gave me one of each shape to taste, and even though they were all baked from the same dough, each had its own special taste, almost like the manna the children of light had in the desert.

I ate, ate, and ate. I nibbled and ate greedily.

Then my mother arranged a plate of cookies of every shape—flowers, crescents, triangles, circles, stars—and asked me to take it to Pani Mleko. I was glad. I'll play with Bobi, I said to myself. I took the plate brimming over with cookies and went out to the balcony on my way to the old lady's apartment.

When I reached her kitchen door, all the cookies had the same shape. They were all round. I gave the old woman the cookies, told her that my mother had sent them, and went to play with Bobi.

When the giant grandfather clock chimed five, I ran and skipped home. I loved to make the rickety iron balconies and stairs shake and feel the tremors that spread in waves through the iron and the whole building until they stopped.

Less than an hour later, the old woman, Pani Mleko, who'd been so nice and friendly until then, appeared at the door to our room, stumbling and dripping with sweat. Her gray hair, almost always gathered in a neat bun, was flying wildly around her head, and pink bald spots showed through it. She was furious, her face was red, and she was holding the plate my mother had sent her, a plate brimming over with lovely round cookies. N-i-b-b-l-e-d cookies!

On my way to the old woman's apartment, I had decided that nothing terrible would happen if all the cookies had the same shape, the purest, most perfect shape, and I nibbled all around them very carefully. The flowers, triangles, stars, crescents—they were all circles.

I'd done such a beautiful job that I was amazed to see that old Pani Mleko had figured out what the cookies' original shapes had been.

I was amazed and ashamed.

My mother apologized.

It took a while for the old woman to be mollified.

But nothing between me and Pani Mleko was ever the same again. Even the grandfather clock in her apartment had taken on an admonishing tone. Only Bobi didn't change. His cheery tail kept wagging rhythmically, left, right, left, like the metronome in the living room of that renowned pianist, Madame Halina Czerny-Stefanska, winner of the Chopin Competition prize, who would determine my fate in Krakow.

I HAD THAT URGE, THE URGE TO NIBBLE, AN URGE THAT IS hard to control.

I used to nibble on the loaves of bread my mother used to send me to buy. I had a system. I would make a small hole in the crust and take the soft part out through it, and by the time I got home, I'd eaten about half of the inside of the bread. Bread was plentiful, so my mother asked me to buy two loaves, and after all, two half-nibbled-away loaves are like one whole one. It wasn't hunger, it was a game. I believe that if I'd really been hungry, I would have controlled my nibbling urge. In our family, it was actually hunger that made us so restrained. To this day, I can't resist the temptation to nibble the heels of breads.

I still saw Bobi, old Pani Mleko's dachshund, when he strolled around the third-floor kitchen balconies. And since he didn't know how to climb up or down the steps, I used to go down to his floor, pet his long back to the tip of his cheery tail, and roll his long, soft, warm ears. He wasn't my dog; he was old Pani Mleko's dog. I wanted so much to have a pet of my own. Until my dream finally came true.

My first pet—the first one after the war—was a dead rat. I found it in the square inner courtyard of the huge apartment building we lived in after the liberation, next to a pile of garbage that was near the metal pipes in the corner that were used to beat rugs on.

I was very happy.

I picked it up.

I ran my fingers through its damp, unkempt fur, petted it and kissed it, hugged it and played with it. The rat was mine and mine alone, and I was so happy all day. I didn't even go to play with Bobi.

In the evening, my mother called, *Ilusia, chodz do domu! Ilusia, chodz do domu!* Ilusia, come home! Ilusia, come home!

I climbed the shaky iron stairs that connected the floors. Pani Mleko's angry clock chimed six times, six admonishing chimes. On my way up, I didn't even look for Bobi, even though I was always glad to see him and pet him. I betrayed our friendship. I was so busy with the precious new rat in my arms.

Before I went into the kitchen, I smoothed down its hair, messy from so much playing, and stood proudly in front of my mother, who was impatient because she'd had to call me twice.

I stood in front of her, opened my arms slightly so she could see my soft, adorable, furry treasure. My little pet that was mine alone.

Hideously repulsed, my mother snatched the rat with its smooth, brushed fur out of my arms and threw it out the kitchen door into the courtyard.

It had started to rain. And the level of my tears rose once again.

I cried, cried, and cried.

It rained all night.

In the morning, when I went out to play in the cobblestone inner courtyard, my rat was lying on its back in a puddle, gritting its teeth at me. It didn't look adorable. I didn't feel like playing with it anymore.

And then, right then, the sun came out, and in my rat's puddle I saw the most beautiful thing in the world. More beautiful than greenish fairy corn silk. More beautiful than blue cornflowers or the red poppies in a wheat field. More beautiful than storks landing. More beautiful than a ladybug.

I saw a rainbow, a rainbow in the puddle.

Pure beauty.

Beauty that needs nothing else.

It was the rainbow from the story my father whispered to me in the hiding place, the story about the man who built a wooden ark and hid all the animals in the world in it and saw to it that they all had enough food, not like in our hiding place, and when the terrible rains stopped, that rainbow appeared—a sign that they could come out of their hiding place.

That the flood was over.

That they didn't have to hide anymore.

That no one was hunting little girls anymore.

WHEN I WAS SEVEN, A MAN CAME TO VISIT US IN THE ROOM in Lvov. He had a blue number tattooed on the skin of his inner arm. That man with the painted number astonished me. It was the first time I'd ever seen a man who'd been written on. He rolled up his sleeve and showed my father the number. I didn't look, but I saw.

That man wore a hat, and when he took it off, a kind of black saucer made of cloth remained on the top of his head. It was Uncle Isser Laufer. He was the first of all the people who came to our room, came, came, and came, told us their stories and sometimes cried. I never listened, never looked, but I saw everything and I heard everything.

That man told my parents everything. They sat around the table under the shade my father had made from a piece of tin and affixed to a bulb, and the man talked about a camp they brought people to, where they strangled them and then burned them.

Strange stories.

Did it happen to children too? To little girls like me?

That man said that he saw someone on the street, a man who'd been a kapo in the camp where they exterminated people. That man, the kapo, was Jewish, but he had helped the Germans. He carried out their orders and even tortured prisoners himself, without orders. That man, the kapo, killed Isser Laufer's childhood friend right in front of his eyes. A good friend, from their days in the *cheder*.

Later, my father told me what a *cheder* was, that he'd studied in a *cheder* too, and about the *melamed* who had a very long ruler and taught the little children Torah. Sometimes he'd smack their palms with his ruler, but not really; he actually smacked the table and made loud noises, but he always stroked their curls and gave them pieces of sugar from his pockets, sugar pieces that had scraps of *machorka* tobacco stuck to them. My father explained to me that since his days in the *cheder*, he'd known how to read from every direction. There were so few books that several children would sit around the same one. My father was very proud of that skill, although he'd never had the opportunity to use it.

Uncle Isser Laufer found out where the kapo lived. He wrote down everything he knew about the man and went to the rabbi. The rabbi Isser Laufer went to had also been in the camp where the kapo tortured prisoners. He destroyed the letter of testimony, saying that they should not talk about Jews who behaved wickedly or collaborated with the Germans. Talking about it is forbidden. Only Nazis should be condemned. Nazis, the rabbi said, not Germans, Nazis. And that's how the Germans became Nazis.

After Berlin fell, after victory, that rabbi went to Germany and settled in the city of Hamburg. He married a fat woman who converted to Judaism and had been called Berta before converting. After she converted, they called her Beltcha. My mother thought that story was very funny. That rabbi was not a young man. He'd already had grandchildren before the war. The Germans had murdered all of his grandchildren, children, daughters-in-law, sons-in-law, and the wife he'd married in his youth. They said that Beltcha bore him twins that were as identical as two peas in a pod, and they both looked like their mother—pink, with blond hair and faded eyes, like piglets, but not as nice as my piglets.

My mother said that one day, a woman named Paula was admitted to the tuberculosis hospital in critical condition. Paula was from my mother's town. They'd known each other since childhood. Paula came from an especially wealthy and well-connected family. She married a very rich man and they had a daughter. When the war broke out, she was in Lvov, where she went to live after her marriage. Her husband was murdered; Paula and her daughter survived. People who started coming back from the concentration camps knew her. They'd known her in the ghetto too, before she'd been sent to the concentration camp with her daughter. They said terrible things about her. They said she was a kapo, a collaborator who carried out orders to save her daughter and herself. Some women even wanted to turn her in for war crimes. It didn't happen. Maybe because of the daughter, maybe because they thought she'd die of tuberculosis anyway.

Paula didn't die. She recovered. Like other Jews, she went to Germany after the war, and like the family of my girlfriend Monica Starski, she ran a business and thrived after the Marshall Plan. My father, the Communist, had a lot to say about that plan of the Americans, who'd waited so long to open a second front and now were pampering the Germans.

Paula went to Germany and lived in their language. Every Galician Jew knew German. Many went to universities in Vienna or Berlin. The chances of running into a prisoner from the concentration camp where you were a kapo were probably smaller in Munich than in Warsaw or Krakow. Paula always praised her daughter, Fredrika, saying how talented she was, how beautiful and hardworking. My mother always criticized me, and my father was embarrassed around me.

In our family, children were never praised. It was considered bad taste. After all, the children were obviously gifted and wonderful. Good looks were never talked about at all. It was considered dangerous to give a child the idea that she was beautiful. It might give her illusions and make her think she could indulge herself and not work hard at school, that her beauty, an unearned gift of nature, was enough to get by on.

THE APARTMENT BUILDING WE LIVED IN AFTER THE WAR, IN Lvov, had a very high, wide entrance gate. My father told me that once, carriages hitched to two, even four horses used to enter through it. It had been an exclusive, luxurious building. Wealthy people had lived in the apartments, and their servants—there was such a thing as servants—lived in small alcoves next to the kitchen. Those servants, and other people who supplied the tenants with merchandise and services, never entered through the splendid front gate. There was a back door for them, and they walked up the rickety iron steps and went in through the iron balconies strung along the kitchens. When my father finished building Communism, there would be no such things anymore. Everyone would live in a front apartment, would work according to their ability and receive according to their needs, and their children wouldn't have bowlegs or rickets or tuberculosis. The children would grow straight and healthy, and no German would hunt them or want to murder them. And they would all have books.

The splendid entrance gate to the apartment building still had some of its ornaments from years gone by, plaster reliefs and frescoes. There was always a horrible, nauseating stench of urine, vomit, and excrement at the gate. A permanent, living, relentless stench. I always walked through it like a diver—not breathing, not smelling, not seeing. It was a stench you could see. The ammonia smell burned your eyes, and the strange, ugly charcoal drawings on the walls burned them too. These were drawings in the form of people with strange, prominent shapes between their legs. And incomprehensible words were written there. I didn't know those words from the books I read, and I didn't ask my mother what they meant. Sometimes I'd hear the bigger children, even the grown-ups, saying words like that—words that were never spoken in our home.

The ochre color that covered the staircase walls had peeled in many places, creating strange shapes and exposing red bricks that had melted into the color of clotted blood, just like at the orphanage. The shapes that the peeled paint carved on the walls were like the clouds in the village—existing side by side were horses and dragons, good monsters and evil ones, anything you could imagine. Later, those creatures existed side by side carved on the new wardrobe we had in Krakow that smelled of varnish.

After the liberation, after the Red Army came and saved us, the war continued westward, to Berlin. Meanwhile, the new Communist regime confiscated the rich people's houses and their capitalistic apartments, and as part of their efforts to improve the world, allotted one room to a family. That's how we got our room in the big apartment building that had once been a luxurious home to very wealthy people. Even tall Sergei and sweet Lyuba, both officers in the Red Army, the liberating army we revered, received rooms in the apartment we lived in.

Sergei was Jewish.

I don't know whether any other Jews lived there.

"Jews." That word was never spoken in our home, not in the presence of the girl.

When we lived in the ghetto, no one who came to visit us was allowed to say "Jew" in my presence.

That's what my mother told me, told me, and told me.

Not to say "Jew" in the ghetto?

My mother and father didn't want me to know that word. They didn't want that word to evoke any response in me. So that if I heard the word *Zyd*, "Jew," I wouldn't think it referred to me and I wouldn't respond.

People who hated the Jews used to say *Zydeck* or *Zyduwetska*—"Jew-boy" or "Jew-girl"—and that was considered even more insulting, more humiliating.

In hiding, when my father told me stories from the big black book and I was six, he always said "the good people," or "the children of light." He didn't say "Jews."

What did I understand about that world?

What did I know, what did my heart guess?

Strange. How very strange.

That girl who, until the liberation, never cried.

This girl never cries, my mother said.

Not when they took me from the ghetto to the village, not in the village, not when Hania Seremet threw me out of the village and back to my mother and father, and not when I stood in the closet holding my father's hand, which was dripping cold sweat, the sweat of terror, and the Gestapo came in to search.

Such a small girl. Mother, father, home, toys, treats. And suddenly—war. Escape, bombings, a horse and wagon and a little girl hidden in straw.

Straight from her white muslin bed into the straw.

Hiding in barns during the day, riding, fleeing at night.

Ghetto, *aktions*, children's *aktions*. Children's *aktions*?

Hiding in a bunker you reached by crawling through the door of the stove.

Handed over in the middle of the night to a stranger, a woman with a white face and a clenched jaw, a total stranger.

Forced to be called by a new name.

To take on a new identity, a new God, beautiful prayers.

Abandoned in a village with old people, strangers.

How lucky that the pigs were there, those dear, good friends.

Then taken again, dumped into the hiding place.

Unwanted. After all, her mother and father wanted her to stay in the village, to be like a Christian girl.

A mother and father she no longer knew, whose language she no longer understood.

The hiding place. Don't go out, don't walk, don't look out the window, don't talk, don't laugh.

Whisper, whisper, and whisper.

Sometimes there was no food.

Hiding in the closet, holding her father's hand, cold sweat.

And outside, death.

The whole world quaking and collapsing, torn apart, exploded.

Even the trained mice fled to the Aryan side.

The Russians save her life, and once again she's left with strangers.

People who don't let her play with the yellow clown that's on the sofa.

And then, how marvelous, she cries.

She cries, cries, and cries. At least she cries.

Then abandoned again, dumped into an orphanage built of bricks as red as clotted blood.

A little Jewish girl who doesn't know the word "Jew."

What was all that?

Did it happen?

It did.

That crying will never end.

That crying will go on forever.

THE WAR ENDED. MY MOTHER GOT WELL AND MY FATHER WENT back to work as the chief accountant in the same slaughterhouse and tanning factory he'd been working in when we ran away from the invading Germans. He'd worked there when the city was Polish, continued working there when the Russians came into the city following the Ribbentrop-Molotov Pact, and he'd worked there after Operation Barbarossa too, until the ghetto was liquidated, under German occupation. And now, after the liberation, when Lvov had turned back into a Russian city, my father went back to his old job, and with all the energy and faith he had, he began to build Communism, to build a new, perfect world. The people who ran that factory throughout all the political and military changes—from Polish to Russian to German and back to Russian—were decent people.

Such a strange piece of luck that was.

My mother told me, told me, and told me.

When the Germans came and the occupation began, all the Jews were ordered to leave their homes and apartments and move into a few streets in one of the city's worst neighborhoods. They built a wall around those streets, and the place became a ghetto, the Jewish ghetto. Those people, the Jews, were not allowed to leave the ghetto, and anyone who worked outside of it at a job that was essential to the German war effort had to wear a white cloth or celluloid armband around his sleeve that had a blue star embroidered or drawn on it.

A six-pointed star.

The Jewish star.

It's called a Magen David.

Anyone in the column of laborers leaving the ghetto to work outside had to wear an armband like that.

And inside the ghetto too. All the Jews.

When the war was no longer in the world, I saw photographs of other ghettos, and the Jews there also had to sew a Magen David on their clothes, and sometimes the word *Jude*, Jew, was written inside it.

The pictures weren't in color, but I read that the Jewish star, the Magen David, had to be yellow.

I wonder why it had to be yellow, not blue, like in our ghetto.

German soldiers with drawn bayonets guarded the group of laborers who went out of the ghetto to work. When they left and when they came back, the laborers plodded along in a row, downcast and weary, exhausted and starved. Slaves. That's how it was. Even without the Magen David armbands around their sleeves, those Jews were immediately recognizable when they were on the Aryan side. For Jews, that was the side of death, but the residents there, non-Jewish people, had the right to live. The ghetto was separated from the side of life. The ghetto became a corridor of death. A waiting room for death.

The Jews crowded together in the crumbling old buildings, with the rats and the lice and the bedbugs and their diseases, and with feelings that were as unbearable as illnesses.

They all tried to save themselves. People made all sorts of hiding places and bunkers for themselves where they planned to hide when the Germans came to murder them or send them to concentration camps where they'd work until they died or were murdered.

That's what my mother told me, told me, and told me.

Other people talked about it too, after the war, they talked about it. I never listened to them. I hated those stories they told about the *aktions*, also the children's *aktions*.

They hunted and killed little girls like me too.

The ghetto became smaller and smaller. People died of hunger, disease, despair, or were picked up in *aktions* and sent to death camps, or shot in the street, or tortured in the Janowska camp. Some people killed themselves and some killed the people they loved.

In the end, the ghetto was liquidated. Those who didn't run away died. They burned everything. The liquidation of the ghetto went on for fourteen days.

I was already in the village, a Christian girl named Irena Seremet.

That's what my mother told me, told me, and told me.

There are such things in the world.

Herr Knaup was the name of the good German, the German manager of the slaughterhouse and tanning factory where my father worked as the chief accountant during all those years, during all those occupations and regimes.

The Russian manager was called Bulani.

The good German manager, Herr Knaup, used to compliment my father and tell him how much he valued his work. Without him, Herr Knaup said, he wouldn't have been able to manage with all the primitive Poles and Ukrainians. After all, my father was cultured. He had been educated in Vienna! Or was it Berlin?

When conditions in the ghetto worsened, the good German manager suggested to my father that he come to live in the tiny room next to the slaughterhouse. He was afraid that my father, his right hand, would be murdered leaving or coming back to the ghetto and there would be no one to help him manage efficiently and honestly with all the primitive Poles and Ukrainians.

The war was in the world, and the tanning factory where my father worked contributed greatly to the German war effort.

That tiny room we lived in next to the slaughterhouse saved our lives for a while, and not only *our* lives, but the lives of many other people as well.

There was food in the slaughterhouse; in the ghetto there was hunger.

My father stole entrails and pails full of blood from the slaughterhouse.

The Jews who arrived from the ghetto every dawn would slip into our tiny room and my mother would give them blood from the pails and wreaths of entrails.

They would break away from the line of slaves for a second, get some clotted blood that they drank on the spot and wreaths of entrails that they wound around their waists or hid in their inner pockets, in the hope that there wouldn't be any searches, that they would manage to sneak the food of life into the ghetto for the children, the mother, the wife, the little sister.

Bone-weary people, dead tired after long hours of hard labor.

Those entrails and that blood, the blood of dead animals, was the source of life. That blood saved people from starving to death. They drank that blood. The fact that my mother and father endangered themselves to help those people and even save their lives fills me with pride.

My mother, my father, and I also drank that blood.

If my father had been caught stealing blood and entrails from the slaughterhouse, he would have been murdered right then and there, along with my mother and me.

Even the good German manager, Herr Knaup, who helped my father and admired him so much, would not have been able to save us.

In the end, Herr Knaup had to evict us from the tiny room when the Gestapo ordered him to return us to the ghetto. He was afraid of the Gestapo too, even though he was German. Herr Knaup was a good, decent man, a citizen sent by his homeland to a conquered country designated to be a reservoir of slaves for the superior race, the master race, the Aryan race.

He was a member of that race.

AFTER THE WAR, WHEN I WAS SEVEN AND WE WERE SAVED and remained alive, people began showing up at our house, lonely people, people who'd managed to survive and remain alive. Some of them kissed my mother's hands and thanked my father. They were grateful for the blood and entrails that had kept them from starving during the war.

I saw that.

And there were other people who spent whole evenings sitting with my mother and father around the square table under the light bulb that spread a meager light over the dust, the dirt, and the fly droppings. A long, narrow brown strip dotted with millions of fly corpses hung next to the bulb.

That kind of sticky strip once killed a cat in the courtyard. Someone had thrown the strip into the garbage. When a cat came along and foraged around in the garbage, its paw stuck to the strip, and in its struggle to get free, it got even more entangled and died. It was sad. The cat was a friend of Bobi's, the adorable dog that belonged to Pani Mleko, the owner of the admonishing clock. We couldn't save it. Its name was Mitzi.

Those people who came to visit us—most of them never appeared a second time—used to talk, talk, and talk.

And my mother talked too, talked, talked, and talked. I knew my mother's stories very well.

I lay in the corner, as always. Not in bed and not in a coffin, but in a kind of convertible armchair. When we went back to Krakow, I also had an armchair like that, upholstered in blue velvet, and I used to curl up on it and read, read, and read until I lost consciousness. I read everything written for me by Dickens, Hugo, Jack London, Tolstoy, Kipling, Mark Twain, Gorky, Sienkiewicz, Mickiewicz, Dumas, Zola, Babel, and even Annemarie Selinko, who told me about Désirée.

But for the time being, in Lvov, on the other side of the blanket or sheet that separated the armchair I was trying to sleep in from the room my parents were sitting in with their guests, those people talked and talked and talked. I tried to fall asleep quickly, and I succeeded almost every time. I had ways of curling up that made me fall asleep instantly—quite a useful skill. But still, sometimes, I couldn't help but hear. How the stories and the people telling them repulsed me, especially a man who visited us several times. He used to stretch out his arms, hold up his hands, and study his nails carefully. Then he'd clench his fists and examine the bent fingers. Finally, he'd bring them to his nose and sniff them.

Awful. In our house in Krakow, that was considered a very impolite habit. My mother said that was what fishmongers did because no soap could overcome the smell that clung to the skin of their hands.

They talked, talked, and talked.

Who was murdered, how they were murdered, where they were murdered—many, many stories.

Who was saved, how they were saved, where they were saved—very few stories.

They were saved accidentally, blindly, luckily, miraculously—those were the words that were repeated in their stories of rescue. And there were other words, words I already knew that were burned into my brain: Gestapo, *aktion*, ghetto, liquidation, forged papers, the Aryan side, bunker, hiding place, cyanide, informers, collaborators, hunger, lice, typhus, Ukrainians, the blue police, execution, concentration camp, murder.

And the places, the names of the places.

Oswiencim, the city my mother was born in. Majdanek, Belzec, Bzezinka.

And the names Hitler, Goering, Goebbels, Himmler, Keitel, Ribbentrop, Rommel, Frank.

And the rivers Dnipro, Bug, Vistula.

And our generals: Kuniev, Zukhov, Rokosovsky. And Churchill and Roosevelt and de Gaulle. And Stalin, Stalin, Stalin.

The great Stalin, Stalin the sun of the nations, Stalin the generous, the beneficent, the savior. He saved us, for example.

His picture was everywhere, serene, smiling, understanding, and protecting. So handsome, with that mustache and those angular eyebrows, all those medals on his proud chest, and sometimes a pipe in his mouth.

And I was grateful. I was a little girl.

WE LIVED THERE, IN THAT HOUSE, IN THAT ROOM IN LVOV, until the war ended, until the final victory, until we took Berlin.

Tall Sergei and sweet Lyuba lived in that apartment with us. Sergei was an officer in the Red Army, the army that saved our lives. Sweet Lyuba was an officer in the Red Army too. Sergei told my father that he was Jewish. We were allowed to say the word "Jew" then.

In the evenings, Sergei would visit our room, talk with my mother and father, and play with me. No one had ever played those games with me. I loved Sergei very much. I'd never been so close to such a tall, handsome, and strong person. Sergei wore his uniform when he came to our room in the evenings. He wore an officer's hat with a beautiful red star on it, epaulettes with his rank on his shoulders, and all sorts of medals on his chest, gorgeous jewelry. A brown leather belt lay diagonally across his chest. The brown holster around his waist wasn't allowed to be opened. It held a gun.

Sergei, whom I loved, always made me laugh.

He would grab me with his huge hands that had soft blond hairs on them and the scent of Russian cologne mixed with the smell of *machorka*, lift me high high high into the air, up to the ceiling, and twirl me around like a carousel. I never let him know how much it scared me and how terribly nauseous it made me. I controlled myself. It was a wonderful fear.

I loved tall, blond, smiling Sergei. The painter Jonasz Stern, whom I loved later, in Krakow, was dark and gloomy.

Sergei was always laughing and nice to me. He used to kneel down when he talked to me, and then his face, that lovely, laughing face of his, would be the same height as mine. And the smell he gave off, the smell of Russian cologne mixed with the smell of *machorka*, was like my father's smell. Later, the whisper of a new, unidentifiable scent was added. Did it have something to do with sweet Lyuba?

I loved Sergei. Sergei loved Lyuba.

Lyuba, that adorable Red Army officer, was plump and short, even to my little girl's eyes. She had a blond braid she wound around her head like a crown and the unruly curls that lost their way glowed like a halo—like the Virgin Mary's halo in the picture that hung in Grandpa and Grandma Seremet's house in the village.

Lyuba, that adorable Red Army officer, wore a uniform held tightly in place by a brown belt, and rolls of her lush, plump flesh jiggled. Another belt lay diagonally across her breasts, which threatened to burst out of the green *rubashka*. Sweet Lyuba also had a holster with a gun in it that we weren't allowed to touch, and a beautiful medal glittered on one of her breasts.

Like Sergei, sweet Lyuba wore stiff, black leather boots. Gleaming boots. You could see your reflection in their glow.

Sweet Lyuba was proud of her boots. She took care of them and pampered them with fervent devotion. Lyuba loved her boots.

Every evening, Lyuba would spread a rank black cream over them and polish them with rags. Then she'd spit a generous gob of saliva on each boot and rub it furiously in a frenzy of polishing.

When they were as gleaming and shiny as could be, sweet Lyuba would hold out the boot threaded on her arm up to the elbow, rotate her arm to the right, to the left, and right again, examining with satisfaction the image of her sweet little face with its pug nose and double chin reflected in the boot, and smile.

Lyuba's boots came to right below her padded knees, pink, jiggly, plump, and dimpled under her short skirt.

Sweet Lyuba was always laughing.

Sometimes she didn't smell so good.

Sergei always smelled good.

Until they got together, and then Sergei had that new scent that I'd already smelled.

The boots brought Lyuba and Sergei together. They fell in love because of the boots. Neither one could take off their boots by themselves, not even with the help of the special tool made for that purpose, which, unfortunately, was no help at all. Taking off those boots required the friendly cooperation of another person who stood in front of you, wrapped both hands around the booted foot, placed it between his knees, and pulled hard. Pulled and pulled and pulled.

Until finally, the foot was removed from the boot and the one who removed it would fly backward with a cry of victory: Hooray!

The boot removal ceremony: Hooray! Hooray!! Hooray!!!

Every evening, sweet Lyuba would come and ask my mother or father to help her take off her beloved boots, her pets, her twin babies. I was still too small and weak.

Every evening, tall, fair Sergei would come with the same request: to help him take off his boots.

Naturally and obviously, they started taking each other's boots off and fell in love.

It was wonderful.

My mother and father were proud and happy. I was less so.

Sweet Lyuba and tall, handsome Sergei didn't live in the same room. The entire length of the hallway separated their rooms.

Every night, sweet Lyuba would tap on the floor with her pink, plump bare feet on her way to Sergei's room and back. Maybe it was my mother who advised her that it was better to get up tired but happy, to tap quietly on the floor back to her room and not invite Sergei there. Maybe she said that based on her experience of loving Avreim'ele the idealist, whom she'd followed to blazing Palestine.

Dozing in Lyuba's room were the empty, orphaned boots.

SWEET LYUBA AND SERGEI LOVED TO GO OUT, AND SOMETIMES they took me with them for a night on the town. And so, for the first time in my life, I was inside a theater. The size, the dimming lights, the curtain, the stage, the audience. Later, in Krakow, I saw many huge, opulent theaters, but that theater in Lvov would always be my first. There is only one first theater.

It was filled with the cheerful din of our cherished Red Army and its officers. They were young and lively, although to me they were grown-ups, and the world was divided into two main groups: the grown-ups and me. For the time being, they were all alive; the long road to Berlin still awaited most of them. They wanted so much to be cheerful.

How many of their relatives were murdered when the retreating Germans left behind scorched earth lined with corpses? How many of their relatives died of disease and hunger in besieged Leningrad? How many of their comrades fell in battle? How many of them had an arm or a leg amputated? And how many of them would return to their homeland after flying the red flag with the hammer and sickle over the Reichstag in Berlin?

They would return and continue to build their Communism under the watchful eye of our *batiushka*, Generalisimus Tovarish Stalin. I loved that Stalin very much then.

And how many of them would be sent to gulags by that good *batiushka* and die from hard labor, exhaustion, disease, hunger, and the Siberian cold?

So many of my mother's Communist friends, those who weren't salon Communists like her, went to Russia even before the war to build the just, new world, to build Communism and save people from the shame of hunger and injustice, from exploitation and anti-Semitism, and never returned.

Those lively young soldiers boomed and roared, laughed and applauded. They looked happy.

So did Sergei and sweet Lyuba. So did I.

The performances were spectacular. Dancers in short skirts carrying red parasols, their bare limbs embarrassing me, a dancer with a hundred long, thin black braids and ballooning pants, clowns, singers, recitations of long and short poems that I too would learn by heart so quickly and would love to recite dramatically, with all my heart.

I understood everything. When the Russian Red Army liberated us and saved our lives, I was seven and I learned to understand Russian.

I completely forgot the beautiful Russian language, the language of the victors and liberators, the minute my foot, shod in a high, clumsy brown shoe that had a painful metal insole, kicked an Israeli orange on the vomit-soaked deck of the immigrant ship, the *Galila*.

I sent that orange to the bottom of the ancient sea, and through the rising fog I saw the silhouette of a mountain and white buildings sliding down to the port with its cranes, and in the middle of the mountain, a gold dome.

And a new story began.

The magician's act was the most amazing of all.

Thin, tall, and agile, he looked like Mephisto in paintings. He wore a black frock coat, a top hat, white gloves, and a yellow bow tie. He pulled an endless number of colorful, tied-together handkerchiefs out of his hand, separated shiny, linked metal rings, performed all sorts of card tricks I didn't understand, and hypnotized people.

He asked if anyone was willing to give him a watch, a real live watch. Watches were expensive and important in those days. Sergei volunteered and gave him his watch, despite sweet, frightened Lyuba's objections. I was dumbstruck and paralyzed with terror. Before the astounded audience's eyes, the magician crushed Sergei's watch with a powerful hammer. But he didn't stop at that. He stomped on the watch and jumped on it a few times.

But he was a magician.

That was magic.

To the joyful cries of the admiring audience, the watch was returned to Sergei, completely intact. It hadn't missed even a minute on its way to death and back.

Sergei would fall in the battle for Berlin. I don't know what happened to sweet Lyubitchka.

They were so beautiful, that couple. Sergei, the Jewish Red Army officer, and sweet, blond Lyuba. My mother and father used to gaze at them with the satisfaction of matchmakers when they came to our room to drink tea they sucked through the small lumps of sugar they held in their mouths, making sounds that were considered utterly impolite in Krakow. They told stories and jokes, and they even sang and danced.

Sergei had a small harmonica, and sweet, plump Lyuba danced the *cozachok* with remarkable lightness, stamped her boots, her gleaming twins.

Sergei would sing *cestushka*. He taught me a few lively, clever songs that I've never forgotten. For example:

> Our doll has fallen ill
> I think she's caught a chill.
> Call the doctor, if you will
> So he can give her a pill.

Or:

> A star that fell from the sky
> Landed on a chicken, and it couldn't fly.
> The poor old chicken made such a to-do
> Squawking and clucking cock-a-doodle-doo!

They sang the sorrowful songs of Mother Russia in harmony. Even the lively songs were sorrowful. Liberators' songs.

I loved those songs so much.

Songs about the wide Volga River, songs about the vast steppes, songs about the wonderful Baikel Lake, songs about taigas and happy children.

There was a song about a girl named Kalinka, a song about parting and a blue kerchief. And there were songs about oppressed peoples forging a new and better future, about red flags and longing.

The most beautiful was the one Tovarish Batiushka Stalin loved, and it wasn't beautiful only because he loved it.

It was a song called "Suliko."

I always felt like crying when I heard it. And sometimes I did cry. How beautifully sweet Lyuba and tall Sergei sang it together, she in her high voice and he in his deep one.

It's pleasant to cry because of a song.

Later, on the ship *Galila*, when I was twelve and a half, I heard Tzippi the sabra with the suntanned thighs and her sabra friends try desperately to sing those melodies they had put strange, harsh words to. How pretentious! What did they have to do with my beloved Sergei and sweet Lyuba? What did they have to do with my liberating Red Army? The nerve of them!

Sergei recited Pushkin's fairy tales about Ruslan and Ludmila, about the wise cat that walked silently back and forth on a gold chain.

I would read everything Pushkin wrote and cry endless tears about Tatiana's letter and her wretched fate, and for tall, lively, strong, and dead Sergei.

We won the war!

My mother recovered. My father had a job. Sergei and sweet Lyuba were in love. I had to part from my beautiful dead rat, but I had a doll.

Those were good days.

VERY SLOWLY, A FEW AT A TIME, THE REPATRIATES BEGAN TO return—the Polish refugees who had been deported into Russia before the German invasion. In those distant days, after the Ribbentrop-Molotov Pact but before Operation Barbarossa, the Russians didn't want a "nonloyal element" on their border, a border that rapidly turned into a front.

The Russians didn't trust the loyalty of those Polish refugees who came to Lvov in their flight from the German army, refugees just like us. In many cases, they were right. There were some who preferred the cultured German invaders to the primitive, *muzhik* Russians. Some even wanted to go back to the territory occupied by the Germans, and most of those never went back anywhere ever again.

The Russians didn't want all the Polish officers who came to Lvov, nor did they want the Jews—the intellectuals, the merchants, the capitalists. There were many Jewish officers, some of them high ranking, all German speaking, since Galicia had been part of the Austro-Hungarian Empire for years, and the empire had been good to the Jews. His Majesty, Emperor Franz Yosef, had protected them.

On government orders, Russian soldiers armed with Pepesha rifles broke into people's houses, sometimes at night or at dawn, and ordered them to pack a few essential belongings. That's what my mother told me, told me, and told me.

She told me how one woman, confused and disoriented, took her rolling pin with her when she was deported.

Those people, including the elderly and the sick, babies and children, were ordered to go immediately to the train station.

The train station was still an ordinary place then.

The stunned people went to the train station. Dozens, hundreds, thousands. They squeezed into railroad cars, my mother and I among them. It was a disaster. Deportation into Russia? Who knows where. My mother told me, told me, and told me because, after all, none of the deportees knew that their lives had been saved that day.

The Russian soldiers hadn't yet become the beloved liberators. They burst into our apartment in the morning, after my father had gone to work, and took us—myself, my mother, and her niece, Perelka, her brother Moshe's daughter. My mother had found her and took care of her after her parents were unable to escape eastward, remained in Poland, and were later murdered.

In the end, Perelka was murdered too, in the ghetto in Lvov.

A sweet, beautiful young girl.

A Russian acquaintance of my father's saw us on the train and ran to tell my father. Alarmed, my father came to the train station with Tovarish Bulani, who was the big boss of the slaughterhouse and tanning factory. Tovarish Bulani, wearing a black leather jacket, officer's boots, and a cap, immediately found a way to get us out of the railroad car.

Were we saved?

Perelka, daughter of my mother's brother, had been separated from us and was in another car. Wanting to save her too, my mother ran along the entire length of the train yelling Perelka, Perelka, Perelka, until she found her. Come, my mother said, we're free, and took her off the train. She took her to her death. Until the end of her life, until she died at the age of ninety and a half, my mother mourned Perelka, blaming herself for her death.

Perelka continued to live with us when the Germans came, and she lived with us in the ghetto. When my mother and father made contact with Hania Seremet, they planned to send Perelka to the village with me. I think she was nineteen then. Perelka refused to leave the ghetto. She was afraid. I was sent away, my mother and father escaped to the hiding place in the home of Juzef Juzak, the carpenter and alcoholic, and his wife Rozalia, the primitive Ukranian who believed that troubles brought lice, while Perelka stayed behind. The ghetto was liquidated, and for fourteen days, so they said, it exploded and burned.

With Perelka inside it.

Perelka was murdered too.

Till the day she died, my mother mourned Perelka, tormented herself for not saving her by convincing her to escape from the ghetto before the final liquidation.

Perelka said to my mother, Auntie, I'm afraid. She stayed and was murdered.

My mother told me that she dreamed about her, about her and the two men my mother loved—Avreim'ele, the pioneer she followed to Palestine, where her white skin burned and her teeth crumbled, and Zimek, the handsome engineer, friend of Dov, her beloved sister Minka's husband. Minka, who was an extremely beautiful, hunchbacked woman, had given Dov two daughters, a dark one named Pnina and a fair one named Rachel. That Dov was such a large man that he could walk around with all three in his arms—his tiny hunchbacked wife and the girls, who were stunningly beautiful.

They were all murdered.

My mother loved Zimek, who married another woman, an elegant woman, unlike my mother whose fanciest outfit, in the spirit of Communism, which did not believe in decoration, was a blue plissé skirt and a white blouse. My mother turned down Zimek's marriage proposal. She considered it a bourgeois act. The woman who took Zimek away from her was also a salon Communist, but unlike my mother, she dressed up and wore lipstick and rouge, and didn't consider marriage to Zimek a bourgeois act; on the contrary, she initiated it. How painful that was.

My mother talked, talked, and talked.

I didn't like those stories. I always tried to get away from them. She didn't tell them to me, but to others, and I heard. Obviously, I never asked my mother to tell me about her lovers. That's all I needed, for her to tell me.

Zimek and his bride, the coquette Hanni, went to Russia to build the good, just world. That was before the war. Later, my mother married my father. His good, pure smile won her heart. That's what she said, said, and said.

Zimek and his bride never came back from great Mother Russia, or from great Father Stalin, the *batiushka*.

What were they thinking, those young idealists, my mother, my father, and all the other Communists?

And the trains set out on their way without us, set out in the direction of life. A harsh life, a life of hunger and hard labor, disease, distress, extreme climates. A terrible life—Siberian cold or Asiatic heat and death.

Human, universal death. Not Jewish death. The war was everyone's. It was hard for everyone, my mother and father said, not only for the deportees, but also for the locals—the Cossacks, the Uzbekans, the Tajikans, who suddenly encountered all those Europeans, the Jews, the Poles, the refugees of the great transfer.

The ones who did return from Russia, the repatriates, usually came back with their families, and some had married there and returned with new children, children born in Siberia, in Kazakhstan, in the Urals, in the vast expanses of Mother Russia. Despite the terrible stories those people told, stories about cold and hunger, about disease and death, my mother and father treated them as if they'd come back from summer camp. My parents didn't consider them survivors of war.

No one had hunted them down in order to murder them just because they were Jews. There had been a war in the world, and no one had enough food, not even the soldiers of the Red Army. And after all, they saved us. We owed our lives to the soldiers of the Red Army.

Some of those who returned from exile in Russia were given rooms in the big building we lived in. We lived there together, a large and varied population: natives of Lvov whose families had lived there for generations, like the old woman, Mleko; Polish and Ukrainian refugees; people like us, who had been saved; those who came back from the depths of Russia; Russian officers like tall Sergei and sweet Lyuba; and other officers who brought their wives and children with them to Lvov, and sometimes their *babushkas*. To me, all the women looked like sweet Lyuba, but none were as sweet as she was.

For the Russian officers' wives, the provincial, battered city of Lvov, only just liberated from the German occupation, was the height of Western culture. Those Russian women admired my mother. She was still thin and she was still being treated with the special gas that was injected directly into her lung with a long, hollow needle, but in their eyes she was a paragon of culture and elegance, *kultura* and *elegantsia*.

They would drop in to visit, those plump blonds with belts tied tightly around their waists that divided their bodies into two round sections as if they were hourglasses, wanting to absorb European *kultura* from my mother, the dignified lady, the Polish *pani*. They would fix their blue eyes on her and try to imitate her manners, her walk, her cooking, but what they were mainly interested in was fashion. They were hungry for fashion—the European fashion of Lvov after the liberation. Even though my mother and her snobbish Polish girlfriends were Communists, albeit salon Communists, they made fun of the Russian officers' wives and laughed at them behind their backs. They were amused by their naiveté and coarseness, and especially their desire to be stylish, as stylish as they were. And they considered themselves extremely stylish. They mocked those Russian women when they went to officers' balls wearing embroidered nightgowns of shiny satin that they bought in the markets, believing they had purchased elegant ball gowns.

The women who had originally ordered those expensive silk, satin, or fine linen nightgowns had probably been dead for a long time. Suffocated by gas, their corpses burned, their ashes scattered.

You could buy anything in the markets.

Most of the objects were "after the Jews"; that's how they were described. The belongings of Jews who were murdered. Books, including those that had strange, square letters like the ones in the black book that survived from the Jewish gynecologist's library. Silver goblets, candlesticks, boxes with small, latticed windows. Inscribed bowls, paintings, musical instruments. Violins in black cases lined with red velvet.

You could put a baby in a case like that and escape with it.

Crystal, fine porcelain pieces, delicate and half-transparent. And albums, a great many albums, some bound in velvet with silver fittings, containing photographs of very serious, handsome people.

They were all murdered. People dead forever.

And lamps, furs, whole foxes with luxuriant tails, with legs and nails and glazed looks, silver foxes and red foxes.

There, in the market, my mother once bought a piece of fur, sad Persian lamb they skin from lamb fetuses torn from the sliced wombs of their mother sheep. That piece of fur became the hair of the precious doll my mother made for me.

The belongings of people who once lived and now were dead.

Once, a Polish peddler in the market offered to sell my father fur slippers that had embroidered tops and soles made of parchment from the Torah. My father bought those slippers and they stayed in the family for years.

What a shame it is that I didn't take an interest in those things. I don't even know what chapter of the Torah the soles of those slippers were cut from.

Maybe from the chapter when God tells Abraham to "go from your country"? Or from the Sacrifice of Isaac? Or maybe from the chapter in which the children of light found refuge in the ark and couldn't go outside because death was outside—not German death, but a wet death, death in the water? What a shame. It didn't interest me at all. Or maybe it was the chapter about manna, the manna that fell from the sky, still my favorite story.

AND THEN THE WAR ENDED. WE TOOK BERLIN.

Dear, tall Sergei was killed; he was dead.

Lyuba cried and left. She went back to Mother Russia, her stomach round, a sign that she too would be a mother. A baby was living in her stomach, the son of Sergei, who was blown up.

Poland was divided once again. Lvov remained a Russian city, and a large area that had belonged to the defeated Germans—what a lovely phrase, "defeated Germans"—was annexed to Poland. The border between Poland and conquered Germany was now along the Oder and Nysa

Rivers—also names that echo in memory. Hundreds of thousands of people began wandering from place to place, some of their own volition.

My mother and father packed a few valises and bundles and were at the railroad station again, perhaps at the same station from which the deportees to Russia had left. This time, we were going home.

"Home."

What is "home" anyway?

The trains took off in the opposite direction, westward. This time, west was the direction of life.

The crowd of people gathered on the platform all looked alike—alive, worried, tired, and nervous, and they all had the same color, a kind of monotonous gray-brown. So did we. So did I, and I was eight, still wearing the scratchy jacket that had belonged to the soda factory manager, whose fate we would never know, tied around my waist with a coarse rope, the sleeves rolled up, thick and heavy around my wrists. It was hot. After a few days on the platform, my mother, my father, and I were pushed into a car by those gray-brown people carrying stuffed blankets, sparse pillows, gray sacks, crudely stitched bundles, straw valises, leather valises, and cardboard valises.

Baggage.

The names and addresses of the people who had once owned that baggage were written on the valises, bags, and bundles in indelible purple pencil, if the valise was light colored, and in white if it was dark. I had always known how to read, because in the hiding place, I'd learned to distinguish between the unmoving black marks and the black marks that scurried around on the newspaper spread under my bent head when my mother combed my hair with a fine-tooth comb to remove the lice.

I read all the names and all the addresses on the valises, bags, and bundles. Tall mountains of valises and bundles that had once belonged to people who were murdered and would never go back to the addresses written on the valises or on the bundles, and I saw photographs from the extermination camps—sophisticated death camps. Photographs like that reached our house, and I couldn't avoid seeing them.

Mountains of valises and bundles, a landscape of death. Did anyone ever go and visit those addresses? After all, they were so clear, written in such carefully printed letters. I learned about it, against my will. All those people were suffocated by gas, their corpses were burned and their ashes scattered.

Could it be?

How could it be?

Did it happen?

I heard the stories. I saw the pictures. I read the memoirs and books of testimony.

So many people. All sorts of people, men and women, old and young, children and babies. And little girls, like me. They'd been persecuted, humiliated, starved. Their dignity had been crushed, their spirits trampled upon. They'd been hunted down and crammed into railroad cars, cattle cars.

And transported.

In terrible heat, in biting cold.

Packed together in the dark, no light, no water, no food.

The stench of excrement and urine, vomit and flatulence, fear and sweat. Many died on the way. And the tracks led on and on and on. Do I have to know all this?

The trains stopped and the people were ordered to get off.

To the screams of the German soldiers and the barking of dogs that were set on them, the people were led to a place where they were told to take off their clothes, their heads were shaved, and they were shoved into a large, sealed bunker with small openings in the ceiling.

From those openings above them, crystals the color of fine celadon were sprayed on them. Zyklon B. And the crystals turned into gas that annihilated them all. They all suffocated. They all died. Do I have to know all that?

They suffocated and became a pile of naked, dead people. The small children too.

And little Jewish girls like me.

That's what the few survivors told us and told us and told us. I didn't want to hear all that.

Finally, the person who sprinkled the greenish crystals would look through one of the slits in the ceiling, and when he saw that everyone was completely dead, he would order the gas chamber to be emptied of all those people.

Someone who was there, who survived, told us.

He was a Jew. He wasn't sent to suffocate in the gas chamber. That was his job—to take the dead people out of the chamber. And maybe one of them was still alive?

He had to arrange them in a pile at the door to a large oven with a tall chimney.

A crematorium. Then he and the others who worked with him put the murdered people onto a conveyor belt, one by one, and pushed them into the opening of the blazing furnace.

And the people burned and burned and burned.

That's what the people with the blue numbers on their left forearms told my parents. I heard them telling it. And I read all the booklets and books written by people who were in those camps and remained alive, and I saw the photographs. I know that all those things were in the world.

Could it be?

They scattered the ashes.

I LOVED EVERYTHING ABOUT THAT TRAIN, THE TRAIN OF life that took us back to Krakow. The passing countryside racing backward, the movement of the car on the tracks, the clickety-clack of the wheels, the sharp tooting and whistling of the engine. I spent hours looking out the window that opened differently from all the windows I'd seen before. I counted electricity poles, I counted telegraph poles, I counted semaphores.

I was a giant and the train was a toy that I could lift with two fingers, gently, so the passengers wouldn't fall, and move instantly to our destination, Krakow. That's where I was born, in the most luxurious maternity hospital in the city. My mother told me, told me, and told me.

Most wonderful of all was when the track curved and you could see the whole train, the cars and the engine—a terrifying, noisy dragon that whistled and emitted smoke from a chimney. Sometimes the smoke was white, like the clouds in the sky in the village where I was a Christian girl, and sometimes it was black and thick.

At night, in the dark, sparks shot out of the chimney and my mother warned me again not to stick my head out the window. The warning was even written next to the window; I read it. Leaning out the window is forbidden. A spark might fly into your eye and burn it. Until that was exactly what happened. My eye hurt and teared, but it didn't burn.

The red emergency handle in the car mesmerized me. The prohibition against pulling it tempted me. I longed to pull it almost as much as I had craved evil Mrs. Fishman's clown. They didn't let me play with the clown, and they didn't let me pull the handle. We traveled for a very long time. Our car was sometimes detached from the engine that pulled it and attached to different engines, and the train was lengthened or shortened, and moved on and on and on. My mother recited a poem by Julian Tuwim, and the train clickety-clacked, in the words of that poem.

We could get off for a while at the small stations. My mother would take me to the faucets between the tracks, special faucets for filling the engines' boilers.

I hated it when she undressed me there and washed me. I was so embarrassed that I wanted to disappear. It was terrible. I was afraid someone would see me. I was so ashamed. I hated people looking at me when I was dressed, and there I was, undressed. After all, I wanted to see and not be seen, like that boy in the fairy tale who had a magic hat that allowed him to see and not be seen. That was the hat for me. That was the kind of hat I wanted. I still hadn't been subjected to the terrible pom-pom hat that came in one of the packages from America, the hat that would destroy my life and give me a tic, a kind of involuntary turn of my head.

But my mother had a will of her own. My mother wanted a clean little girl. I still had no idea then how much they'd have to fix me and improve me in the future when my mother no longer had to worry about the war or her illness. She still wore a kind of mask on her mouth whenever she came close to me, a surgeon's mask that was supposed to keep the Koch bacillus from infecting me. I was immune—she knew that, because after the war, they tested me—and she wasn't contagious anymore after all the treatments she was still getting, but that's how it was. The white mask eliminated any risk, any hug, any kiss. Could a kiss be lethal?

We rode on and on and on.

A very long time, too little time. And I was eight.

We arrived.

Krakow.

JONASZ STERN, THE PAINTER, WAS WAITING FOR US AT THE railroad station.

Then, I still didn't know that he didn't know how to draw a camel. I still didn't know that I'd love him. I still didn't know that his ascetic mien—the sensual lips, sunken cheeks, and piercing expression—would be my ideal of male beauty. Fair, glowing Sergei was defeated by dark beauty. Jonasz Stern was my mother's girlhood boyfriend and a Communist, a real Communist, not a salon Communist like her. And now, after the war, being a Communist paid off very well.

Tall, gaunt Jonasz and his beautiful, tormented face. Two deep, marvelous grooves furrowed his cheeks. From his youth, wherever he lived, he established a fighting Communist cell, went to prison, staged hunger strikes, and almost went to fight the fascists in Spain. And now, when he was finally building his new, just world, he found us, his comrades, a place, a room to live in.

A room in Krakow. A room in Krakow after the war was an extremely rare commodity. My mother and father and even I seemed to think that was right. Maybe I didn't think so, only because I didn't think about things like that. The stories I told myself and the books I read were my real life in those days. I saw, but I thought I was invisible. That suited me.

Finally, it paid to be a Communist.

That was also a room in a shared apartment. Those strange combinations of people sharing apartments after the war.

It was a six-room apartment with a communal kitchen and bathroom, in a corner building. One Sobieskiego Street. The former elegant, luxurious entrance. Already former even then.

The apartment was huge. Expensive parquet, wide glass doors, and high French windows. In the past, before the war, an old aristocratic lady, Pani Jaroslawa Morawska, had lived there alone. It was her city apartment. Her small palace was located on a family estate not far from Krakow. The entire estate, including the palace and all its contents, was nationalized after the war, and a strange assortment of tenants was sent by government order to live in Pani Morawska's opulent city apartment. We were the last to come, and we were Jews. The worst of all. As justice and equality dictated, Pani Morawska lived in one room, not even the largest, most luxurious one.

The large, luxurious room, the corner room with the round balcony encircled by an art nouveau grillwork railing, was given to Jonasz Stern's lover, Panna Jadwiga Madziarska, also a painter, who painted my portrait in pastel colors.

Panna Jadwiga Madziarska had fair hair—bleached, my mother declared with the expertise of a natural blond—that she wore in a crown of permanented bottle curls as frizzy as the steel wool used to polish pots. She had a high, shrill, self-indulgent voice and you could hear a question mark at the end of every sentence she spoke. She moved her torso and jiggled her breasts when she talked. She had round, blinking purple eyes. In my mother's opinion, Panna Jadwiga came from an inferior milieu; she was stupid and had never had *kindershtube*. Obviously, my mother didn't think she was right for Jonasz Stern. She used to say that anyone who wants a swan imagines that his goose *is* a swan, but a *goose* is what he has. In Polish rhyme, that sounds even worse.

Panna Jadwiga Madziarska was a talented painter. My mother commissioned her to paint my portrait. I sat for her several times in her corner room with the round balcony and art nouveau grillwork railing, the most beautiful room in the apartment. Panna Jadwiga Madziarska painted with a bird's movements, a bird with permanented blond curls. The portrait was excellent, despite my great disappointment that Panna Jadwiga had left out the tiny black polka dots on my new pink dress with the short puffy sleeves and the ruffles on the bodice that the dressmaker, Panna Zofia Duda of the Paris salon, had made for me.

In the portrait, I'm sitting, rather bored and melancholy, looking at the observer with large, dark doe eyes. The corners of my lips show the hint of a smile and my head is adorned with a pair of silly ribbons in the same color pink as my dress.

I never forgave Panna Jadwiga for not painting the polka dots on the dress. I thought that was a terrible omission. I told her, but nothing helped. I'm the only one who knows that there were polka dots on the fabric of the dress made for me by Panna Zofia Duda, the dressmaker who sewed Paris fashions for all the ladies who could afford the luxury, even the salon Communists. Her only son, Karol, who had an eye covered with an opaque white film and didn't have a father, was run over by a tram. The dentist was run over by a tram too.

Panna Jadwiga painted me again, in the post-Cubist style that was very fashionable in Krakow at the time.

When she saw the post-Cubist portrait, my mother said that I looked like a cross section of a coal mine and she didn't buy the painting.

The government bought that portrait, in which I look like a bisected coal mine, for a substantial sum of money and hung it in one of the rooms of the Polish Defense Ministry. Quite a few Jews worked there, some of them veteran Communists, who shared Jonasz Stern's aims. That's how I reached the highest places.

Panna Jadwiga painted a portrait of my mother too, which she also rejected immediately. In it, my mother is painted as a figure made up of twisted tubes crowded together and pressing against each other, breaking apart and coming together, wound around each other like a noose dangling from a gallows. Tubes with no beginning and no end, an ingenious, many-branched, labyrinthian weave.

How did Panna Jadwiga know all that? How was she able to imagine my mother's tangled, tortuous, manipulative, brilliant character?

The Polish government paid a substantial sum for that Constructivist portrait of my mother, as they had for my post-Cubist portrait, and hung it in one of the rooms of the Polish Ministry of Industry.

In those years, the beautiful, wise years in Krakow, I was introduced to all the arts—museums and exhibitions, concerts and ballets, books, theater and films, luxurious buildings and lush gardens—masterpieces that people wrote, painted, scored, and built before I was born. It was wonderful. But especially distinctive, more distinctive than the others, were the paintings done by the live, dark, gloomy-looking Jonasz Stern. He didn't know how to draw a camel when I asked him once. But he painted unusual pictures that were all titled *Composition—Composition No. 1, Composition No. 5*. They were all very similar, and even after long, intense observation, you couldn't identify a single familiar shape in them. It was abstract painting, Jonasz told me. Modern painting, my mother said, and despite her reservations, she took me to every exhibition. It was considered the bon ton. I'll always remember those new shapes that I saw in Jonasz's paintings. I'll always be interested in them.

I WAS LESS INTERESTED IN THE PEOPLE AROUND ME.

People like Pani Jaroslawa Morawska, for example, the elderly aristocrat, who used to wear dresses with stand-up lace collars with a jabot of ruffles that curled and cascaded like whipped cream on a cake, pinned with a cameo showing the glittering silhouette of a young goddess in translucent mother-of-pearl. She wore pearl necklaces that wound around her neck three times and rose and fell on her heaving chest when she bumped into me in the hallway. Then she'd run off to her room in a panic.

Such *degradatsia*! Jews in her apartment! A little Jewish girl in her hallway!

My mother said she was an anti-Semite. I didn't think about things like that. I saw and was invisible. Maybe she just hated everyone, the whole world, and the Jews were no exception? All I sensed was the intense embarrassment she exuded, the evasive glances whenever she met me in the communal hallway.

And her hate was justified. Everything had been taken from her.

Her entire world had collapsed.

Everything had been taken from her: her title, her property, her honor. And worst of all—her son.

Her only son, the son she bore late in life.

Her son, an aging bachelor, an officer in the Armiya Krajowa, the underground "Home Army" that fought and killed Germans during the occupation, fell in the Warsaw uprising. That mighty, failed uprising the Poles staged as the Red Army approached Warsaw in the hope that they, the patriotic Poles, the Home Army, would liberate their capital themselves.

It didn't happen that way.

By stopping and waiting on the far side of the Vistula, the Red Army allowed the Germans to suppress the uprising and kill the rebels. The capital was bombed for weeks. Almost no building was left standing. Warsaw was flattened into a desert of ruins. Thousands were killed, underground fighters, citizens, children, weakening the Poles until they were defeated. Only then did the Red Army renew its attack and liberate the ruins that were once Warsaw from the German occupation.

Stanislav, Pani Jaroslawa Morawska's officer son, was buried under a sea of smashed buildings. His body was never found. They said he died near the ruins of the ghetto, whose uprising had already been put down.

The day before we left our homeland for Palestine, my mother, my father, and I stood on those heaps of rubble near the monumental statue erected in honor of the ghetto rebels. There, the taxi driver told us that the guards at the foot of the statue, the armed soldiers with glittering bayonets protruding from the ends of their rifles, had been stationed there after Jew haters repeatedly vandalized the statue. The story saddened my father greatly: for more than four years, Communism had been trying to improve the world and destroy anti-Semitism in the process, and they had still not succeeded!

Friar Marek, the Capuchin monk, told us about Pani Jaroslawa Morawska's son, Captain Stanislav Morawski. They were fellow students in the same gymnasium in Krakow and were friends even though the monk came from an inferior family. Marek and Stanislav fell in love with the same girl; Maria was her name. Maria loved them both, and they lived in a paradise for three. Maria left them both and went to Paris, studied classical languages at the Sorbonne, and never went back to Poland.

After the tragedy of her departure, Stanislav wanted to become a monk, but he became an army man instead, while his best friend, who'd always wanted to join the army, became a monk. Marek, the monk, had an enormous amount of love in him, and he was the lover of one of the women who lived in our apartment. That's how we met him.

His lover was a teacher, a pious spinster.

She might have been thirty. To me, anyone over fifteen was old. I thought that love between two such old people was impossible, repulsive and unreal, just as the idea of physical contact between my parents was out of the question. All my father did was stroke my mother's soft, straight blond hair with his soft, warm hands, nothing else. And even that was too much and went on for too long.

The pious spinster, the monk's lover, always wore shapeless, baggy dresses in gray or navy blue with dazzling white starched collars and cuffs. She always seemed to be moving inward, and even when she extended her hand, she seemed to be withdrawing it. She had sparse, dark hair streaked with gray. She rolled it over her ears into two ponytails the thickness of thin mouse's tails, as thin as the tails of Mysia and Tysia, my beloved mice from the hiding place. She spoke quietly and wore a beautiful medallion embossed with a picture of the Madonna and her baby, sweet Jezusik, hanging on a thin gold chain.

Her lover, the monk, would visit her at least two evenings a week, and sometimes he even stayed till morning. More than once, I met him in line for the toilet or the bath. Friar Marek, lover of the pious teacher, Panna Kristina Kowalski, wore a long brown robe called a habit, made of thick, coarse material that looked scratchy, like the soda factory manager's jacket whose rolled-up sleeves weigh heavily on my wrists to this day. The robe had a hood, and a thick white rope with several knots in it was wound around his waist. His black hair was shaved in a perfect circle on the top of his head, and amazingly enough, his beard was red. He wore sandals with rubber soles on his bare feet, in winter too, even when it snowed. He walked quietly and spoke quietly in a pleasant voice. He would come into our room to visit and tell my mother and father about the Warsaw uprising and the Warsaw Ghetto uprising. He'd been there through the whole war. He lived next to the ghetto and saw and heard everything. The shelling, the murders, the deportations, the *aktions*. He heard the people screaming, the children sobbing, the babies wailing. He told us about the people who jumped from the top floors of burning buildings, throwing down their babies wrapped like bundles, running out of cellars, bunkers, and sewers, hunted down, murdered, until the liquidation was complete. He told us that the members of the Polish underground tried to smuggle weapons to the Jews who revolted in the ghetto. He told us that some of them were saved.

The pleasant monk, the lover of our neighbor the pious teacher, also told us about the bald, bespectacled pope in Rome and his friendly relations with the Germans.

I didn't listen to those boring conversations. That was after I saw the photographs in a large, flat, black book, which I read, just as I read all the books my father brought me. Thin little books bound in cardboard that fell apart instantly, books in which people who had managed to remain alive told horrendous, inconceivable stories. And they told them all in simple, ordinary words.

Could it be?

I saw and was invisible.

Invisible and guilty. My mother had already managed to hang the Damocles sword of guilt over my head.

She didn't give birth to me only once. Every time I was saved, she was the one who saved me, gave birth to me once again. What would have happened otherwise? Otherwise, might I have been one of the small figures with twisted limbs in those photographs?

I liked the pictures of the pink, sweet, good baby Jesus better than those black, evil photos. Even though he came to a bad end.

THE WORLD WAS FULL OF IMAGES OF THE SWEET, GOOD BABY Jesus. Christmas was coming. There were decorated pine trees, glittering and enchanted, in the churches, and a kind silent play going on under them: plump, smiling, pink Jesus extending his round arms from a straw-filled manger, and bending over him with an expression of gentle wonder on her face was Mary, his mother, Joseph the carpenter at her side. Juzef Juzak, the alcoholic who hid my mother and father and finally me, was a carpenter too, and in his apartment in Lvov, while the war was still in the world, I saw that scene set in a ruined stable. In the corner next to the wall were animals—a cow and a donkey. I didn't see any pigs, and they'd been my favorite animals. Such a familiar place: a stable, animals, and sweet Jesus sleeping on a pile of straw just like the straw I slept on in the village. I could smell the odors. A gold star with a tail hung over everything, and in the distance, three magi were approaching. One of them had a black face. It was so enchanting. The star led them to Bethlehem, the place where baby Jesus was born. And that place was in the Holy Land. Palestine was in the Holy Land too. My aunt Salka, her husband Moshe, and their two children, Danny and Ruthie, were also there.

Salka was the only aunt from my mother's family who survived, the only sister left. The Germans murdered all the others.

It's very hot in Palestine, my mother told me. And she knew, because she'd been there once, before I was born. Jews lived there and they had problems. Later, there'd be war there too, and the Jews would have an army called the Hagana.

They'd win that war, but it wasn't the Germans they'd defeat.

The Germans were already defeated.

My father, who knew everything and could do anything with his hands, taught me to paint a blue star called a Magen David, the symbol of the Jews in Palestine. That blue star had been drawn on the white armbands the Jews in our ghetto in Lvov had to wear. In Lvov, it was blue; in other places, it was yellow. I decorated the blue star I painted with letters and greetings I wrote and painted for my mother and father. They were very worried and were always talking, talking, and talking about what would happen to the Jews in Palestine.

They still hadn't told me that we had to go there too.

How beautiful that gold star with the streaming tail was, the star that led the magi to the manger where sweet Jesus lay! Much more beautiful than the Jews' blue star.

And there were songs and ceremonies and meals and midnight masses. We were Jews, but I also had a tree, a tree someone gave my father. He brought it home to me and Friar Marek helped me decorate it. We didn't believe in any god, not in little Jesus either, but it was so beautiful. Everything was so beautiful.

I painted the nativity scene; I colored and cut it out myself. There was little Jesus with the Holy Mother Mary and Joseph the carpenter, his father, and all kinds of animals. Of course, I added a pig, my favorite animal, and a cat, because I knew how to draw cats the best. I could never draw cows, for example. I pasted all those figures on the cover of a cardboard box and added a few shepherds kneeling and praying, and on the side I added the three angels, one of them black. Over everything, I hung the comet with the tail, which I had cut from cardboard and covered with the gold wrapping of a chocolate bar I'd received in a package from Switzerland, from Uncle Goldman—a very distant relative of my father's. That very distant relative and his family had been living in Switzerland for years, even before the war that was in the world, and they were very religious and very rich. We were his only relatives outside of Switzerland that the Germans hadn't managed to murder.

Not very often, he would send us a not-very-large package. He's a miser, my mother said. And because he was religious, he certainly wouldn't have been pleased to know that the gold paper wrapping of the Swiss chocolate bar he sent us, Lindt chocolate—the finest there was, my mother said—was adorning the comet heralding the birth of Jezus Cristos, the Messiah and Savior, the tiny baby lying on a bed of straw just like the straw I slept on in the coffin when I was a little Christian girl in the village.

Baby Jezusik lay there with his arms reaching out to bless the entire universe, and then died, and in his suffering on the cross, alone and abandoned, he atoned for all the sins in the world. What hope, what promise, what a wonderful story!

Communism was also hope, promise, a wonderful story.

The story of Jezusik was a sort of continuation of the stories my father used to tell me when we were in the hiding place on Panienska Street. My father whispered those stories to me. We always whispered in that hiding place. If anyone heard us and informed on us, the Germans would come and murder us. My father whispered those stories from the Torah, the book of the Jews, about Jesus's real father, who wasn't Juzef the carpenter but God, the God whose name was Jehovah, the God of the children of light, of the good people, as my father called the Jews, because we weren't allowed to say the word "Jew" in our home.

AFTER THE WAR, THE GOOD PEOPLE WENT BACK TO BEING JEWS, although some of them weren't good at all. Occasionally, people would come to our house, people who survived by chance, by a miracle, by luck, and they would talk.

They talked, talked, and talked.

One of them told us about Srulik, the son of Malvina Gotfreund, a lovely young man who was recruited into the Jewish police and became an enthusiastic follower of the Gestapo's orders. Many people suffered and were murdered because of him. One of them came to our house, sat frozen, didn't eat or drink anything, and talked about Lodz. He was from Lodz. He talked about the Judenrat in the Lodz Ghetto. And there was one who came back alive from an extermination camp and talked about the Jewish kapo, Yeshayahu, who made the prisoners quake in fear. He was a hideous nightmare who beat and murdered them.

Some of those collaborators were identified, caught, tried, and even executed. Many escaped and continued to live among ordinary people.

Those were the kinds of stories I didn't want to hear. They didn't interest me.

The people who came and talked to us were ugly and wretched, and not always clean. Some spoke a different language, similar to German—Yiddish—an unpleasant language, and when they spoke Polish, they distorted it painfully.

I had learned about the Jewish holidays when I was back in an orphanage in Krakow, an orphanage for Jewish children, run by Jews and funded by Jewish money—the money of wealthy American Jews. It was probably very unpleasant for them, those American Jews, to learn that most of the Jews in Europe had been murdered.

In that Jewish orphanage, they taught us songs in a foreign language—Hebrew—without explaining the meaning of the words. They taught us the way you teach animals to do tricks. I used to explain more to my trained mice in the hiding place.

My mother also knew a few words in that language. She learned them when she was in Palestine, where she'd gone to be with her beloved Avreim'ele and to live out her ideal. The blazing sun, the malaria, and maybe the cooling off of love in a tent after a hard day's work drove her back to her native country, to Poland, to Europe, to bourgeois salon Communism.

My mother even sang a few songs to me in that language—sad songs about a shepherd, a shepherdess, and howling jackals.

They sent me to that orphanage when my mother had to go to a sanatorium to continue recovering from her tuberculosis. And there, in that orphanage, they celebrated strange, unfamiliar holidays.

On one of those holidays, they decorated the walls with paper clowns and all sorts of masks and dolls: the mask of a fat king, the mask of a crooked man with a beard and big ears whose name was Haman, the mask of a Jew with a white beard and a blue dress, and the mask of a young girl wearing a gold crown who looked like the Holy Mother, but her name, they told me, was Esther, Queen Esther. Ester'ke, like the lover of good King Casimir, who invited Jews to his kingdom and admired and protected them.

Then they taught us all the incomprehensible songs that had the word "Purim" in them.

Those decorations and songs couldn't compare to the wonderful decorations and songs about plump, pink Jesus who extended his arms in a gesture of acceptance and forgiveness and was crowned with a glowing halo. They couldn't compare to the fragrant Christmas tree decorated with paper chains, fragile glass balls, small flickering candles, and giant, golden walnuts. And they couldn't compare to the Lamb of God made of white sugar that carried a cross on its back, or the brightly painted Easter eggs on the holiday celebrating Jesus's death and resurrection.

Jesus was born and died, was resurrected and then disappeared again, but promised to return. And when he did, the world would end and all the dead people would be resurrected.

Even the ones who'd been choked to death by gas, their bodies burned and their ashes scattered.

You could drink the blood of Jesus and eat his flesh during Mass, in church. And there were processions and hymns, and the priest carrying the host, walking through the streets on his way to give extreme unction to save the soul of someone who was dying, accompanied by two boys wearing white lace dresses swinging incense burners. Those dresses were so beautiful. And the scent was so wonderful, like a gust of wind from a field of ripe wheat, leaving behind a trail of kneeling people with bent heads, their palms pressed together in submissive prayer. And I, a wandering, curious, enthralled little girl, observed the holiday makers, the mourners, the rituals, in that new city where everything was so ancient.

KRAKOW. GRAND, MAJESTIC BUILDINGS, HEAVY GATES, A castle where poets and kings are buried, latticed metalwork, dark stairwells, inner courtyards with a round well in their center, locks, carriages, windows, iron bars, theaters, museums, parks, boulevards lined with chestnut trees blooming with white candlestick flowers in the spring, purple lilac bushes with the sweet fragrance that had not yet become so sad, black horse-drawn carriages.

A carriage like that had taken my mother, my father, and me, when I was still in my mother's belly, to the new, elegant, and most expensive maternity hospital in Krakow, on Garncarska Street.

That's where I was born.

Churches. Enormous buildings, both seductive and frightening, impervious, severe and gloomy, darkness permeated with the scent of incense, shafts of light filtering in through the stained glass the colors of precious stones—ruby, sapphire, emerald, and topaz.

The heavy odor of dripping candles. So very much dripping.

Gold, wax, tears, blood.

And the statues—Mary, Jadwiga, the melancholy, beloved queen of Poland, who knew what was, what is, and what would be. The bereaved, beautiful young mother, forever a virgin. What's a virgin? Her white dress covers her divine feet, which stand on a golden crescent. Why doesn't she fall? She's so firmly planted in her grief.

Her turquoise gown, dotted with golden stars, flows from her shoulders. Her head, crowned with a glowing halo glittering with precious stones, pearls and diamonds, bouquets of stars, and the plump, pink bottoms of little angels hovering around her.

So many gaping, dripping wounds flickering in the dark.

Crucified Jesus. The crown of thorns piercing his ascetic forehead. Large, lush, heavily ripe drops of blood drip from it.

His hands and feet are nailed to the cross. Tossed at the foot of the cross is a skull with dark, staring eye sockets, and next to it, crossbones, apparently from an earlier crucifixion.

I'd seen a skull and crossbones in photographs on the elegant hats of ss soldiers standing on a ramp, legs spread, shod in gleaming leather boots.

And the skulls in my mother's picture, taken in one of the sanatoriums she went to, as usual, to treat her tuberculosis. I most probably was sent to camp again or an orphanage. In the picture, you see her against the background of a chapel built entirely of people's skulls and thighbones. People who had once been alive.

Under Jesus's ribs, on the right side, was a gaping wound, staring like an eye. Carved clusters of blood drops bubbled from the wound in his chest and the wounds on his hands and feet, from the holes made by the nails. The drops had been meticulously designed and polished, painted blazing red and polished with shiny lacquer. Spectacular.

Most interesting of all were the paintings of Judgment Day.

The sinners sentenced to roast until the end of time in vats full of boiling oil and blazing tar. Breathtaking, fascinating demons, so strange and diligent, running around and torturing tiny figures of naked sinners. They used all sorts of impressive accessories no less horrifying than the apparatus made, at my mother's request, by the orthopedist with the yellow hands and the pleasant voice, Dr. Marian Klon. That apparatus was a match for any of the ones used in the Spanish Inquisition, which I had already read about. Then came the tortures inflicted by the eye doctor and the dentist. No more. That was more than I could bear.

The demons and imps were all male, and they had wonderful names: Beelzebub, Lucifer, Mephistopheles, Asmodeus, Boruta, Rokita, Paskuda, and just plain Demon. The angels had first names too, but despite the halo, the golden hair, the drawn sword, and the wings, the demons were much more interesting.

The name of one of the important angels was Daniel, like the name of the beautiful little boy Hania Seremet dumped at the gates of the ghetto, where the Germans murdered him.

I knew them all, all the demons. You could make excellent deals with them. I knew that from stories and legends. Pan Twardowski and Faust. And there were rumors about Niccolo Paganini too.

The dark entrance to the church, permeated with the smell of incense; the cool, moist rim of the basin of holy water polished smooth by the touch of believers' hands. "In the name of the Father, the Son, and the Holy Ghost, amen."

I too dipped my hand in the holy water and crossed myself. I was a little girl and I had to stand on my tiptoes. It was a game. It had nothing to do with anyone's God. I didn't believe in God. Religion, my father said, is the opium of the masses. Opium was what the poor Chinese from Pearl Buck's books smoked.

I knew the prayers. My mother taught me my first prayer then, long before, when the war was in the world and I became a Christian child overnight—no longer Ilona, Ilonka, Ilusia, Ilka, Ileczka Goldman, but Irena Seremet.

It was so beautiful in the church. Sometimes they sang or played music, and the prayer was a melody too.

I saw, I smelled, I felt everything. Krakow gave me that as a gift, in addition to the colors of the rainbow in the puddle in which my dear dead rat rotted.

How wonderful.

MY MOTHER TOLD ME, TOLD ME, AND TOLD ME HOW SHE GAVE birth to me and how she almost died giving me life. It happened in the newest, most luxurious hospital in Krakow, on Garncarska Street, the maternity hospital for aristocratic women, although rich, Jewish women and salon Communists, like my mother, gave birth there too.

You're the child of my sorrow, she said. *Du bist mein Sorgenkind.*

She always said that in German. Why in German?

Several days before I was born, my mother and my father came to Krakow from Bochnia, where they lived in the most beautiful modern house in the city, the house my father built for my mother and that the gypsy woman predicted he would lose. That's how it was with us, dignity and a high standard of living, not like it was with some people who came back alive from the war, talking suddenly about how respected and wealthy they'd been before the war, how they'd been heroes during the war, fighting with the partisans against the Germans. Stories, stories, and stories, my mother mocked with forgiving kindness: he was just a smelly fishmonger, he never read a book in his life; she had no *kultura* at all, and her father, back in their small hometown, used to blow his nose between two fingers. And now? Where are they and where are we?

My mother and father planned very carefully for my birth. They went to live in the most lavish and expensive hotel in Krakow, the Under the Rose Hotel, where Balzac met his Madame Hanska. Those Polish women. Napoleon also had a Polish lover, Maria Walewska. Maybe it's good that I'm a Polish woman.

Then, at dawn on June 27, 1937, my mother began having labor pains. Her water burst and her uterus decided to deliver me into the world. That's how it was. It couldn't have been otherwise.

My father ordered a carriage. In wonderful Krakow, the taxis were carriages. An enchanted black carriage harnessed to an enchanted horse, driven by an enchanted coachman, as the poet Konstantom Ildefonse Galchinski wrote, and so began my final journey through my mother's womb, in a carriage clattering along cobblestones—the same kind of stones that paved the square courtyard where I saw the rainbow in my dear, dead, wet rat's puddle.

That's where I was born, in the best, the newest, the most private and most luxurious maternity hospital in Krakow—a tiny, Jewish baby girl, all of two kilograms and seven hundred grams, hairy and ugly, with an elongated, crooked skull. My mother counted five fingers and toes on each hand and foot. They promised her that elongated, crooked skulls almost always sort themselves out with time. With regard to how ugly I was, they didn't promise anything.

From the first minute, something was wrong with me.

Later, after the three of us went back to our home, the newest, most modern and expensive one in the provincial town of Bochnia, my mother began hemorrhaging terribly, developed a high fever, and had convulsions and spasms. The family friend, the gynecologist, Dr. Fishler, who performed abortions on many Communists, including salon Communists, and on many pioneers who came especially to him from Palestine to get rid of unwanted pregnancies, saved my mother. It was a true miracle: a part of the placenta had remained in the uterus and caused severe infection. Such was that much-praised modern hospital, the hospital where the most well-connected noblewomen and rich, Jewish salon Communists went to give birth.

My life almost killed my mother. That would have made my father a widower, for the second time. And I would have been an orphan, or I might not have been at all.

That is something I cannot understand. Is there something I *do* understand? I don't understand anything.

Years later, I found out that my mother hadn't been my father's first wife. Before her, he'd had a small, very young, and very sick wife from a poor family.

They met at Communist Party secret meetings. Maybe they fell in love, maybe they became lovers. When they found out that she had a fatal, incurable kidney disease that left her only a short time to live, my father didn't withdraw or turn his back on her. My father married her.

I didn't like the idea that my father had been so in love with a woman I hadn't known, even though she was already dead. But from the moment I heard that sad story, my admiration for my father grew, that noble-spirited man with the skilled hands that could do anything: pull gold teeth out of my mother's mouth so they could be sold to buy me another few days of life; and make tiny cups out of the silver paper wrapping of cigarette packs—cups for my trained gray mice in the hiding place.

Maybe that small, dead woman—I think suddenly—took my father's budding love with her when she died, and that's why he was always so embarrassed in my company, why he never kissed me or gave me a big, simple hug?

Simple.

Hugging is simple.

More than once, I had the fantasy that I might not really be my mother's daughter. After all, I'm so different from her, with her alabaster skin so delicate that tiny veins show through it. Maybe I'm the daughter of that small, sick, dead woman, my father's first wife?

My father took her to famous doctors and professors in Berlin and Vienna—to no avail. It had been clear from the beginning. There was no hope.

Dr. Fishler, a friend of the family, told my father that her days were numbered.

Only a small number remained. She died.

I never knew her name. I didn't ask.

My mother told me, told me, and told me.

She told me how she forbade my nanny to take me for walks in my carriage near the home of the bereaved mother of my father's first wife.

She told me how the mourning mother was always standing at the door of her low, humble house staring stonily at my carriage—the carriage that held the baby of her former son-in-law, her small, dead daughter's former husband.

Even though I was an ugly, hairy baby with a crooked, elongated skull, I was nevertheless alive. My mother, the salon Communist and declared atheist who read all the books in the world and was so modern and progressive, was afraid of the evil eye, that sad mother's evil eye. And maybe it's not so strange that her daughter died so young, for the Germans would probably have murdered her in the war anyway, just like they murdered almost everyone, dozens, hundreds, thousands, hundreds of thousands, millions.

We were saved. The Red Army and my mother saved us.

We owe our lives to Tovarish Stalin and my mother.

THE MINUTE I WAS BORN, MY MOTHER BEGAN HER EFFORTS to improve me, to improve my intellect, my mind, and my tiny body, which weighed only two kilograms and seven hundred grams.

According to the theory in fashion at the time, the mind of a child is a soft, delicate thing that should be allowed to develop, grow, and strengthen in absolute silence. Therefore, a baby should not be overburdened with intense impressions, so that its mind can develop in peace and quiet. Stimulation should be kept to a minimum, and everything around it should be white, quiet white, clean white, and anonymous. Only that way will the mind fulfill its potential.

And so it was.

They put me in my own large, pretty, well-lit room painted all in white oil paint. They called that color *shleif laque*, a matte paint that wouldn't, God forbid, capture dangerous reflections that might distract me from my peaceful, quiet development. The windows were covered with starched white linen curtains so that even changes in the weather would not upset my soft, developing brain. Sky, clouds, sunrises, sunsets, storms, rain, hail, snow, birds—so many dangers to be avoided.

They put me in a crib that had the hardest, most orthopedic, most modern, and most expensive mattress. Naturally, the bed was painted matte white and the mattress was covered with a tight, starched white sheet. They diapered me with white diapers, dressed me in little white dresses, and covered me with a white blanket.

My sterile white room, my tabula rasa.

My mother told me that I was a good baby, a baby who didn't cry.

I never cried.

When I did actually cry once, they summoned Dr. Fishler in a panic. It turned out that I had a terrible abscess.

Dr. Fishler was our family doctor and a family friend. He had scraped a considerable number of gifted sabra zygotes from the wombs of hardworking pioneer women in Palestine, my mother's ideological comrades who came to Poland to have abortions. She helped them and put them up in our house—to her displeasure, it must be said, because they used to leave bloodstains on her embroidered silk nightgowns and the fine linen sheets elegantly monogrammed in decorated lace with the initials G. G., Gusta Goldman, white on white.

Dr. Fishler also escaped with us in the wagon when the war broke out. Two years passed.

For the time being, I had nannies and nursemaids and toys. In photographs, you can see a ball, a little duck, and maybe blocks, a teddy bear, a basket, a pail and shovel, a doll, and a little horse on wheels. There was also a truck and a velvet dress with a lace collar. Could the dress have been red? Yes, of course it was red. Even in the black-and-white picture, you can see that it was deep red, like wine.

The war came. All that was lost.

Who knows how I might have turned out in that sterile environment if the Germans, led by Hitler, had not decided that there was no room in the world for so many races, and therefore no room for a little girl whose skull had straightened and who wasn't so ugly anymore.

The war started, and I was two.

THE ESCAPE, THE WAGON, THE ROADS.

Entire countries drowned in blood.

And the magnificent, blond, blue-eyed German army, so straight and proud, mechanized and organized, flooded Poland in a mighty, deadly wave, sweeping through it with remarkable elegance. The Third Reich had taken on a mission—to hunt down a little Jewish girl and murder her.

Or had the war saved my mind? It was so urgent just to stay alive that there was no time to worry about my developing mind. No more white on white.

We ran away in a wagon filled with straw, harnessed to a huge workhorse. We ran away to the east. We ran away from the Germans. But the front followed us; the Third Reich had decided to solve the Jewish problem. And the Jews were not enough. They also had to murder the gypsies, the intellectuals, the homosexuals, the philosophers, the Communists—a great mission that required ideology, determination, devotion, and meticulous planning.

Hunted like animals, we fled, hid, disguised ourselves—hateful days, my mother said.

And finally, after long, hateful, terrible years, the war ended.

By a miracle, by luck, by chance, my mother, my father, and I were alive when Tovarish Batiushka Stalin and his entire Red Army came, liberated us, and saved our lives.

Only then, when the war was no longer in the world, and we were saved and not murdered, and we took Berlin and went back to Krakow, only then did the work of improving me begin.

The war ended, and finally there was time to look at me, at my body— the body that held a mind that saw everything but thought the body itself was invisible.

My mother looked, looked, and looked. Suddenly she was giving me the same piercing glances I remembered from the night Hania Seremet threw me out of the village and dumped me at the hiding place. She looked at me, her lips covered with a mask like the kind surgeons wear in the operating room, so that she wouldn't, God forbid, breathe her Koch bacillus, that lethal tuberculosis bacillus, on me, even though she was no longer contagious and I was immune.

My mother spoke a great deal. Quite a great deal. She spoke in her rhythmical, authoritative, suggestive voice, the voice of a teacher or a preacher who never doubts the absolute rightness of his words. My mother was not a person with doubts, and I provided a fertile field for passing judgment and conducting rescue operations. Even though I thought I could see and not be seen, I was constantly being criticized.

That was it, there was no choice, the sword of Damocles hung over my head. The accusation—my ingratitude, my lack of seriousness. Your father had no initiative. If I hadn't been who I am, none of us would be alive today, my mother said.

Maybe I took after my father?

THE IMPROVEMENT CAMPAIGN BEGAN. THERE WAS NO ESCAPE. And from whom, from what? From my mother, who gave birth to me not once, but many times, again and again, every time her intelligence and ingenuity saved my life, again and again?

The first thing that caught my mother's attention was my posture.

She looked at me and saw that it was very ugly. My stomach protruded more than usual anyway; I bent my back and my shoulder blades weren't the same height. The right one—or was it the left—was too high, or maybe it was actually too low.

We went to an orthopedist.

The orthopedist was ugly. Greenish gray hairs, not particularly clean, grew out of his nose and ears. His hands were yellowish and his nails cracked. There were brown nicotine stains on his right hand. He was very thin, as if he were hanging from his shoulders inside pants that were too large for him. The pants were made of material shiny from use, a dark, damp stain spread across the front. Sparse hair of an indeterminate color, which slightly resembled the color of the soda factory manager's scratchy jacket whose rolled-up sleeves weigh my wrists down to this very day, was stuck to his temples, and a few very long hairs that had been separated from the hair on his temples were combed over his bald skull from left to right, a pathetic hint of a part. Every time he moved his head, that rebellious group of hairs would move from its place, scattering a flying shower of greasy dandruff, and the orthopedist, looking oblivious, as if that bald head were not his, would return the hairs to their place with a surreptitious, well-practiced movement.

The orthopedist's office smelled of rubber and something else equally disgusting. Strange objects—I had no idea what they were used for— were hanging standing upright or just strewn around. They all reminded me of the torture instruments from paintings of the lives of the saints, or the Grand Inquisitor's tools. Different from these were the prosthetic hands and feet of various sizes that were actually frighteningly realistic and left no doubt as to what they were used for. Later, on the immigrant ship, *Galila*, which took me across the ancient, stormy sea to Palestine, a huge male prosthetic leg, filled with Polish salami and raspberry jam, swayed right in front of my nose, hanging from the bunk above me, dripping raspberry jam that smelled of kielbasa and had the color of clotted blood, like the bricks of the orphanage.

Through the glass doors—one of which was cracked and pasted together with a pink Band-Aid—of a metal closet painted in peeling white varnish you could see grown-ups' and children's limbs of various sizes made of white plaster, with names written on them and sometimes numbers, which were nothing like the blue numbers on the arms of the people who used to come and tell all the stories I didn't want to hear.

And there was a mask. The face of a young woman, her eyes closed, the hint of a smile at the corners of her mouth. Such a beautiful smile. So sad. Did they also make prosthetic faces?

The orthopedist had a quiet, modulated voice. He was a nice man.

His yellow hands weren't cold, like I thought they'd be. He asked me nicely to take off my blouse and bend forward. He tapped my back and checked all the vertebrae in my spine. Then he asked me to walk back and forth, away from him and toward him, and stand in different positions. My mother was there the entire time, her fisted hands under her chin and two alternating facial expressions: embarrassment because her child, the child of sorrow, was such a damaged creature in need of improvement, and deep satisfaction for having caught the problem in time. Maybe something could still be salvaged. An I-told-you-so expression.

After the nice yellow orthopedist nodded and scratched the top of his head, scattering a soft cloud of dandruff around him, my sentence was pronounced.

An orthopedic corset.

Just as my mother had expected, and apparently had secretly wished for.

Extremely urgent. Preferably right away. Otherwise, the girl might become crippled, crooked, grow a hump on her back, who knows what.

And after all, my mother already had a humpbacked sister, Minka.

The horror of Minka's humped back haunted my mother all her life. Minka, her oldest sister, her most beloved sister, her smart, good, educated sister who had the face of an angel illuminated by a halo of golden hair, was a humpbacked dwarf. When she was a child, she rolled down the stairs in the house and something inside her broke. She stopped growing, her back was twisted, and she grew a hump.

Minka's parents, the grandparents I never knew, the beautiful Rivka and the distinguished Gruber—the Germans murdered them both—went to the most famous orthopedists in all the capitals of Europe. To no avail.

Dov, a bald, bespectacled giant with the face of a kind, gentle child, fell in love with the beautiful, generous, smart Minka. They met at the university. Dov was from Prague, a friend of Zimek, my mother's first, unforgettable love.

Minka and Dov got married. Dov was a professor of chemistry, a gifted scientist with a bright future. They predicted that he would win a Nobel Prize. Meanwhile, before the war, he spent his spare time devising small, amusing inventions to improve everyday life. Ink for a stamp pad that never dried up, dishwashing detergents, iridescent paint, silver polish, and stones for cleaning cloth shoes. That small, minor invention—the stones for cleaning cloth shoes—saved my mother and father from a good number of hungry hours in the hiding place when the war was in the world. My mother and father mixed together ingredients that Juzakowa gave them, and according to the formula Dov had once dictated to my father, they prepared a white mixture and poured it into round shoe polish tins. When the mixture hardened, they'd take the round white lumps out of the tins and give them to Juzakowa to sell in the market. White cloth summer shoes were quite fashionable then, the round lumps were sold, and there was money for another slice of bread or a cigarette.

My uncle, huge, bearlike Dov, used to carry delicate Minka in his arms everywhere they went, and after the birth of Pnina and Rachel— one dark, the other fair—he'd carry all three of them, Minka and Pnina in his arms and Rachel on his shoulders.

They were inseparable.

The war separated them.

They were murdered separately.

WE WERE TOLD THAT THE ORTHOPEDIC DEVICE ORDERED SO urgently was ready and we went to the orthopedist's office, which looked like an Inquisition torture chamber.

While the orthopedist was measuring the new back-straightening device, he told us that I was also flatfooted, something else wrong.

I needed insoles. I'd never be able to wear sandals or even low-cut shoes. I would have to wear high, laced, low-heeled shoes with insoles till the end of time. Stiff leather shoes in the winter, and in the summer, as a kind of concession or compromise, shoes made of thick, white cloth. Intimidation and threats: if I didn't wear insoles for the rest of my life, not only was I in danger of becoming a hunchback, but I would also probably limp.

Meanwhile, I tried on the orthopedic corset. It was a kind of armor, a cage made of stiff, leather-lined metal ribs. The inner parts, the parts that came into contact with my body, were covered with light suede, and the outer parts with yellow pigskin, stiff and smelly, like my schoolbag. The pieces of leather that protruded around the ribs were cut in a decorative zigzag. That armor was wound around my torso and fastened with a belt that had a metal buckle. Straps made of more flexible leather were pulled over my shoulders and fastened with buckles located on my back, slightly below my armpits.

Those straps held two padded oval pillows against my shoulder blades, guaranteeing that my shoulders would be pulled down and back.

I couldn't move. Even though the belts were padded, the corset dug deep, painful red furrows into my flesh. And the smell, the stench of pigskin, overwhelmed me. And while I was still trussed by that orthopedic corset, the yellow orthopedist took measurements for the insoles. I had to step into a whitish dough and leave the imprint of my feet—a mold for the insoles that would be supplied as quickly as possible, because you don't see such a terrible case of flat feet every day.

Mein sorgenkind, my mother occasionally uttered.

In the evening, when I took off the armor, the furrows on my body were already red, deep, and very painful.

At school the next day, my eraser fell and I was so tightly trussed in the smelly Inquisition corset that I couldn't bend down to pick it up.

The second evening of the corset, when I was extricated from the cage of torture, the furrows in my flesh were even deeper and more painful than the day before. There were sores in some places. My mother was alarmed, sorry, and embarrassed. The corset was consigned to the high shelf in the closet, never to be worn again. In the end, because the pigskin smelled despite the small cloth bundles stuffed with lavender my mother put on the shelf, the orthopedic corset was thrown into the trash can that stood in the inner courtyard of the building we lived in on Sobieskiego Street in the beautiful city of Krakow, a cobblestone courtyard like the courtyard in Lvov, and furnished like it with garbage pails and a stand to beat rugs on. A tree even grew in the courtyard in Krakow, although I didn't find a dead rat there. Nor did I look for one.

The insoles remained. We went back to the nice yellow orthopedist. The damp stain on the front of his pants was slightly larger this time. When he wasn't busy fitting devices of torture on little girls, the orthopedist grew hairs in his nose and ears. Even they, especially the ones that grew out of his nose, were yellow from the cigarettes.

Hallelujah. The insoles were ready. They were waiting for me quietly and peacefully, secure in the potential for suffering they held for me and me alone.

We didn't say a word to the orthopedist about the armor consigned to the closet shelf. I was seated on a chair and took off my shoes, and the insoles were brought. They were brown pigskin soles that had the same familiar smell as the corset of torture. That smell stayed with us for years, when we were driven out of Poland, our homeland, and sailed to Palestine. My luxurious new suitcase, so luxurious that it was lined with thick linen designed to protect it against the hardships of the journey, also had that pungent smell of pigskin. Live pigs smell much nicer.

The insoles were inserted into my new, high, brown leather shoes ordered especially for the occasion. I put on the shoes with the insoles and tied the long laces that wound through an endless number of shiny metal eyelets, got up, and started to walk.

It was terrible. Every step hurt me. But after the Inquisition corset mutiny, I didn't have enough courage left to object and complain. So I became the little mermaid whose lot it was to suffer when she was finally given feet.

I never got used to those high, stiff leather shoes and their thousand holes. And we still haven't talked about the dentist.

In the summer, the brown shoes were replaced by clumsy, ugly cloth shoes. I had to clean them with a rag steeped in a round lump of white paste similar to the stones for cleaning cloth shoes that my mother and father prepared in the hiding place according to the formula Uncle Dov invented, and that Juzakowa sold in the market. Those white shoes used to leave white stains on everything they came into contact with, so you could trace all the places I'd walked in.

I wore the high brown shoes with the torturous insoles for the last time when I kicked a sabra orange from the deck of the immigrant ship *Galila* down into the depths of the ancient sea straight to angry Poseidon's trident, right in front of the moist eyes of his Amphitrite and all the ambrosia-eating, nectar-drinking Nereids, nymphs, and sirens staring in amazement. How much I loved those Olympian gods, those marvelous heroes, the Titans, the monsters, and the demigods of ancient Greece! I knew all their loves, hates, whims; I knew their names and remembered their stories.

And we still haven't talked about the dentist.

MEANWHILE, THE IMPROVEMENT CAMPAIGN SWEPT ON, THIS time focusing on my eyes.

My dark, slanted eyes, which attracted so much attention wherever they were noticed, always evoking such dubious compliments as, "Tell me, little girl, did you forget to wash your eyes today?" Even though they were good-natured, genuine attempts to express admiration, I still hated finding out that I not only saw, but was also seen. Even my mother said that I had beautiful eyes, and to the end of her life, she was sure that all the worthwhile things in my life happened because of my beautiful eyes.

Beautiful and weak, very weak. How did they find that out? Maybe in school. We had another problem. We went to the eye doctor. My mother and her child of sorrow. Me.

The eye doctor's office was dark. Maybe there were no windows. When my eyes got used to the dark, several forms took shape, mainly furniture that resembled giant, dark, unmoving animals, perhaps mammoths, and between them, chairs upholstered in cracked leather with horsehair sticking out of the cracks like springs.

I was well acquainted with mammoths. The mighty heads, the curved white tusks, the fur. They were extinct. Once, they actually lived here, in Krakow, on the street where the eye doctor's office was, back when an evergreen forest still grew here. How did something so substantial, so huge and heavy as a mammoth, disappear off the face of the earth? How strange. Would cats disappear too? And pigs, my dear friends? And what about people? Jews, for instance?

I felt sorry for those mammoths when I saw drawings of how they were hunted. Trapped in an enormous pit, skewered on sharpened tree trunks, and all around them, on the rim of the pit, small, ugly, primeval people wearing fur stabbed them with flint-tipped spears, cavorting wildly with joy.

Primitives.

The first thing to float out of the dimness was a massive desk similar to the one my mother hid under while my father and I hid in the closet when the Gestapo searched our hiding place. Back then, the war was still in the world, and there was no time to take care of my eyes. Saving my life was more important.

A lamp with a celadon shade cast a circle of light on a worn and elegant green leather blotter decorated with a golden Greek frieze. I knew from books that beautiful leather like that was made in Morocco. Next to the blotter, the greenish light reflected an alabaster pen holder with slots for pens and two inkwells with polished metal covers.

The alabaster gleamed in the reflected light. My mother told me that once, her two loves, Zimek the Czech engineer and Avreim'ele the pioneer, told her that her stomach was made of pink alabaster. I didn't like that story.

The eye doctor was tall and thin. There was a button missing on his shirt, and through the slit I could see a potbelly as solid and compact as a ball, with a navel that looked at me like an eye, adorned with curly gray hair. Would the young lady be so kind as to sit, the eye doctor asked politely. He addressed my mother and me in the third person.

I sat down on the high spinning chair. The doctor lowered it a few turns, and that was fun but also a bit frightening. I've always despised swings and merry-go-rounds, and after spinning around once, sliding up once, and sliding down once, I used to throw up.

On bus rides too. I couldn't control it, and the future held a nightmarish sea journey for me on the immigrant ship, *Galila*, where I suffered the worst nausea imaginable.

But the eye doctor's spins were few and gentle. He turned on another light that illuminated a piece of hanging cardboard with letters of various sizes printed on it. I knew letters very well from my time in the hiding place when I watched the lice scurrying around on newspaper.

I saw a large E, and a P and F under it, then T O Z in a row below them.

The lower rows weren't clear. My mother was standing next to me, the same expression on her face that she'd had in the orthopedist's office. My child of sorrow. Maybe something could still be salvaged?

And we still haven't talked about the dentist.

If the young lady will allow me, the eye doctor said, putting a pair of heavy glasses without lenses on me that pressed against the bridge of my nose and pinched the skin behind my ears. The eye doctor with the protruding ball-belly peering at me with its navel eye put an opaque disk into the frame, blocking one of my eyes, pointed a ruler at the illuminated piece of cardboard with the letters, and asked me to read row after row.

Then he asked me to read the letters again after he blocked my other eye.

The frames dug painful indentations into the bridge of my nose and behind my ears. I was sure that all the mammoths were commiserating with me and feeling sorry for me. The pain didn't keep me from being deeply impressed when the eye doctor opened a marvelous leather satchel that held row after row of lenses in round, yellow metal frames, each with clasps, lying in slots in the wine-colored velvet that was as luxurious as the velvet dress worn by Milady, the bourgeois schemer in *The Three Musketeers*.

The examination to determine the seriousness of my condition began. Various lenses were fitted into the heavy frames, and the examination continued without a break until I could read the bottom row of letters. How terribly disappointed I was when I found out the letters didn't say anything. They were just letters. I mean, they could have written something nice there, or at least something interesting.

The doctor turned on another light. The office was now dimly lit, and I could see all sorts of fascinating objects. Watching over everything was a kind of bisected Cyclops eye with red and blue tubes representing blood vessels, and muscles and fiber after fiber in various shades of pink.

The examination ended. The heavy frames were removed, the lenses were returned to their home—the slots in the artificial wine-colored velvet—and the satchel was closed. The indentations on my nose and behind my ears hurt me for a long time afterward.

The eye doctor sat down at his massive desk, put his cigarette out in the alabaster ashtray fitted into the blotter next to the inkwells, and wrote down the results of the examination. The previous cigarette had smoked itself while he was examining me and had turned into a column of light ash that scattered and vanished when the doctor touched it.

I remember his handwriting. It was remarkably illegible—a strange sort of privilege that doctors have. It was even more illegible than my mother's illegible handwriting. My father had the clearest, most beautiful handwriting in the world, and mine looked like chicken scratches. That's what my mother said, and she even wrote me this in a letter when I was in one of those summer camps and she was in a sanatorium: Ilusiu, your handwriting looks like chicken scratches and your spelling mistakes scream out for divine vengeance.

My mother waited tensely for the doctor to pass sentence. In our family, doctors were respected.

All I wanted was to see and not be seen, and my nose hurt and I had pain behind my ears. Sentence was passed. The doctor said that my vision was very problematic and very weak, perhaps as a result of poor nutrition while I was growing, even a bit of hunger, one might say. The doctor added that in the future, during adolescence—I didn't understand exactly what he meant—when the body is renewed and grows in leaps and bounds, the situation might improve and there might be regeneration. Such miracles have occurred in the past.

But by then I'd be thirteen, an old lady. Meanwhile—glasses.

Strong glasses. Four and a half diopters. I had to wear them all the time. I couldn't take them off even for a minute.

And we still haven't talked about the dentist.

A WEEK PASSED, TWO WEEKS PASSED. THE GLASSES ARRIVED —thick glass framed by iron hoops joined by an arched bridge, and flexible metal springs at the ends of the earpieces.

I put them on.

The world became enriched with details I'd never imagined I was missing.

The glasses were very heavy and I couldn't blink with them on. My lashes were too long and brushed against the thick lenses.

I had no choice. Using the scissors from the elegant manicure set my mother bought at one of the markets that sold the belongings of murdered Jews and deported Germans, I cut off about a third of my long, thick black lashes. Only then could I blink freely, with nothing in the way.

Over the years, my lashes grew back somewhat, but they were never again "black velvet curtains," as my mother used to call them. She called my eyebrows "squirrels' wings."

Before I started wearing glasses, people in the street, on trams, in restaurants and shops used to notice me, look at me, and say, Little girl, could you please tell me why your eyes are slanted? And why didn't you wash your eyes today? I hated those questions. I preferred seeing and not being seen. But grown-ups thought they were complimenting me on my beautiful, dark doe eyes, my long, thick black lashes, and dark eyebrows. People said, Maurycy Gottlieb should paint you. You have Ester'ke's eyes!

Ester'ke, the beautiful Jewish woman, the good king's beloved.

People who'd grown used to the blue, green, and gray eyes of sweet blond Polish girls were delighted to see dark, Jewish eyes. There weren't many Jewish eyes left in Krakow after the war.

The Germans had murdered most of the little Jewish girls.

They also murdered the Jewish girls who had blue eyes, like Rachel, the blond, blue-eyed cousin I never knew.

And now, with my eyes hidden behind thick lenses, no one gave me those dubious compliments on their shape and cleanliness anymore.

While the new glasses added a great many details to my world, they were first and foremost an instrument of torture. They were horrible. The lenses weighed heavily on the bridge of my nose, digging a deep notch that grew deeper and redder and hurt constantly all day long, day after day, week after week, month after month, year after year. The springs of the earpieces hurt where they pinched and pierced the thin, delicate skin behind my ears, and the round frames pressed on my high cheekbones. At the end of the day, deep, red grooves bisected my cheeks.

I wound padded bandages around the arch that connected the round frames and around the springs of the earpieces. It didn't help. It just looked very ugly.

And we still haven't talked about the dentist, or the children who ran around half-naked, their bodies covered with bloody sores, and urinated on the trays of drying spaghetti near the sewers of the port city of Bari where we boarded the immigrant ship, *Galila*, and sailed to Palestine.

I CONTINUED TO WORRY MY MOTHER. AFTER THE TERRIBLE years of war, after the horror and the fear, my mother apparently wanted to make up for the childhood that had been stolen from her only child, to atone for the harsh years, to improve my body. As a result of a test I took, she decided that her child of sorrow had to begin attending a remedial rhythmic class without delay.

I had no idea what that was. I hadn't read anything about it in my books. What a shame that my mother didn't just ask me how I felt.

My mother signed me up for the rhythmic class. She said I needed special gym clothes for it and immediately set about finding a suitable outfit for me. She found an old shirt of hers, orange with green polka dots, which had shrunk in the wash and fit me perfectly. She also found flannel bloomers she'd worn after the liberation when she was sick and thin and almost died of tuberculosis. Meanwhile, she'd gotten healthy and fat, and the bloomers were small on her. They were in the classic flannel bloomers color—ghastly pink. My mother threaded rubber bands around the leg openings and tightened the elastic waistband. The bloomers were still big on me, but my mother said that gym clothes had to be roomy. Loose. That's what made them comfortable.

There was me and there was the world, the grown-ups. Strange things went on in the world, and I thought that's how it was. That outfit didn't seem unusual to me until we got to the hall where the rhythmic class was held—a spacious hall that looked particularly vast to me, until I realized that one of the walls was a mirror. We had only one, very high mirror in our house, in the bathroom, which I had difficulty looking into. There was a mirror on one of the closet doors too, but I didn't like to open that door because it squeaked, and in general I wasn't too fond of closet doors. I never looked at myself in the mirror to evaluate my appearance. It didn't interest me. I saw and was invisible.

And then, in the hall where the rhythmic class was held, I saw, I saw myself in the orange shirt with the green polka dots and the pink flannel bloomers held in place with rubber bands that were slightly too tight, digging into the flesh of my thighs and cutting off my circulation. And all around me, along the length of the walls, the other children arranged themselves at the bar. They were very "other," those other children. They were all wearing pretty, short gym pants made of navy blue satin, and white or turquoise undershirts.

I looked like an existential error. Like dissonance.

The teacher had a long pointer and she signaled to the somber-looking man sitting at the piano in the corner. Everyone launched into all sorts of ridiculous movements. So did I. The tight rubber bands around my thighs cut off my circulation and dug painfully into my flesh. The elastic waistband loosened and came undone, and the pants started falling. I tried every way I could to execute those stupid, pointless movements, and at the same time to hold the pink flannel bloomers with my free hand so they wouldn't fall off.

I never went back there.

Even I, who never paid attention to what I looked like and who always felt like that boy with the magic hat who saw and was invisible, even I couldn't bear my image in the mirror next to all those other children, so charming, so properly dressed, and so beautiful.

I decided that if that's how one is supposed to look, if that's how it's possible to look, and I didn't look like that, then I wouldn't go there.

And we still haven't talked about the dentist.

UNTIL THEN, I'D RECEIVED ALL MY CLOTHES AS GIFTS. THEY were used clothes or new ones that came in packages from America. It was in one of those packages from America that I received that horrific hat with the pom-poms and a kind of navy blue sweatsuit made of poor-quality flannel. Until there was more money and my mother decided that the time had come to order clothes tailor-made for me from the dressmaker.

First came the school chemise.

Panna Zofia Duda, owner of the Latest Paris Fashions for Ladies salon, made the blue satin chemise for me when they found out I didn't know how to write and sent me to school. I was eight.

The second item was a *demi-saison* coat for transitional seasons, the first coat ever made especially for me.

The Parisian dressmaker's salon was located on the third floor of an old building not far from the Rinek and from the house where my friend Celinka, later Tzippi, lived.

The sign affixed to the entrance had a drawing of a lady wearing a wide-brimmed hat covering half her face, her hand placed gracefully on her waist. The bottom part of the lady's skirt and her hair had peeled away.

I couldn't keep myself from breathing on the stairs leading to the third-floor salon, so I had no choice but to expose myself to the disgusting mishmash of smells that always filled the air there—cooked sauerkraut mixed with the stench of rancid lard, penetrated by the occasional waft of faint perfume worn by one of the Parisian dressmaker's customers. I hope today's bath day, I always thought as I climbed the stairs to the salon, and my mother fills the tub with hot water and sprinkles gentian violet crystals into it. They melted quickly and produced wonderful, curling miracles, floating on the surface of the water, spinning around in amazing spirals that faded until the water became purple and had a metallic smell—and all in the name of sterilization, of course, because the bath, like the kitchen and the toilet, was shared by all the tenants.

Sometimes, when we climbed the stairs to the Parisian dressmaker's salon, one particular smell floated above all the others—the smell of Pani Helena Finkelstein's perfume. Helena Finkelstein was my friend Celinka's mother. People said she was young, they said she was beautiful, and they said she had a lover. My mother told me about a woman she'd actually met who told her that her husband had a lover, so she cut something off his body, the thing on statues that's always covered with a big leaf or else completely broken off. And my mother knew another woman who told her that her husband and her best friend were lovers, so she poured some acid on her and the rest on her husband. That woman, the one who poured the acid, was a painter, even a good painter, who later became very successful and famous, and not because of the acid.

My friend Celinka, along with her mother, Pani Helena of the perfume, her father, Dr. Phillip Finkelstein the Zionist, and her mother's lover, who had very white skin and straight, thick, greasy black hair, sailed to Palestine with us on the immigrant ship, *Galila*, but nothing was cut off or poured there, except for raspberry jam when the jar broke, filling the hollow prosthesis stuffed with Polish salamis that dangled above my bunk.

And so, on our way up to the Parisian salon, I always knew whether Pani Helena was there. The Parisian dressmaker Panna Zofia Duda was always stuffed into a purple georgette crepe dress whose seams were about to burst. It had damp stains under the armpits that spread during the fittings. I always held my breath when she lifted her arms. Her small face was surrounded with tiny curls that were like the wool of the Easter sugar lamb, Agnus Dei. Her shiny red cheeks looked like Cupid's buttocks and her tiny pug nose was stuck between them like a miniature sex organ. Her small eyes were piercing, bright purple. The fuzz of a little mustache was golden above her cherry, doll lips, which always had a hundred pins stuck between them. An endless flow of chatter cascaded from those lips, always interspersed with code words common in conversations ladies had with their dressmakers:

Yokes, décolleté, darts.

Ruffles, slits, bodices.

Paris, Dior, New Look.

Plissé, pleats, lining.

My mother and I waited our turn sitting on the sofa in the corner next to the sewing machine, its graceful curves gleaming, looking like a chess queen lying on its side, the name SINGER decorating its stomach in gold letters. My indigent grandmother, Rachela Goldman, probably had a sewing machine that was much less elegant than that one.

The couch was soft, draped with a threadbare cover patched with scraps of different fabrics. Actually, I thought it was pretty. It reminded me a little of my wartime patched underpants, which my mother said looked like the atlas of an unknown country. Curious, I surreptitiously lifted the edge of the cover to find out what kind of fancy upholstery it was supposed to be protecting. Under it was another tattered cover, and another one under that. I didn't continue the geological examination of the couch to the end to find out how many threadbare covers were piled on one another. And if they were all peeled away like an onion, would the couch disappear completely?

And so we sat on the multilayered couch in Panna Zofia's Parisian salon waiting for the first fitting of my first coat.

No more scratchy, soda factory manager's jacket tied around my waist with a rope, the weight of its rolled-up sleeves bearing down heavily on my wrists to this very day. No more used, strange rags I received as gifts.

This time, it was something tailor-made for me. True, they'd probably leave a sizable hem so the coat could be lengthened to fit next year. After all, the girl was always growing. It would be a thin wool coat, a *demi-saison* coat, woven from threads of various colors that joined together to make the ugliest color imaginable—something between cadmium yellow, ochre, and brown. It was a color I found particularly repulsive, almost like green—not the green of plants, of course, but the diarrhea-green of clothes.

My mother chose the pattern. It never entered my mind to express a wish about what I would wear. You wore what there was, and usually, there wasn't. I didn't object or suggest something I liked better. I didn't know that little girls have a right to their own taste. I didn't know I could have taste.

My mother was the one to decide on the kind of fabric, the color and design of the coat. My mother said that some people had taste and others didn't. My mother had taste, others didn't. My little coat would be a cloche cut, have a baby-doll collar and, naturally, a lining. A good piece of clothing must have a lining. The lining was made of shiny satin the same color as my cousin Felix's diarrhea. Felix was the smelly greenish son of my father's brother, Uncle Henryk, and his bucktoothed wife, Malvina. It was during a conversation with her that I first realized—how puzzled and disappointed I felt at that moment!—that there are stupid adults.

The slightly puffed sleeves had cuffs.

It's the day of my first fitting.

My mother and I are waiting on the couch. Meanwhile, Panna Zofia is dancing around her customer, Pani Helena Finkelstein, the mother of my friend Celinka, who would later transform herself and become Tzippi.

Tzippi—the same name as the sabra with the tanned thighs had, the one who, together with her sabra friends, threw sabra oranges from the command bridge of the immigrant ship, *Galila*.

Pani Helena was having a taffeta evening dress made in a very deep blue color, the ultramarine of the crystal-fragile sky.

The design was gorgeous. The New Look of Christian Dior, Paris. It was going to be a strapless dress with a fitted waist, though despite all the pathetic, fruitless efforts, it wouldn't be Scarlett O'Hara's wasp waist. A full, pleated cloche falling almost to the ankle. Actually, Pani Helena had narrow, graceful ankles.

The rest of her abundant flesh was pushed and squeezed and crammed into a shocking pink satin corset reinforced with whalebone and kilometers of pink laces threaded through a hundred small metal eyelets.

I'd already seen her encased in that corset when Celinka and I once went into her boudoir and I saw my first lady's toilette and all the cosmetics and implements of beauty, like in books, like in movies.

Pani Helena was standing there in her boudoir looking at her reflection in the mirror. Her lips, smeared with crimson lipstick, were pursed like the hole that chickens lay eggs through and she was turning her torso left and right, probably to check the effectiveness of the pink corset. Now too, with the most concentrated look imaginable, Pani Helena Finkelstein was staring at her reflection in the large oval mirror in Panna Zofia Duda's salon—a product of carpentry genius, since the mirror could be moved up and down in its frame.

There's a hint of criticism in Pani Helena's expression. Not self-criticism, of course, but criticism of the handiwork of Panna Zofia, the Parisian dressmaker who is showering attention on her customer, an endless flow of chatter cascading from her mouth, which worries me a great deal because of the dozens of pins stuck between her cherry lips.

Those pins still worry me.

Embarrassed, I try as hard as I can not to see Pani Helena's body, which occasionally shows through the corset and the dress. My eyes wander around and around the walls of the salon, over the peeling wallpaper that exposes green walls—a kind of celadon that reminds me of the color of the Skoda my father was given for his important job, driven by a chauffeur who'd had his ear eaten and his nose squashed when he was a boy.

I forgot to bring a book. Disaster. I always take a book. Nothing can be so terrible if I have a book I can disappear into.

I browse through the stack of damp, crumpled magazines. They smell of mold and something else unpleasant. Maybe the cat pees on them. The magazines have drawings of very tall, slender, beautiful women in frozen poses—sometimes their hands are on their waists, sometimes they hold their hat brims. They stand with their legs close together, one always extended slightly forward. They wear gloves, sometimes long enough to reach their elbows.

I once saw gloves like that in a movie. How I loved to go to the movies. A promise that we were going to a movie filled me with joyous anticipation and boundless excitement. Oh, the sweet longing for something that ultimately comes to pass!

Sometimes there were drawings of little girls next to the elegant women in the magazines. They were tall and slender too, not like me, who walked through the world flatfooted, with a protruding stomach, glasses, ugly ears, short thin hair, asymmetrical shoulders, and a million holes in my teeth. And I don't know the multiplication table, and my spelling mistakes cry out for divine vengeance!

But I know how to draw very nicely; everyone says that.

Those girls in the magazines don't forget the multiplication table and they know how much time you have to leave the faucet on in order to fill the pool so that two trains leaving at exactly the same time from two completely different points can crash and sink in it together. Let it be over with already, I say to myself, so we can go home and I can bury myself in my book, but not before I wash my hands in the hope I can wash that smell off them.

ANOTHER LADY COMES INTO THE SALON. SHE'S WEARING A turban like the Turks in museum paintings, and her dress has a hundred tiny round buttons down the front.

My mother knows her too. From before the war.

Oh boy, this is the end of me. I have no book and they start to talk. The stories begin. How were you saved and where were you?

Well, my mother says, that was lucky. You're looking good.

The lady with the turban was saved thanks to forged Aryan papers, like me.

Enough, let them stop with all that. Home, a book, and that's all.

I'm afraid she'll ask about the family.

I don't want to hear. I don't want to know. I don't want to see.

They're talking about fabrics.

English wool is the best. They make reasonably good wool in Lodz too, but nothing compares to the real thing. Speaking of which, do you know about the Lodz Ghetto? the lady with the turban asks. Here they go again.

How can you tell if it's real wool? You pull out a thread and set fire to it. If it's real wool, the thread gets scorched but doesn't burn. Real wool doesn't burn. That's a fact.

Did that help anyone during the war?

They talk. I fix my eyes on the damp magazines. Names and kinds of fabric are spread all around me, streaming like waves from the long bolts of cloth, one meter and sixty centimeters wide.

And the talking flows too. Rayon, shantung, tweed.

And the regal fabrics, from books: plush, velvet, lace, silk, brocade, satin, muslin, chiffon, tulle.

And the simple, proletarian fabrics, the inferior ones: pique, cotton, percale, flannel, perhaps even gabardine. And perhaps not. After all, my mother had a tailored, elegant fur coat that was gabardine on the outside.

The fur was inside.

Ladies from Krakow who weren't just ordinary nouveau-riche women, but were truly wealthy, even before the war, wore coats like that, with fur inside and not outside, so as not to show off with fur because that was in poor taste. My mother was very pleased with her supposedly modest fur coat. Rather thunderous modesty, it must be admitted, for a Communist, even a salon Communist.

The third fitting for Celinka's mother's magnificent evening gown is over. Not a single pin was swallowed. They're all back in the red plush, heart-shaped pincushion. I'm asked to pick up the pins left on the floor with the help of a horseshoe-shaped magnet. That's an entertaining, enjoyable job, like a game, a kind of competition with myself: how many pins can I pick up at once, stuck together by the force of the magnet?

Like my private spitting Olympics, which I'd recently limited slightly because of the unfavorable reaction of the people who watched me doing it.

Panna Zofia helps Pani Helena take off the ultimate, ultramarine, night-blue evening gown and put it on the stained mannequin standing on one leg that splits into three prongs close to the floor.

The mannequin has a narrower shape than Pani Helena, and the dress hangs half-empty on it. It's marked with white lines made by a special chalk, not like the chalk in school, but hard, flat, tailor's chalk.

I am very relieved when Celinka's mother is finally dressed like a person, or more precisely, just like Celinka's mother, in a suit with very wide shoulders and a short, narrow skirt. A jabot of copious, lacy ruffles flows from the décolleté, and the cuffs peering out from under the jacket sleeves are made of the same lace. The suit is navy blue, and like many women's suits in those days, it was a man's suit in its previous life.

Maybe that man is already dead and they've unraveled his suit and turned the cloth—the finest English wool that does not wrinkle, that's flexible and as soft as flesh—into a suit for Madame Helena Finkelstein.

Madame Helena was not a poor woman, quite the opposite, but in postwar Poland, you couldn't buy English wool, and so men's suits were turned, in both senses of the word, into women's suits.

My mother also had a suit like that, with shoulders like a boxer's, her soft, plump, pink knees peeking out of the narrow skirt. Even my mother, who thought she resembled Marlene Dietrich, admitted that she didn't have beautiful legs.

Women with pretensions of elegance wore all sorts of astonishingly ridiculous hats with those suits. My mother also had monstrous hats like that resting in their own special, round cases.

IT'S MY TURN FOR A FITTING. LUCKILY, IT'S FOR A COAT. I'D never agree to undress. As it is, I'm terribly shy with the three women looking at me.

To my embarrassment, my mother comes out with an old peasant saying, vulgar and mocking: Mother, mother, the chicken is looking at me and the rooster is laughing.

The women giggle.

I want so much not to be here. Home, a book, and that's all.

After Panna Zofia drapes me in what will eventually be my new coat, but for the time being is nothing but pieces of cloth loosely basted together, she kneels down. Dangling from her neck is a tape measure, yellow on one side and white on the other, its waxy coating cracked and peeling, and a hundred pins are once again stuck between her lips. And she talks and talks and talks, and the pins stay stuck to her bottom lip like the chewed-up, damp butt of the *machorka* cigarette that was always stuck to the bottom lip of Juzef Juzak, the carpenter and alcoholic, who hid us when the war was in the world.

Panna Zofia pins up the hem, a generous hem, so there'll be enough to let down next year. After all, the girl is constantly growing.

They talk, but luckily not about the war.

Panna Zofia isn't Jewish, she's Polish. Her clientele has thinned out quite a lot during the war years, most of it gone forever.

They talk about the latest fashion.

Demi-saison. Demi-saison?

Paris, Dior, the New Look.

Plissé, pleats, lining.

Chinese collar, *bébé* collar, Slowacki collar, cowl collar.

Cuffs.

Yoke, décolleté, bodice.

Slips, petticoats, girdles, brassieres.

Silk stockings, nylon stockings, where can I mend the runs?

Scissors. Where are the scissors?

A thorough search for the scissors.

Panna Zofia bangs hard on the table. Where are the scissors?

The scissors, hiding on the table covered with patterns cut from brown paper and newspaper, pieces of cloth and rags, make a sound that gives away their location. Like in the old saying: "Bang the table and the scissors will answer you." Those words are resurrected like Jezus Cristos.

A wrinkle on the little coat I'm trying on has to be ironed. Panna Zofia takes it off me and several of her pins, which were not stuck properly in the cloth, scratch me. She puts the coat—more accurately, the promise of a coat—on an ironing board padded with countless layers of scorched cloth, almost as thick as the couch we sat on. Maybe the ironing board would also disappear when all the layers were peeled away?

She takes the pins out from between her lips and moves them close to the horseshoe magnet, which drags them away. That's just plain cheating, I think; that's not a real horseshoe. It's nothing like the horseshoes my horse in the village had when I was a Christian girl there. This only looks like a horseshoe. I was always disappointed when I found out that something wasn't real, that it only seemed real.

Panna Zofia picks up the cup that's on the table and brings it to her lips, fills her mouth with water, and with a sudden, fine, powerful spray, wets the scorched rag lying on top of the coat. Steam rises when the blazing black iron comes into contact with the wet rag, and the special odor of damp wool being ironed by a blazing iron spreads through the room.

The odor is mixed with the smells coming from the closet whose doors were half-open, a massive closet replete with carvings, engravings, and elaborate locks. Clothes of all sorts hang in it. Some are probably waiting for first fittings, some for second, some for third, and some are even finished, waiting to be taken. And maybe there are even finished dresses that no one will come to take. A white wedding dress, for instance, all foamy chiffon. Maybe the client was murdered in the war?

A cat comes out of the closet, a red shoulder pad in its mouth. A large spotted cat with a weakness for French magazines. A strange smell, concentrated and foul, fills the room. It might be perfume, perhaps lavender, mixed with naphthalene and women's stale sweat, and I can also smell the obscene odor that sometimes comes from my classmate, Yolanda, the fat, overgrown girl who nauseates me, and despite my objections, is always trying to be close to me.

Panna Zofia puts the basted coat on me again, and now it's warm from the iron and smells of damp wool. That's how I would smell every time a sudden rain surprised me while I was wearing it. And after all, it was a *demi-saison* coat!

A few more pins are stuck into it, and none of them, I must admit, into me. Panna Zofia gets up from her kneeling position surprisingly quickly, sighing deeply.

The first fitting is over.

Finally.

NOW IT'S THE TURN OF THE WOMAN WITH THE BUTTONS AND the Turkish turban, the attractive one. My mother is in no hurry to leave. The three of them are in the middle of a conversation, the cascade of words flowing:

Suit, dress, blouse.

Zipper, buttonhole, button.

Skirt, coat, jacket.

Snaps.

Potbelly.

Trousers, vest.

Sporty, *demi-saison*.

Gray goes with everything.

Black goes with white.

Brown with yellow, and preferably no orange. Orange isn't elegant!

Red goes with gray, although gray, of course, goes with everything.

Green and blue? God forbid!

Blue goes with white.

And green possibly with brown.

And yellow? Yellow is also undesirable.

And red and orange should never be worn together, or orange and green. That's a crime, a real crime. A *scandale*! What are we, circus acrobats?

Purple! Maybe with gray. Although gray, of course, goes with everything.

The attractive lady with the turban is getting ready for her fitting.

To my astonishment, she takes off the dress with the hundred round buttons in a single motion. The buttons are a complete fraud, like the drawers in the closet my father and I hid in when the Gestapo searched our hiding place.

The dress opens with a long zipper in the back, and there she is, standing in a lace-trimmed beige slip and nylon stockings, one of them with a long run in it, held up by a garter belt. I wonder what time she left, how quickly she drove, and into which pool she would fall and drown, like the trains in the math problem.

The attractive lady isn't wearing a corset or even a bra, and looking at her isn't all that embarrassing. None of her flesh jiggles or quivers like jellied chicken feet or my mother's white-pink pudding breasts. On a piece of paper torn from a urine-damp Parisian magazine, my mother writes down the address of a lady who picks up stitches and mends stockings with runs. She can be found in a small alcove under the steps of an ancient house next to the Rinek, and she spends her days stopping runs from running any further. My mother gives the piece of paper with the address on it to the lady with the turban and the run in her stocking.

The attractive woman is having a suit made. A man's suit made of fine English wool, as flexible and soft as flesh, has been unstitched and turned inside out. Navy blue with a white pinstripe. The inside is like new.

They pick a design—there aren't many to choose from. They make a skirt out of the pants. The jacket: a Chanel collar, two rows of buttons, flapped pockets, square shoulder pads. And the skirt has a slit in the back. All lined, of course. The most important thing is how the suit is finished on the inside.

Too bad it wasn't checked cloth. Checks are very stylish.

But the fabric is like new.

I hope they don't talk about who once owned the man's suit. I hope they don't start talking about those things again, about the war. Home, a book, and that's all.

The curly-haired Panna Zofia with the little face that looked like Cupid's buttocks later made me some new and surprising clothes. I never liked any of them, although I never thought about what I was wearing and how I looked anyway. I didn't look in mirrors.

I especially disliked the pink dress with the tiny black polka dots, the short puffy sleeves, and the ruffles on the bodice. I wore that dress for my portrait painted by Panna Jadwiga Madziarska of the permanented, bleached-blond hair, the goosey lover of our family friend, Jonasz Stern, the painter who didn't know how to draw a camel, although he once drew me a tomb, Rachel's Tomb. A dome and a palm tree. Later, I drew a tomb like that.

Rachel's Tomb is in Palestine. People were going there, even non-Zionists like Pani Helena's husband, Dr. Finkelstein, my friend Celinka's father.

There was another ancient structure in Palestine where people went and cried. It's called the Wailing Wall. The Jews say that it was once a wall of their Temple, the Temple I read about in Feuchtwanger's book on Flavius Josephus and the Jewish wars in Palestine. They lost then too, and they keep on crying next to that wall of their Temple, its stones soft from the tears. It didn't help them in the past and it won't help them in the future. Crying doesn't help anyone.

And we still haven't talked about the dentist.

THERE WAS A HAT TOO, A HORRIFIC HAT, A HAT OF HORRORS that, unlike the magic hat, made me doubly visible, not invisible.

I developed a tic because of it.

The horrific hat came to us in one of the wonderful packages from America. Distant relatives sent them to us, because the Germans had murdered all their close relatives. The packages were enormous events in my life. Everything was different in those packages—the wrapping paper, the imprint, the markings, the addresses, the smell. Another world, distant and intriguing. A foreign culture. All so extravagant, so different and amazing, so American!

I knew the Americans. I knew them from books. I read about Tom Sawyer and Uncle Tom and I knew about the poor slaves and about the Indians. I was surprised to learn from my parents that when the war was in the world and the Americans took so long to open a second front, they were fighting another war with Japan and defeated them with the help of an atomic bomb, or maybe two—a special bomb, the atom bomb.

There were fantastic things in those packages from America, the likes of which I'd never seen before. All sorts of very strange objects: narrow, shiny, turquoise satin shoes that were thirty centimeters long and had stiletto heels; gleaming wide belts so short they could only fit around Scarlett O'Hara's wasp waist, made of a strange material called plastic, with glittering gold, diamond-studded buckles. And there were strange wallets, also made of plastic, and strange things to eat, and strange powders.

Everything was strange.

That word, plastic, was always spoken with a kind of pretentious, mocking tone. "American taste," they'd say, meaning bad taste. The handbags were made of clear plastic shot through with artificial flowers, beads, sequins, and other silly things. I once received a blouse with a wonderful button, a small, round, glass ball imprinted with an amorphous shape in ultramarine, purple, and turquoise—a shape and colors like the ones I used to see when I pressed a damp thumb against the lashes of my half-closed eye. A marvel! That little button became the king of my treasures and was added to the frog pin given to me by Monica Starski, the girl who knew arithmetic and went to Germany with her rich parents—a small green frog climbing up a shiny, silvery metal ladder. I kept that button among my treasures for years.

I always remembered and always will remember my lost treasures, the red thread the mice stole and the picture of the pretty girl with the ribbon on the skewered piece of torn newspaper in the filthy bathroom of our hiding place, when the war was in the world.

My father said he knew someone who once received a package from America that had a pair of highly polished, elegant patent leather shoes, Sunday shoes, in it. Even though they were pointed and very narrow, he wore them to the May 1 parade. A few drops of spring rain were enough, and the soles of the fancy shoes were left behind in the first puddle. My father's friend, also a hardworking, methodical accountant, lost no time in writing to the manufacturers at the address stamped on the inside of the shoes in striking gold letters. A reply from the American shoe manufacturer arrived months later. It expressed its astonishment. Its factory had been manufacturing burial clothes for sixty years without a single complaint.

Those clothes and accessories came from another world. They were so strange. The glitter, the vivid colors, the peculiar shapes, the new materials, all that plastic. Who were those people who produced them? And who were the people who wore them? Were they all so tall there, so thin and narrow? And what kind of taste was that, the glitter, the transparency, and the shiny colored plastic?

Sometimes packages of food arrived. What joy, what a surprise, to unwrap the package—carefully, of course, because we saved the thin string; we'd probably need it sometime—and discover all sorts of wonderful round and square cans and tins.

Sometimes there were cardboard boxes too, with cubes of white sugar in them, gleaming like the alabaster of the sweet Madonna in church. Sometimes there was also chocolate. My mother and father were happiest about the coffee. A whiff of the wonderful aroma when they took the cover off.

ONCE, THERE WAS A SMALL BAR OF CHOCOLATE IN ONE OF the packages that had an especially attractive wrapper. This is only for the girl, my mother decided. After all, I was the child of her sorrow, her *sorgenkind*, who had to be compensated and improved because her childhood had been stolen from her. I devoured the small bar of chocolate and was sick for three days. I didn't leave the toilet for three days, to the great displeasure of the other tenants. The toilet, like the bathroom and the kitchen, was shared.

The chocolate was a laxative. That most certainly must have been written on the wrapper, but in English. In our family, only Aunt Minka and Uncle Dov knew English, but they'd been murdered along with their daughters, Rachel and Pnina. The Germans murdered them when the war was in the world.

The square tins held a strange kind of meat in the shape of the tin. You might think that there were lots of small square or rectangular animals running around in that amazing, distant America located on the other side of the world, the country that waited for our Red Army to win at Stalingrad before they opened a second front, and defeated the Japanese with the help of one or two atom bombs. They hunted those animals, and after they cut off their tails, ears, and legs, squeezed them into small cans and sent them to distant relatives that the Germans hadn't managed to murder, in Krakow, Poland, Europe, on the other side of the world.

The meat was very delicious.

But most wonderful were the cans of fruit.

Drawings on the outside of the can showed what was inside. Or maybe they were photographs. Squares of orange, yellow, and white fruit were interspersed with shiny circles of red cherries. I always picked out those cherries and ate them. I was an only child and I had no rivals. My mother and father watched me happily as I ate those canned cherries. We're alive. The girl is eating.

There were round slices of fruit with a hole in the middle. The word ANANAS, pineapple, was written on the can. I read that word and understood it. I recognized letters on other labels, but I didn't understand the words. That was the language of the Americans, the language the British spoke too, the language used by Dickens, Kipling, the Brontë sisters, Walter Scott, and that poet, Shakespeare, whose name I learned to spell and write. Such a strange name and such strange spelling: so many letters you don't pronounce.

I went with my mother and father to see many plays that Shakespeare wrote. They were entertaining, like the plays about the king of the fairies and the queen who fell in love with an ugly donkey, and a little elf called Puck danced around her, scattering magic dust. And there were very sad plays, like the one about the king whose daughters betrayed him.

I cried at that play, and so did my mother. I liked to cry at sad plays and when I read sad books. It wasn't like the crying that came out of me after the war and has never stopped. It was crying that passed and was almost pleasant.

The most amazing cans were the ones that held food in the form of powder. Powdered milk, powdered eggs. Strange new tastes. My mother would fry the powdered eggs with browned onions. No one liked those omelets. We weren't hungry anymore. We were much more spoiled.

The soup powders weren't bad, but they didn't even come close to the wonderful taste of the soups my mother cooked, those golden soups with the floating circles of shiny, golden fat, sometimes with thin noodles, sometimes with giant, flat white beans, and sometimes with tiny egg yolks from eggs that hadn't yet hatched and were inside the chicken's stomach.

I hadn't liked to think about chickens since the time I was a Christian girl in the village and saw what they ate, for example, Grandpa Seremet's tubercular lungs.

What a shame that I wasn't allowed to read while I ate.

My mother's soups. The beet borscht whitened with sour cream— what a spectacular purple color. Pickled cucumber soup. Potato soup spiced with flakes of fried lard. Cabbage soup with smoked ribs or salami. Tomato soup with crunchy white rice. Were the recipes for all those soups written in the book my father gave my mother as a wedding gift, the book from which she'd borrowed a year's worth of menus when we were in the hiding place? And perhaps those were soups whose secret my mother managed to wheedle from the cook we had in Bochnia, Pani Patrycia, before the war was in the world?

We weren't the only ones to get packages from America. There were other people who were saved and had rich, distant relatives in America. Was everyone in America rich? There were strange stories about those packages from America. Not just the story about the elegant walking shoes. There was also the soup powder story.

Someone, my father told me, had received a package of food from his distant relatives in America. Canned foods, sugar cubes, milk powder, and egg powder. One of the boxes of soup powder didn't have a label. They ate the food from the cans, the pineapple, the fruit salad; they ate the square meat from the tins that had an opener attached; and they made soup from the soup powder. Finally, only the box of soup powder without a label was left. They cooked and ate the contents.

Weeks later, a letter arrived from the distant relatives who had sent the package, and in it, the last request of their distant aunt, Aunt Fanda. She asked that her ashes, in the sealed box, be scattered over the Vistula River, the river of her childhood, her beloved river, the river on whose banks she'd had her first kiss from Uncle Mundek on the shortest night of the year, the night bouquets of flowers and lit candles are thrown into the river, and the illuminated bouquets float downstream with the current in memory of the Virgin Wanda who refused to marry the German Knights of the Crusade and drowned her youth, beauty, and virginity in the waters of the Vistula. That was the night when the fern bloomed, the flower with a heart of gold.

Aunt Fanda had been eaten. I'm not sure that my father believed that story.

And once, we received a crate of oranges. I still didn't know that those were sabra oranges sent by my aunt in Palestine. Bright round suns. Everything about them was wonderful. The shape, the color, the peel, the dripping slices, the juice, the pits, the soft white covering. They were so delicious. It was a pity to wash my hands afterward.

I used to inhale the aroma, save the peels, scrape off and eat the white covering. The whole orange, the whole little sun, was wrapped in thin, rustling paper. I smoothed out those papers and pressed them between the pages of my books. They kept their fragrance for a long time. Beauty has a smell. So does fear, I remember.

THAT HAT, THE HORRIFIC HAT, THE HATED, TORTUROUS HAT, came in one of the first packages of clothing. It had been knitted by a machine and tended to ride up. Its dominant color was red, with a white and blue pattern. It was a kind of stocking cap, closed on the top, with large white pom-poms attached to the two corners. They stuck up from either side of my head and swayed with every movement I made. That hat was grotesque and hideously ugly.

It was clearly a girl's hat, and I was the girl in our little family. I was given the hat and I had to wear it. It was winter and it was cold. But no matter how much I pulled it down, all the way to my eyes, to the tip of my nose, the hat would ride up. That was its nature—to ride up more and more until it came off my head and fell. There was a moment—recognizing it required a remarkable intuitive sense that bordered on foresight—when there was still a hope of setting the hat firmly on my head and preventing it from falling, and at that moment, I had to execute a particular movement, a complex, rapid jerk of my head. I developed exceptional skill at it, and whenever the hat started riding up over my straight hair, threatening to fall off, I would jerk my head quickly and put it back in place.

That jerking became a tic, my own private movement. I'd jerk my head when I was wearing the hated hat, and I'd jerk it when I wasn't. I'd jerk it in the morning, I'd jerk it at noon, I'd jerk it in the evening. I'd jerk it at home, I'd jerk it on the street. I even jerked it at the school they finally sent me to when they accidentally found out that I didn't know how to write.

No one ever thought that a girl who takes books out of three libraries, a girl who'd finished reading all of Victor Hugo, didn't know how to write.

In the all-girls' school, they laughed and made fun of me, calling me *kreciglowka*—the girl who turns her head. In Polish, that's one word. In Polish it sounds much worse.

And we still haven't talked about the dentist.

Maybe it's time to talk about the dentist.

THE DENTIST WAS A FRIEND OF MY MOTHER'S BROTHER, UNCLE Leibek, who was also a dentist. They went to dental school together, maybe in Berlin, maybe in Vienna.

The Germans killed Uncle Leibek, my mother's brother.

The dentist couldn't sleep at night, and he talked a great deal about that with my mother. My mother had insomnia too. She used to read all night. My white nights, she said. A wonderful book, she'd add.

The situation was at its worst after the treatments she had, when they injected a huge hollow needle between her ribs into her lung, filled with special gas to shrink the lung with the hole in it gnawed by the tuberculosis bacilli.

I always tried not to listen to my mother's stories about her illness. Those stories repulsed me and I wasn't interested in them. I tried not to hear or understand anything.

Sometimes she wouldn't fall asleep until dawn. Then my father and I would tiptoe around and whisper. We did everything very, very quietly. We knew how to do that very well from the hiding place during the war.

In the future, the dentist would try to kill himself. Twice. He wouldn't succeed.

A terrible accident would happen. In the late afternoon, he would be run over by a tram on its way to the Wawel Kings Palace, which stood high on a hill above the Vistula, the river that never received the ashes of Aunt Fanda from Brooklyn.

He would die.

My father had gleaming white teeth. You could see them when he smiled, although he didn't smile much, and when he did, he kept his lips closed. He was usually tired and he had digestive problems. He had pains in his stomach and intestines.

My mother said he ruined his digestive system when he was a poor student and ate potato soup thickened with burnt flour every day in a restaurant owned by a dirty widow, Frau Sharmantska.

Dirty old Frau Sharmantska was saved in the war and again opened a small restaurant in her basement room, again poisoning the stomachs of poor lonely students. Above her, under the steps, lived the woman who picked up stitches and stopped the runs in stockings from running any further up the legs of elegant ladies. She lived in a tiny alcove, and on her left was the watchmaker's alcove. A kind of small telescope called a loupe stuck in one of his eyes lent his face a permanent expression, an eternal, twisted smile drawn to the side. Millions of beautiful, gleaming items rolled around in the circle of light cast by the small, bright lamp— gearwheels, springs, astonishingly tiny screws. Pan Zenon Kornowski, the watchmaker, fixed my first watch.

A very small watch I received in Lvov, after the war ended.

Written on the face of the watch was the word DOXA. It was made in Switzerland, the country my distant Uncle Goldman sent chocolate from, wrapped in rustling, useful golden paper, the country that chose never to get involved in any war, just to sell, sell, and sell. Watches, chocolate, rifles.

Distant Uncle Goldman from Zurich also liked to sell. He had a shop that sold sewing accessories and equipment for tailors. How happy the Parisian dressmaker, Panna Zofia, would have been if Uncle Goldman had been her uncle!

On the left of the watchmaker's alcove, in a slightly larger alcove with a small dirty window, worked Jacek Kowalski, the shoemaker.

The watchmaker and the shoemaker were friends, always talking loudly to each other. The shoemaker yelled with his mouth full of tiny nails and a cigarette butt, usually unlit, and the watchmaker yelled without looking up from the watch he was fixing, the skin around his eye pressed tightly against the loupe.

The shoemaker, Pan Jacek Kowalski, made me the pair of high shoes that we put the torturous insoles into.

The watchmaker and the shoemaker were nice people, and both hated the man who repaired pens. They didn't talk to him.

The man who repaired pens, who also had an alcove in that cellar of alcoves, was bald and had blue spider's hands. He smelled blue. His name was Pan Lech Podwiarski, and he repaired my first fountain pen, a magnificent pen. It had a real fourteen-carat-gold nib with an engraved inscription, and the handle had a marble pattern in deep ultramarine.

I got that pen from Uncle Isser Laufer, who wore an upside-down velvet saucer under his wide-brimmed black hat. Every once in a while, Uncle Isser Laufer brought suitcases full of wonderful things to our house. Silver lamps, candlesticks, paintings, books, and once—pens.

He bought and sold those things, the "after-the-Jews" things, the murdered Jews.

He'd bring his suitcases in the late evening, almost nighttime, and ask my mother and father—who, as veteran Communists, were above suspicion—to hide them in our house for a night or a day. Dealing in those things was illegal, and he put himself and my parents at risk.

They never said no to him.

Before the war, Isser Laufer had had a young wife and a baby. The baby's name was Adam. I don't know what the wife's name was. After the war, he had neither baby nor wife.

Isser never talked about it. I was grateful.

My mother and father were very glad when Isser Laufer found a woman and got married.

It was at his wedding that I first saw people with beards and sidelocks wearing black clothes and hats that had small, velvet, upside-down-saucer hats under them, just like Uncle Isser Laufer's. I'd seen Jews like that in the photo album my father once brought home. One picture showed a German cutting the sidelocks off someone like that, a Jew.

The Jews at Isser's wedding had shawls with fringes at the corners and black stripes on the sides. They affixed square black boxes to the middle of their foreheads and wound black leather straps around their forearms. Wrapped in their white shawls, they all faced the same direction, and as they swayed, they mumbled things in an incomprehensible language.

My father said they were religious Jews, not like us. We were nonreligious Jews, Communist Jews. He told me that they were saying very ancient Jewish prayers in a very ancient language, Hebrew, to a very ancient God, the God he'd told me about in our hiding place.

Isser Laufer's bride was much younger than he was. They met at the Jewish Komitet, where they'd gone in the hope of finding relatives. Isser Laufer's future bride was hoping to find someone there—maybe her father, maybe her mother, or her brother. Someone.

She was the only one in her family who survived.

Her mother had shoved her hard out of the line of people being led to the transport, toward the crowd of Poles watching them. A Polish couple had caught her, took her home, and raised her till the end of the war.

If the Germans had known she was Jewish, they would have murdered not only her, but them too, and also their new baby.

They were noble, they were heroes. They saved her, loved her, made her their daughter. Isser's young bride was named Eva. My mother's dressmaker, Panna Zofia Duda, made her a generous trousseau, paid for by Isser, who was growing rich. Buying and selling the possessions of murdered Jews was a thriving business.

One of the dresses was as beautiful as a dream: a Christian Dior design called the New Look. Deep ultramarine, like the color of Celinka's mother's dress, like the color of the pen Isser gave me, like the color of the number tattooed on the skin of his forearm. It was made of soft, thin wool and had long, narrow sleeves, a fitted waist, a very wide, military stand-up collar, a wide skirt, a full cloche. Two strips of ruffles flowed down the front of that cloche.

It was gorgeous. Not even in movies had I ever seen anything so spectacular. The wedding took place in the somber hall of the Jewish Komitet.

Men and women sat separately at two long tables covered with cracked oilcloth. That was strange. I think I was the only child in the hall. So few Jewish children were saved in the war.

Eva, the bride, wore a regular-length white dress and a crown of starched tulle. The scent of her bouquet of white carnations overcame the smells of the gefilte fish, the jellied chicken feet, the chopped liver, the eggs and onions, the horseradish, the chicken soup, the tzimmes, and the compote. The sweet challah was delicious, and there were pieces of herring rolled into small snails, and a colorless drink. The man who poured the drink smelled like Juzef Juzak, the carpenter and alcoholic. My mother said that was special Jewish food, and the Jews didn't cook meat with milk or eat pigs.

How nice the Jews could be—they didn't eat pigs!

One of the carnations from Eva's wedding bouquet was pinned on the lapel of Isser's elegant jacket, the lace as white as his face. Eva looked very pretty, even though she was usually ugly.

They stood together under a piece of square material stretched onto four poles held by four men with funny curled beards. One man, dressed like them—a rabbi, my father whispered to me—spoke and cried, cried and spoke, mumbling incomprehensible words. Then we couldn't hear him anymore because everyone was crying very, very quietly.

They gave me a candle to hold, and it dripped on my hand, burning painfully.

A small glass was wrapped in newspaper and Isser Laufer smashed it with the heel of his shoe. Everyone cried out with joy in their strange language.

My mother told me that the rabbi who sanctified the marriage between Eva and Isser, the one who spoke and cried, cried and spoke, was the older brother of Isser's first wife, mother of the baby, Adam.

After the wedding, Isser and Eva went to America and there, in New Jersey, they had an egg farm. They sold eggs to the Americans and lived in peace.

WHEN MY FATHER SMILED, IT WAS WITH CLOSED LIPS. HIS WHITE teeth didn't show and didn't gleam. It was a pensive, rather sad smile.

My father's beautiful teeth were healthy. They didn't have even one filling. Not so my mother's teeth. They had been ruined back in her road-paving pioneer days in Palestine.

My mother was the first patient after the war to be treated by our family friend, Uncle Leibek's fellow student at dental school. He pulled out all the poor little stumps left in her mouth after my father, with his skilled hands and the help of his amazing Swiss pocketknife, pulled out all her gold crowns when they were in the hiding place and I was still in Marcinkowice. Those gold crowns bought me a few more weeks of freedom, air, sun, food, life.

The dentist made my mother false teeth, which, from then until her last day, sat grinning in a glass of water every night. She never got used to them.

Then it was my turn.

It's time to talk about the dentist.

It began with the smell. The first sign was the nauseating smell.

The dentist sat me down on a kind of chair, more precisely an armchair, with the arms upholstered in green leather under my elbows and a stiff, round headrest, like a pillow. He raised the armchair and tilted me backward. The footrest, made of shiny metal and decorated with a strange kind of embossing, rose along with the armchair. My head spun, like it did when I was on a swing or a bus. I felt nauseous.

A powerful lamp switched on above me, assaulting my eyes. On the left was a small, cracked porcelain bowl, with all sorts of horrifying tools hanging around it. The dentist tied a stained, peeling oilcloth bib under my chin as if I were a baby who drooled and spit up. He aimed the blinding light into my mouth, opened wide at the dentist's command.

I closed my eyes and tried not to faint.

My mother stood there, that familiar, righteous expression on her face. *Mein sorgenkind*, my child of sorrow.

The nauseating smell, solid and steadfast, filled the air around me. Only the dentist's hands had the mild smell of a clothes closet. The examination began.

With a sharp instrument, the dentist probed all my teeth for holes and found them easily.

Holes, holes, and holes.

A nightmare.

My mother clucked with her toothless mouth. The false teeth were not ready yet. So worrisome. Her child of sorrow. The dentist said that the appalling condition of my teeth was the result of malnutrition and hunger. He had to fix and save whatever was possible.

Fillings, fillings, and fillings. A million fillings.

There was a horrifying, deafening sound. The drill had been turned on, and the dentist's hand, with its delicate, clothes-closet smell, armed with a drill, invaded my open mouth and started drilling into my brain.

Into my face. Into my soul.

It was horrible.

Ghastly.

Unbearable.

I'd never felt such pain in my life.

I pushed away the dentist's hand, which was armed with the terrifying torture drill. I leaped out of the Inquisition armchair and closed my mouth.

None of the pleas, threats, or intimidation helped: my teeth would fall out; I'd never be able to smile.

As if I had reasons to smile.

They explained that the pain would get worse if we didn't take care of those wretched holes now, but no explanation convinced me.

I stood my ground.

I won't mention the dentist again.

I much preferred the dead grandfather from the village of Marcinkowice, where I was a little Christian girl. I had fond memories of old Grandpa Seremet, who spit up his lungs till he died. He rescued me from terrible toothaches with a pair of huge, rusted carpenter's pliers he held in his crooked fingers with their long, black nails. He put the pliers in my mouth, pulled out the tooth, and that was that.

I won't mention the dentist again.

MY BEST FRIENDS IN THOSE DISTANT DAYS IN KRAKOW WERE the cardboard dolls I drew, colored, and cut out. They were no more than fifteen centimeters tall, and their underwear was drawn on their bodies. Each one had a name, a personality, a biography, and based on their developing life stories, I'd make cardboard clothes and accessories for them—dresses and belts, hats and shoes, parasols and fans, everything drawn, colored, and cut out. Every article of clothing and accessory had little tabs that held them on the doll's shoulders or against her body.

I remember nine dolls—girls, boys, men, and especially the beautiful, elegant women like the ones in the magazines in the Parisian salon of my mother's dressmaker, Panna Zofia Duda. The dress that Eva, Isser Laufer's bride, wore served as a model for many of my dresses.

The tabs wore out quickly, and I often had to make maintenance repairs—paste on new tabs and disguise the scars—a great deal of work. But even if a doll or a dress was worn out beyond repair, I didn't part from it. I always had a shoebox that I used as a coffin for my used dolls and dresses. Dolls might actually be resurrected. I had to find a new shoebox every now and then because my mother would decide to throw out the one I had.

Who could have imagined the calamity that would suddenly befall the dolls and their wonderful life stories that intertwined in a mighty saga?

When I came home from school one day, I heard children's voices in our room, unfamiliar voices. They were the voices of two girls my age, perhaps twins. Their parents had come to visit my mother and father and brought their daughters with them. They came from Warsaw, the capital. The girls were wearing shiny black patent leather shoes like the ones I had seen on dolls in a toyshop window. I'd never had such a wonderful doll.

I loved my plain cardboard dolls, the dolls I made. I loved them the way I loved the dolls I'd made for myself in the village from a stick and an apple for a head that my good friends, the pigs, always gobbled up. I loved them the way I loved the wonderful doll my mother made for me after the war, the one that the children and I played with in the square cobblestone courtyard, the doll they coveted and finally stole from me.

The two girls I didn't know were playing with the dolls I'd drawn, colored, and cut out, my dolls. They were playing with their elegant clothes, with their stylish hats, their fancy wallets, their fans, their parasols.

Luckily you can't play with a doll's life story. Or can you?

Horrified, I watched the two girls I didn't know touching the delicate dolls. Some of them were so delicate that they could only be handled with the greatest care, and some were so worn out and frayed that they could be easily torn. Now their lives were in the hands of those girls I didn't know.

When the guests were finally about to leave, my mother, in an appalling and ridiculous attempt to ingratiate herself, gave them all my dolls, gave them my dolls as a gift!

Their clothes, their hats, their fans, their parasols, everything.

Even their life stories, the essence of their lives, their pasts, presents, and futures till the end of time.

I didn't protest, I didn't cry, I didn't say anything. Maybe I thought that's how it was in the world. My mother was very pleased. She was proud of me and my dolls and she told me how much those girls liked them, those girls with their fancy clothes and black patent leather doll's shoes, the daughters of the Polish Council of State chairman, Edward Ochab, and his wife, Rachel, my mother's childhood friend from the Hashomer Hatsair youth movement.

What an honor. My dolls had been kidnapped and given to such a prestigious, distinguished family.

I stopped drawing, coloring, and cutting out cardboard dolls.

MY MOTHER WAS BORN IN A LITTLE TOWN CALLED OSWIENCIM in 1904, and even though she was still a child during World War I, she remembered how the Austrian officer burst into her parents' wholesale wine store on his horse.

An officer on a horse in a wine store. My mother remembered that.

So do I.

I remember the Polish woman.

Her name was Hania, Hania Seremet.

We were in the ghetto by then. There wasn't much food, but I wasn't really hungry. The period of plenty in the slaughterhouse and tanning factory where my father worked as an accountant was over. The good German manager, Herr Knaup, was very pleased with my father's work, so he let him, my mother, and me live in the tiny room next to the slaughterhouse, as long as it could be kept hidden from the Gestapo, of course.

In the end, we were thrown out of the slaughterhouse back to the ghetto. The era of pails of blood and wreaths of entrails was over.

There were constant *aktions* in the ghetto, even children's *aktions*. Someone told my mother that the Germans had set up a playground to lure the children into going there, making it easier to hunt them down and murder them. And there were other places that had large concentrations of children—schools, orphanages, hospitals—and that fact also made hunting them down and murdering them much easier. That's what my mother told me, told me, and told me. We have to get the girl out of here, she decided. We have to escape, get away, hide on the Aryan side, the side of life.

They said the ghetto was going to be liquidated. That all the Jews would be exterminated.

My mother and father already had a hiding place, with the Juzaks on Panienska Street, very close to the ghetto, but Rozalia Juzakowa, wife of Juzef Juzak, the carpenter and alcoholic, had laid down a condition: they could come, but without the girl. I was that girl. So they had to find a solution for me.

And that's how they found Hania Seremet.

My mother told me, told me, and told me.

Murderess, she called her.

The Polish woman, Hania Seremet, appeared one night in our little room in the ghetto.

How did she manage to get through the gate, past the armed guards, the walls, the fences?

My mother said she had a lover in the Gestapo.

She came into our tiny room in the apartment inhabited by many people, most of them strangers to each other, an apartment that was divided into little alcoves, sometimes by curtains or rags—flimsy illusions of privacy, patched and teeming with lice.

There was a stove in that apartment. The stove was in the kitchen. It was a kitchen stove for cooking. It had an opening for coal. That stove was never lit.

A fairly sophisticated bunker was dug behind the stove. My father planned it. My father could do anything with his hands. He knew how to plan bunkers, pull out gold teeth, make miniature goblets out of silver paper for my sweet little trained gray mice, Mysia and Tysia, start a fire with a magnifying glass and the sun's rays, forge papers, draw Magen Davids on fake armbands, and a million other useful and wonderful things. When the war was no longer in the world and we lived in Krakow, he knew how to do my arithmetic homework for me.

I have a diagram of the bunker my father drew. I don't know whether he made that diagram during the war, when he planned the bunker, or after the war, to add to the testimony he gave at the Jewish Komitet.

To get inside the bunker, we had to crawl through the opening for the coal. I remember the smell, the dark smell of coal powder. Years later, in Krakow, on days when I was sick, how pleasant it was to lie in my muslin bed while the frost drew wonderful flowers on the windowpanes and Pani Wyrzguwa stoked the giant porcelain stove in the corner—a stove-altar. But that was when the war was no longer in the world.

Once, before the ghetto was liquidated, when there was a children's *aktion*, I wasn't home and it suddenly became very urgent to get me back there and hide me in the stove. My father, who was still working for the good German, Herr Knaup, had forged papers saying that he was a worker absolutely essential to the Third Reich. Those days, such papers saved the lives of people who had them. That was a special *aktion* to catch children, so the adults weren't in any danger. And my father was a father, not a child.

I was a child.

My father was afraid to go into the street and bring me home.

My mother, who had no papers, went out and walked to the friends' house where I was, two alleys away. Two alleys between life and death.

My mother said, If I weren't who I am, you wouldn't be alive today. None of us would be alive.

I'd gone to play with the son of my parents' friends. He wasn't the beautiful boy, Daniel, who Hania Seremet left at the ghetto gate where the Germans murdered him. He was a different boy. My mother went out into the streets of the ghetto, which had emptied out, walked to their friends' house, and brought me home. The friends had already hidden their son, the boy I'd gone to play with, in a suitcase full of cloth remnants. The boy's mother was a dressmaker, and I'd gone there not only to play with her son, but also to try on a new dress she was making from the remnants of an old dress of my mother's—she'd turned the material inside out and chosen the pieces that weren't torn.

When we came home, my mother told me to crawl into the stove. Behind it, a few children who shared our apartment and a mother and her baby were already crowded into an amazingly small alcove. That was my first hiding place, if we don't count the hiding place under the straw in the wagon we rode in to escape from the Germans when the war broke out. There were a great many hiding places after that—closets, boxes, beds, hiding places within hiding places.

The woman with the baby who was in the hiding place with us always made the tenants in our shared ghetto apartment nervous. Her baby was shriveled and greenish.

My cousin Felix, Henryk's son, who was born after the war when there was plenty of food and no one was hunting down children anymore, looked like him.

After the Red Army liberated us and saved our lives, sad, lonely people who sometimes spoke that unpleasant, incomprehensible language came to visit my mother and father. They talked about the children who'd been hidden in bunkers when the Germans, armed with rifles, came to look for them, and what happened to those children if they suddenly burst out crying.

The greenish baby in our bunker in the ghetto didn't cry or scream, and the Germans passed by our house, didn't even come inside. I was saved again. My mother saved me.

IT WAS NIGHT, AND THERE WERE FOUR OF US IN OUR LITTLE room in the ghetto: my mother, my father, the stranger, and I. This is Hania Seremet, my mother told me. Ilusiu, *kochanie*, she said, from now on, your name is Irena Seremet.

Not Ilona, not Ilka, not Ilonka, not Ilusiu. From now on, I-r-e-n-a S-e-r-e-m-e-t. Irena Seremet f-o-r-e-v-e-r. And then she said,

> Our Father who art in heaven,
> Hallowed be Thy name;
> Thy kingdom come,
> Thy will be done,
> on earth as it is in heaven.
> Give us this day our daily bread,
> and forgive us our trespasses,
> as we forgive those who trespass against us;
> and lead us not into temptation,
> but deliver us from evil.

Repeat after me, my mother said.
I did.
Again, she said.
I repeated it again.
Again.
I repeated it a third time.
My father stood looking out the window at the night, his back to me.
I already knew the words in the right order.
Now on your knees, my mother said, you have to kneel and put your hands together. Like this.
My mother bent over me and positioned my limbs as if I were a doll.
Bend your head, my mother said.
Again now, for the last time, say it again.
Our Father who art in heaven . . .
I didn't make even one mistake.

I opened my eyes for a minute, kneeling with my head bent over my hands, and out of the corner of my eye caught my mother's expression of satisfaction. She was looking at Hania Seremet as if to say, Well, didn't I tell you? I promised you the girl would learn, and learn quickly! I know my girl.

My mother and father already knew Hania Seremet. They'd made the deal with her: such-and-such a sum of money for my life.

Hania Seremet must have doubted that a little girl like me could learn the Lord's Prayer so quickly. A lovely prayer. For me, it had only words and sounds.

It was all very quick.

And I believed that's how it was in the world.

What was I thinking? Did I think at all?

I stood up. Hania Seremet took some papers and a bundle from my mother. Later, I learned that my rags were in that bundle, along with a dark red velvet dress with white collar and cuffs.

I wore my only pair of shoes.

The papers were my forged documents. They had apparently been ordered earlier and cost a great deal of money. Hania Seremet must have received a great deal of money too, and a promise that she would keep getting more and more money as long as she took me out of that ghetto, a ghetto about to be liquidated, and hid me in a village with her parents as a Christian girl with a Christian girl's name.

My mother and father didn't tell me anything about the stranger who would come in the middle of the night to take me to a strange place.

The deal was carried out.

And what did I think, what did I feel?

A girl.

The four of us, my mother, my father, Hania Seremet, and I, walked quietly into the dark, narrow, short hallway. The heavy smell of sleep, the murmurings of dreams and waves of fear came from both sides of the hallway.

At the door, a whiff of that nauseating stench, horrible enough to bring tears, burned our eyes again. The latrine. The last door on the right.

A stinking latrine, filthy and dark: the toilet bowl broken, the glaze cracked, and what might once have been white had turned brown. There was no seat. I was so afraid I'd fall into that foul hole that I held onto the rim of the cracked bowl although it really repulsed me, and the smell, or the memory of the smell, stuck to my hands and pursued me everywhere.

The iron water tank was hung high up, under the ceiling. Its paint was also peeling. A kind of logo was imprinted on it, a drawing with oval writing, but no matter how much I looked at it or how hard I tried to understand it, I couldn't figure it out.

All sorts of things were tied to the handle of the water tank to make it longer: ropes, a bit of chain, a thin string. They were ripped off time after time because they were pulled so hard, and then something new had to be improvised to lengthen the handle, which always hung out of reach.

Layers of olive green paint and plaster peeled from the leprous walls, exposing bricks in some places. The walls were spotted not only with a mix of oil paint, plaster, and bricks, but also with brown smears in all directions.

I could easily make out animals, people, castles, monsters, and flowers—wonderful, fascinating shapes—between the peeling layers and brown smears.

MY FATHER OPENED THE DOOR. WE WENT OUT. WE WALKED down the wooden stairs. A step creaked, the iron railing was damp and cold. The smell of the railing clung to my right hand for a long time afterward. That smell had a heavy taste, dark and stinging. When we lived in Krakow and the war was no longer in the world, the frozen copper bars in the trams had a similar taste.

We went out. Into the street.

Left behind us was an ancient smell, layers of the putrid stench of cabbage and pork.

I'd tried not to breathe.

You can close your ears. You can close your eyes.

But it's very hard not to breathe.

We went outside.

The stench of poor people's food trailed behind us.

It was a wet night full of air.

I breathed.

We walked quickly in single file close to the walls of the buildings. The farther away we got from the building we lived in, the lower the buildings got.

No one held my hand.

We hurried along.

Hania Seremet, my mother, my father, and I, and numerous huge, squat rats. We slipped away.

The rats were also slipping away, in the opposite direction.

It was a dark night, and from a distance, probably from the direction of the ghetto guard towers, we heard laughter, and long shafts of light probed the area. I didn't cry.

We reached the place that might have been the end of the ghetto. An ordinary, unremarkable fence.

I didn't cry.

We stopped—Hania Seremet, my mother, my father, and I. No one held my hand.

I didn't cry.

Hania Seremet pushed me through a hole in the fence to the other side and squeezed through after me.

I didn't cry.

I didn't turn around.

I was abandoned.

My mother told me, told me, and told me about the way back to the ghetto. How I hated all those stories.

She told me how she cried, cried, and cried.

After Hania Seremet took me.

After I was abandoned.

She told me how she could barely drag herself back to the ghetto, leaning against my father.

My father never told me anything.

That's how they handed me over, my mother told me. We handed you over to Hania Seremet, to almost sure death. To Hania Seremet, the murderess.

When we handed you over to that murderess, my mother said, I cried all the way back. As if I were coming back from a funeral. My daughter's funeral. My only child.

I didn't think I'd ever see you again.

That's what my mother told me.

I so hated to hear her tell the story of that night, of going back.

Years later, many, many years later, I asked my mother, Mamusiu, please tell me—I always addressed my mother politely and never raised my voice or used a word considered rude—why did you hand me over to that woman, to that Hania Seremet, if you thought you were handing me over to certain death?

But *kochanie*, we had no choice, no other way, my mother replied impatiently, surprised that I didn't understand the situation as it was then, Hania Seremet was the only one who agreed to take you; the hiding place with the Juzaks on Panienska Street had already been arranged; and you know that they absolutely would not take a child!

We had no choice.

We were all helpless.

That was absolutely clear.

And it was after all the *aktions*, right before the final liquidation of the ghetto, the last minute!

Little girl,
I want to tell you a story,
My little girl,
The girl I was
The girl I am
The girl inside me.
I reach out to you.
Come to me.
Ilona, Ilka, Ilonka, Ilusia.
My little one.
I take you in my arms.
I embrace you.
I hold you close.
You are inside me.
You were a little girl,
You were me.
My two sons were born of you, of me.
They were inside you, inside me.
And in them, the grandchildren
And great-grandchildren that would come.
I reach out to you,
Little girl,

Come to me.
I take you in my arms,
I want to embrace you,
Take care of you,
Be with you,
Look at you,
Listen to you,
Touch you,
Protect you,
Comfort you,
You
You
You.
I want to stroke your head,
Your hair,
Your face,
Forever
And lull you to sleep in my arms
With warmth and compassion.
Curl up safely
Little girl,
In my arms,
In me,
Rest.
Don't worry! Don't worry! Don't worry!
I'll never leave you.
I'll never leave you as long as I live,
For we shall die together,
You and I.
I want to tell you a story
About what was.
What I remember of what was.
I want to tell you a story.
And I'll weep,
And so will you,
You'll weep without fear.
You'll weep openly.
It's a happy end.
That's how it will be.

TALL, THIN HANIA SEREMET, WITH THE SKIN OF HER GLOWING
white face pulled tautly over her high cheekbones and her square jaw
clenched, with her flashing green eyes and her pitch-black hair, eyelashes,

and brows, with her mouth as narrow as a well-healed scar, beautiful, elegant Hania Seremet was a criminal.

A murderess, just as my mother said.

She was well known in the ghetto.

She had good connections. She had an in with the Germans and the Gestapo. She did a lot of business. She promised to help many of the Jews in the ghetto, to arrange hiding places on the Aryan side.

She would take them out, whole families, only the richest families, with their diamonds, their furs, their money, their jewelry, with forged papers that cost a fortune, with promises and hope that they would have a hiding place, a future, life. Many of those people were dumped back at the ghetto gates stripped of everything. No one knew what happened to the others.

My mother told me, told me, and told me.

She was the only one willing to take me. For money, of course, quite a bit of money.

That was a lie, the money.

My mother and father lied to Hania Seremet about the money.

There was no money. Only a small amount, a very small amount. Certainly not a fortune, like they promised to Hania Seremet. After all, my father had filled his warehouses with merchandise right before the Germans invaded.

My father never had debts. My father paid cash for the merchandise he bought. The warehouses were bursting with building materials at the very time they began to destroy everything, and we, my mother, my father, and I, fled with one suitcase and no money.

Everything was lost, just as the gypsy woman had predicted.

Hania Seremet, the murderess, left people to die.

But not always. Not everyone.

For example, she didn't leave me to die.

We went through the hole in the fence, Hania Seremet and I, just the two of us.

We were outside the ghetto, on the Aryan side, the side of life. Suddenly there were no rats. An enormous, empty area spread out in front of us. A square? A field? A triangular, corner house stood on the far end, two parallel streets on either side of it.

We began walking, the stranger, Hania Seremet, the woman I'd seen for the first time that night, and I. We stepped onto a sidewalk lined with very tall trees. The streets were very wide. There were no rats. A dog stood there. The street was paved with oval stones called cobblestones.

The carriage that took my mother and father to give birth to me in the prestigious hospital in Krakow had clattered along cobblestones like that, and I found my dear dead rat in a puddle on cobblestones like that in the inner courtyard of our building in Lvov.

It was a wet night. Every now and then, blue light flashed from the tram tracks. It was spectacular.

The dog standing there suddenly began to walk. From the direction his stooped body was taking, you could distinguish between his head and his tail.

The night was becoming lighter, fading.

A man, his head lowered between his shoulders, his collar raised and his hands deep in his pockets, walked in the opposite direction to the dog. A trickle of people and rain began. A two-car tram passed by, vibrating noisily, and lightning flashed on the electric cables.

Beautiful, happy sounds.

Sparks flew from the tracks, fireworks. The lit windows of the cars were empty. Only three of them showed silhouettes drawn into themselves.

The train driver was standing in the first car.

Later, when there'd be no more war and I'd remain alive and the Germans wouldn't murder me, how much I'd love to stand behind the driver and watch his clever, precise movements with admiration as he played on the beautiful, shiny copper handles, pipes, wheels, levers, and brakes.

The night grew lighter and lighter.

The wind began to stir, bringing with it the smells of horse, straw, souring milk, and people's drowsiness. I heard a train whistle, not far off, innocent. Still innocent. A milkman's wagon passed by us, a hot white smell wafting behind it.

The melody of horseshoes clacking, the clatter of wagon wheels over cobblestones, the rattle of full milk pails banging against each other, the sound of milk splashing against the inside of the pails. The figure of the wagon driver, the milkman, his head lowered between his shoulders, like the dog, like the passerby, like the tram passengers.

The stranger, the tall, thin woman named Hania Seremet, and I reached the train station. It was no longer night.

The car Hania Seremet and I rode in was filled with soldiers. German soldiers. They'd been there quite a while before we boarded.

They were handsome and clean, and smelled of the wool their uniforms were made of, of boot polish and soap. They were amiable and cheerful. They flirted courteously with Hania Seremet and played with me.

They gave me sugar cubes. They said I was as pretty as a doll.

I remember that.

Hania Seremet wrote proudly to my mother about how I stole the heart of the *Wehrmacht* with my beauty and charm.

My mother repeated that story endlessly; she told it, told it, and told it.

How I hated all those stories.

I always felt guilty and put off by the fact that my mother thought the German soldiers' compliments were so important.

The train rode on, not for a long time. It wasn't raining anymore. It grew light, turned into a beautiful day.

We reached the village, a tiny station. We walked along a dirt road, the stranger carrying my bundle of rags, my forged papers, her shiny black bag, and me.

I didn't cry.

She didn't hold my hand.

I continued to not cry.

I must have thought that's the way it is in the world.

We walked along the dirt road, we arrived.

The name of the village was Marcinkowice. The tall, thin Polish woman, Hania Seremet, and I reached her parents' house in the village where she was born. Or maybe it was her grandparents' house, I don't know. What do I remember? What do I really remember? Maybe I only remember a story I was told? Or a story I made up? Or just dreamed?

The smell I remember is real.

You can't tell anyone a smell.

THE HOUSE IN THE VILLAGE I LIVED IN HAD A STRAGGLY, gray straw roof with a red brick chimney sticking up from it. Fragrant white smoke rose from it. The stranger, Hania Seremet, left me, my forged papers, and my bundle of rags there, in that house, with Grandpa and Grandma Seremet.

Hania Seremet, the stranger, went away quickly.

I was left with those two people, also strangers. Before leaving, Hania Seremet told me to call them Grandpa and Grandma—*dziadzio* and *babcia*. They were shorter than other grown-ups I'd known, and they were old and ugly. They gave off a different smell, heavy but not repulsive. Pleasant, even.

The grandfather was bent in two. He had a sparse beard and long yellowish white hair.

He didn't have much longer to live.

The grandmother usually sat in the door, on the threshold, on an unplaned wooden bench. The splinters of that wooden bench pricked my hands more than once, and even worse, under my nails.

The grandfather coughed, coughed, and coughed, long, deep, echoing coughs that ended with wheezes, grunts, and spitting. He spit dark red blood and lumps. Maybe pieces of his lungs. The lumps were pink.

Sometimes one of the stupid chickens that ran around the entire yard and house discovered one of those pink lumps and started pecking at it, even though Grandpa Seremet tried to cover what he spit up by kicking sandy soil over it with his foot.

Grandma Seremet was missing a front tooth, and all the words that had an "s" or "sh" sound came out of her mouth like a whistle. Her sparse hair, gathered into a thin bun, resembled the color of the straw roof of the house. Every once in a while, for no apparent reason, Grandma Seremet would lift her arms in a panic and pull out one of the many pins stuck in her bun. She would put the pin between her lips and her face would take on a strange expression because her mouth, tightened around the pin, would stretch sideways crookedly, like a forced smile, making me afraid that she would swallow it. With a rapid movement of her arms, Grandma Seremet would wind the bun on the back of her neck, hold it there tightly with one hand, and with the other, pull the pin out of her mouth and stick it in the bun. The other pins loosened immediately, but Grandma Seremet didn't know that, and she was satisfied. Her expression remained pleasant and optimistic until the next dramatic moment of emergency occurred.

The grandmother wore several petticoats under her skirt, and an apron with a torn pocket in an unidentifiable color was tied around her thin waist. An eternal, damp spot of dirt adorned her stomach.

The inside of the house was dark. The stupid chickens ran around inside the house too, climbed onto the beds, the chairs, ran into the closets, and climbed on the tables. I never encountered a cooked chicken on the table.

There was a large stove in one corner. I'd already known one stove—in the ghetto, I'd smelled the stove from the inside. They were very much alike, the stove in the ghetto and the stove in the village, but in one respect, they were totally different. The stove in the village was always burning, and the steam that rose from the pot on the burner gave off a delicious smell, the smell of potatoes.

On the wall hung a picture of a bearded man, the hint of a smile on his face, holding open his shirt to show a red heart painted on his chest, golden rays spreading outward from it. And there was a picture of a woman in a white gown that came down to her feet, with a blue robe and flowing golden hair, balanced admirably on a crescent, a yellow circle of stars around her head. Candles were burning under the picture, maybe candles in red cups—I don't know if there was electricity—and vases of multicolored paper flowers in many different colors stood on either side of the candles. The candles and vases of flowers were on a wooden shelf covered with a stunningly beautiful white lace doily. The man with the red heart looked sad, but the hint of a smile on his lips was pleasant and promising.

Most wonderful of all was the smell of potatoes. Oh, potatoes!

I smelled it the minute I arrived there. I still didn't realize how important potatoes would be in my new life.

I still didn't realize that you had to peel potatoes before cooking them.

I still didn't realize that you had to grate them on a sharp, rusty grater if you wanted to make pancakes out of them. They were a delicacy, those potato pancakes. Maybe a bit of blood from my knuckles added flavor.

I still didn't realize that potato grating would be one of the many jobs to fill my new life. That I'd be a potato peeler, a horse shepherd, a goose shepherd, a carrot picker, a corn peeler, the one who swept the house and yard, who brought the boiling pea soup from the church's soup kitchen and handed pails full of smelly, unidentifiable slop to the pigs, my amiable friends.

The grater was sharp and rusty, and no matter how hard I tried not to let it happen, at some point a scrap of potato would fall out of my hand and my fingers would slide down the grater, cut so badly that they bled. Those poor fingers. My knuckles were scraped almost to the bone, and they were scraped again before they had a chance to heal.

Knuckles without skin, without flesh. Over the years, those wounds seeped down into a deep place where they could not be seen. It was so unpleasant to discover those things. To know that they existed, to remember.

EVERYONE IN THAT VILLAGE WORKED VERY HARD. I DON'T believe that they made me work harder than others worked. I don't believe that they would have treated me differently even if I'd been their flesh-and-blood granddaughter, not a Jewish girl the Germans wanted to hunt down and murder.

They were quiet people. They never touched me, not in a good way or a bad way.

The grandfather even helped me sometimes. When I had splinters in my hand or under my nails from the unplaned wooden bench that stood at the door of the house, he would dig them out with a needle.

Once, he simply saved me.

I was suffering the torments of a horrendous toothache. It was torture. And that grandfather gently pulled out the tooth with a pair of huge, black carpenter's pliers and saved me.

That's the kind of person that grandfather was.

Later on, he died.

A mighty torrent of blood erupted from him and he died.

I was very sorry that he died.

At his funeral, I was constantly afraid that I'd burst out laughing. I wanted so much to laugh during the funeral procession, which moved slowly along a path that crossed the field of tall, ripe wheat. I walked between the heavy, golden stalks of wheat bowing down against the dark background of the azure sky.

Blue cornflowers and occasional red poppies glowed on the ground between the stalks.

The priest walked at the head of the procession. I knew him from the soup kitchen that gave out boiling pea soup.

Our horse, my horse, the horse I shepherded, pulled the wagon that carried the dead grandfather in a coffin that looked very much like the box-bench-coffin I slept in, but was completely new. It smelled pleasantly of wood.

The grandmother, Hania Seremet, and some village people trailed behind the wagon. I walked with them too, keeping myself from jumping and skipping, terrified that I'd burst out laughing.

I controlled myself. I managed not to laugh. Maybe only a little, into my balled fist. I almost choked.

I had that urge, the urge to do the opposite of what was expected. I was very sorry that the grandfather had died. Grandpa and Grandma Seremet were quiet people. They hardly spoke to each other, and almost never to me.

I don't remember myself speaking to anyone until I was quite a bit older.

But I must have spoken a little because when Hania Seremet dumped me at my parents' hiding place after it became clear once and for all that there was no more money to pay for saving my life as a Christian girl in the village, my mother and father didn't understand me at all. We spoke a kind of strange dialect they found hard to decipher.

Hania Seremet took me to the village, to Grandpa and Grandma, and left. The grandfather and grandmother, whom I was seeing for the first time, took me into the small hallway that connected the house to the cowshed and the stable. Grandpa and Grandma Seremet must have known that I was coming and that my name was Irena. Maybe they didn't know that the night before, my name had been Ilona.

A small hallway. There was a wooden bench in it, a kind of box. The seat was attached by hinges, and Grandma Seremet opened it. There, inside that box, which looked very much like a coffin, was where I had to sleep.

Grandpa Seremet brought a sheaf of golden, fragrant straw from the stable and lined the bottom of the coffin.

By day, the lid was closed and the coffin became a bench.

At first the straw pricked me.

I got used to it.

I slept.

Maybe they covered me with a sack.

I was very sick once. I remember the pain. Terrible. Everything was on fire. The straw was wet, squashed, and sparse from my fever and sweat.

They changed the straw.

I got better.

When I was sick, maybe because of the fever, I saw all sorts of things that didn't exist, frightening, awful things, and also wonderful things.

And outside, when I recovered, there were totally real, wonderful things.

The clouds, the horse, the pigs, the geese, the sunflowers, the corn with its perfect, matching rows of yellow beads enveloped in soft celadon fairy hair as shiny as the yellow fabric of the unattainable clown in the home of the monster, Mrs. Hela Fishman, when the war was no longer in the world.

The sweet, orange carrots, with their wild, lacy green heads of hair that I could pull out of the garden bed, wipe with my sleeve, and eat.

Wonderful, stunningly beautiful things. All taken from me the day Hania Seremet dumped me at my parents' hiding place.

That's what my mother told me, told me, and told me: she dumped you back with us. The ghetto was gone. It was certain death. She dumped you into certain death. Juzak and Juzakowa didn't want to hide a little girl. She took you, then tossed you away.

SHE DUMPED ME INTO A SMALL ROOM IN AN ORDINARY APART-ment on Panienska Street in the city of Lvov. A high parterre apartment in an apartment building in a commonplace, respectable neighborhood. Before the German invasion, before the war was in the world, before the Germans decided they had to exterminate all the Jews, gypsies, homosexuals, and Communists, it had been the apartment of a Jewish gynecologist and his family.

His office was also there.

The hiding place was in the room that used to be his office.

The Jewish gynecologist, his mother, wife, two daughters, and baby son had been thrown out of the apartment right after the Germans invaded. The Germans murdered them. Now the Juzaks lived in the apartment: Mr. Juzef Juzak, who was a carpenter and an alcoholic, and his wife, Mrs. Rozalia Juzak, Juzakowa, a very religious Ukrainian. She was always crossing herself quickly, mumbling, "*Hospodin . . . Hospodin. . .*"

Years later, after the war, Juzakowa joined the Jehovah's Witnesses, and instead of saying *Zyd*, the Polish word for Jew that sounded insulting, she would say "Son of the Old Testament." In Polish, that's a single unwieldy and strange word.

And there was a child, the son of Pani Juzakowa and Pan Juzak. His name was Edjo, six years old, like me. Handsome, quiet, kind, and shy. He had dark golden hair, dry, brittle, and very, very straight, like the sheaves of fresh wheat Grandpa Seremet occasionally brought to line my coffin. Edjo's golden hair sometimes fell into his eyes, and when it did, he would push it back with a graceful toss of his head, a movement that was the epitome of beauty, until the next time it fell, which was not long in coming.

Ania, their daughter, was already dead. She was sixteen when she died.

My mother and father hid in that room from the time the ghetto was liquidated until the Red Army liberated us after heavy bombing. Batiushka Stalin's promise, "We shall celebrate in our streets too," came true and there really was a celebration. My mother and father hid in that hiding place for eighteen months. In the end, I hid there with them.

The room had two windows.

Hanging on the windows were curtains called *dyskretki* in Polish. They discreetly hid the bottom half of the windows so that no one could see inside. It was, in any case, a very high parterre apartment, far beyond a person's height. Those curtains had hung on the windows even before the German invasion, and in order to downplay the sudden changes that had been made in the room, they were left there after the room became my parents' hiding place.

Any change in the curtains would have meant certain death for my mother and father. And after Hania Seremet dumped me back in their hiding place, for me too.

That room, once the Jewish gynecologist's office, had two entrances. One door, always closed, sealed, and locked with a lock and a chain, led from the hiding place to the staircase of the building. It was through that door that Hania Seremet pushed me into the hiding place when everything was gone—my parents' money, the gold crowns my father pulled out of my mother's mouth with his skilled hands and the amazing Swiss pocketknife, and all the promises.

No more village, air, sun, carrots, horse, pigs, geese, or coffin on the Aryan side, the side of life.

The other door led into the Juzaks' apartment through a dark, narrow hallway. In the hallway, on the right, was the toilet, not as horrifying as the toilet in the ghetto, but it too stank of eye-burning ammonia, and it had a chain attached to a belt tied to a bit of string that hung from its tank, and there too, it was beyond my reach. The ceiling of that toilet was high, very high, and its walls were painted pink, peeling oil paint on the bottom half, and above that, up to the ceiling, peeling white plaster. Dividing the two halves was a strip printed with a repeating pattern of spirals, branches, trees, and other shapes I couldn't figure out. That was all very beautiful.

Stuck in the wall to the right of the filthy, cracked toilet was a large, crooked nail, deliberately bent. Usually speared on the nail were scraps of newspaper that had been torn into more or less equally sized squares. Despite the darkness, I always thumbed through those pieces of newspaper looking for pictures.

The toilet in the village was a kind of square, wooden shed that had a bench with a large round hole in it. I had to be very careful not to slip and fall inside, into the full cesspool. While there was no nail with square scraps of newspaper and the hope of finding pictures there, I could see the sky and the earth through the slits between the boards, and sometimes a beetle glowing with all the colors of the rainbow would crawl inside. And there were swarms of buzzing blue and green flies. The stench was less oppressive.

The pictures I found among the scraps of newspaper in the toilet of our hiding place were few and far between, and usually uninteresting—maps with arrows, airplanes, men in helmets, men in suits and hats, men encased in tight uniforms.

Those were scraps my father waited for eagerly. He would piece together the map from them, and with his stump of red pencil he would mark the Red Army front line.

And what would happen if the battles continued for a long time and the red pencil wore completely down before the Red Army liberated us? Would we die of hunger here, in this hiding place? Or maybe we would be found and murdered.

How anxiously my father waited for the Allies to open a second front. That didn't happen until after Stalingrad, when the victory of Tovarish Stalin and the Red Army was assured.

Once, in the toilet, I had wonderful good luck. I came upon a beautiful, rare picture of a girl with curls. My mother said that they were called bottle curls. The picture of the girl was continued on another square— her forehead, the top of her head, and in the center, a large, magnificent ribbon, like a butterfly, like the ribbon Hania Seremet tied in my hair when we went into town to be photographed so she could send the pictures to my mother and father, proof that I was alive.

I drew girls with ribbons like that in the rare empty spaces in the booklet of menus my mother dictated to my father in the hiding place when they had very little to eat.

There were menus for every day of the year, day after day after day, and no menu appeared more than once. For inspiration, my mother used the big black cookbook my father bought her when they moved into their new house in Bochnia. That cookbook went with my mother and father every time they ran away, was with them in the slaughterhouse and in the ghetto, and now it was with us in the hiding place. Another source of inspiration for my mother were the dishes prepared by Pani Patrycia, my parents' cook during the few years between their wedding and the German invasion. Pani Patrycia kept her recipes a secret, and only rarely, after listening to my mother's pleas spiced with flattery, did she give away a recipe or two.

We had no food in the hiding place. We were hungry. Maybe not very hungry, but never full.

I pulled off and saved those two newspaper scraps showing the girl with her ribbon and bottle curls. The precious picture joined my dearest treasure, the red thread that was eventually stolen by my sweet trained gray mice, Mysia and Tysia.

Rolling around in the muck on the filthy toilet floor in the hiding place were butts of the *machorka* cigarettes Pan Juzef Juzak used to roll from newspaper and smoke constantly, almost without a stop. The drunker he was, the more he vomited and spit, the less frugal he was, and the longer those foul, damp, chewed-on butts were, to my parents' great happiness.

My mother would lie in wait for Pan Juzef to go in and out of the toilet. When he came out, she would collect the precious butts quickly, before he sobered up and collected them himself. Then my mother and father would carefully, gently unroll the butts, empty the remains of the smelly, nauseating *machorka* onto a piece of newspaper, flatten them into a thin layer, and leave them to dry.

Later, my father would roll those dry remains into new cigarettes—a treasure.

My father had a kind of miracle tool, like a magician's, for rolling cigarettes, but sadly it didn't work with newspaper. That's what my father said. So he had to manage without it, and with his skilled hands he prepared rectangular pieces of newspaper, arranged a level row of *machorka* in the center, lifted the edges of the rectangle, and rolled it up tightly. While still holding it between his fingers, he would run the tip of his tongue along the edge of the paper, licking it quickly and evenly with just the right amount of saliva for the edge to stick to his tongue and not tear, but to stick nicely onto the thin cylinder of the cigarette. A masterpiece, magic.

And there was a new cigarette. Success! Joy! A treasure.

My mother and father smoked to the end of their lives. My father till he died at fifty-eight. My mother till she died at ninety and a half.

There was another problem, which had to do with lighting the cigarette. My father was a clever match splitter. A champion match splitter. With his skilled hands and the help of his amazing Swiss pocketknife, my father could split one match into four, even six smaller matches.

There was a shortage of everything, even matches. I think cigarettes were no less important to my mother and father than food.

In addition to his amazing Swiss pocketknife, my father had a magnifying glass.

It was a kind of metal box painted black, about six centimeters long, four centimeters wide, and a centimeter and a half high. The box was made of two parts: the top was actually a kind of cover, and the inner part sprang out of it like a telescope. The inner part was a round, folded magnifying glass connected by a spring, and it jumped out when the outer part of the box was moved. It also had a notch you could stand a 35-millimeter contact print in, to look at its details. It was a photographer's optical instrument.

That was my father's treasure—a gift from giant Uncle Dov, husband of my mother's beloved sister Minka, father of the girls, Rachel and Pnina. The Germans murdered them all. Uncle Dov, who was a gifted scientist, was also an avid photographer.

That was a treasure. My father used it to steal fire from the gods, like Prometheus.

My father would trap every ray of sun that came through the windows of our hiding place. He would aim the magnifying glass and focus the ray of sun on the newspaper, trying very hard to keep his hand as steady as possible. We all shook a little from weakness, maybe even from hunger. The focused ray of sun would darken the paper until the golden spot turned brown and the pleasant smell of scorched newspaper rose from it. Then the brown turned into black and a small flame burned a hole in the paper.

From that stolen fire, my mother and father would light their precious cigarettes with enormous satisfaction. They had saved a sixth of a rare match.

THE SHORT, NARROW, DARK HALLWAY LED INTO THE APARTment. The Juzaks lived in the apartment.

Sometimes, when we were very hungry and my mother and father were sure that Juzakowa was deliberately starving us so that we would die already, my mother would crawl into the kitchen inside the apartment, grab a potato, sometimes only half-cooked, from the pot boiling on the stove, and come back to us with burns on her hands and a triumphant smile on her face, and feed us crumb after crumb.

"Mother bird," my father used to say. My mother always tried as hard as she could to feed us.

My father and I were inside the apartment only once. At Christmas.

Perhaps Juzakowa invited us to sit around her holiday table in the kitchen because of the holiness of the holiday and all the forgiveness and love, or perhaps it was because most of the tenants in the building had gone off to celebrate with relatives in the provinces or in villages.

How different that place was from anything I'd ever seen. How splendid, how bright and warm.

In the corner stood a small Christmas tree hung with colored balls and tiny, lighted candles. There was a small wooden structure under the tree, very much like the stable in my village, Marcinkowice, except that part of the roof of the small stable was destroyed and the straw covering had gaping holes.

In one corner was a tiny, beautiful woman wearing a white dress and a blue cape; she was kneeling over a tiny box filled with straw, and inside the box, lying on that straw, was a sweet little pink doll, a baby. I thought to myself that my father, with his skilled hands and the help of his amazing Swiss pocketknife, of course, could have fixed that little stable of theirs to look like new. They only had to ask.

I only thought that, I didn't say it.

I must have believed that I saw and was invisible, and I didn't want to destroy that illusion. I never considered the possibility that my words could have any effect or could resonate.

And the aromas coming from the stove!

Hot, mysterious aromas, delectable, delicious aromas, and rising majestically above them all was the sweet perfume of the cake.

That was just too wonderful.

It was like the fairy tale of the boy who was given a table of wonders covered with all the dishes he wished for, everything he desired. It was like those wonderful flakes of manna that God scattered from the sky to the children of light so they wouldn't be hungry, and when they ate it, each one could imagine the most delicious taste he wanted.

I was in a fairy tale.

Our hiding place, which was so close by, right at the end of the short, narrow hallway, seemed so far away, as if it were in a different world.

And the light, how much light there was.

A lamp hanging over the table spread enormous light.

The hiding place was always so dark. And the food in the hiding place, if there was any, was always eaten immediately. There were never any leftovers, except for the breadcrumbs, of course, that I collected and saved to mold delicacies for my gray mice, the little mice my father and I trained, Mysia and Tysia.

Everyone sat down around the table, we on the side of the door leading to the backyard, and across from us, Juzak, Edjo, and Juzakowa, who was working at the stove. That was a real table, an actual table. It was very strange. And there was food on the table, real food.

It was a fairy tale.

It wasn't really happening.

An upside-down world.

Worrying.

I didn't want to be there.

Suddenly we heard a knock on the door behind us, the door that led to the inner courtyard, and before any of us could pull ourselves together after the fright of that surprise, the door was thrust open and on the threshold, flushed and nervous, was a neighbor holding a cobalt blue enamel cup. She walked right in.

Fear and trembling walked in with her.

My father, who was sitting with his back to the door, immediately dropped his head to his chest and covered it with his hands. Then he jumped up, shoving his chair aside and sending it clattering to the floor. Folded up like his amazing pocketknife, or like someone having a sudden convulsion, he slipped quickly into the hallway, to our hiding place.

My mother sat fixed to her chair, turned into stone, displaying her good, Aryan looks. I didn't want to be there. I believed I was invisible.

"Good evening, good evening, Pani Kowalowa. May God bless," said Juzakowa.

"Forever and ever," the neighbor responded.

"A guest in the house, God in the house. How can I be of service to my lovely neighbor?" Juzakowa continued as if nothing unusual were happening, as if finding the Jews hiding in her house didn't mean the end of us and the end of her.

Right now.

The end of us all.

"As you can see, our cousins are here for a visit," Juzakowa continued in her soft, heavy Ukrainian accent.

"I really need some milk. The bastard broke the jug," Pani Kowalowa said politely.

"Natural, very natural, dear lady. Of course, I'd be delighted to help you."

The thin, bluish milk that the farmers mixed with water, even though doing so had been strictly forbidden by generations of regimes, was poured into the cobalt blue mug, its glaze cracked in several places, exposing dark gray metal.

The neighbor turned her fat rear end with a rustle of starched underskirts and left, accompanied by a whiff of her caustic sweat and the aroma of holiday food.

She smelled of something else too, an obscene smell that only later would I realize was the smell of menstrual blood. Yolanda, an overgrown, fat girl—breasts, buttocks, arms—with blond hair and freckles, who was in my fifth grade class and always insisted on coddling me and sitting me on her lap, against my will, smelled like that. That was in Krakow, after they didn't murder us, after the Red Army liberated us, long after the war. And I was ten, maybe more.

Yolanda even invited me to her home. Actually, she kidnapped me.

She and her family lived in one of the most opulent palaces in Krakow's central square, the Rinek. The palace where the Czartoryskis, or maybe the Potockis, or the Radjiwills, had lived: gleaming parquet floors, thick carpets that absorbed the sound of your steps, carved doors in white and gold, paintings on the wall and stucco friezes, huge crystal chandeliers hanging from ceilings painted with skies, angels, flower bouquets, and half-naked creatures wrapped in pastel-colored rags. All moving about and circling around, none of them falling.

There were tall French windows with thin muslin curtains that streamed to the parquet floor, wooden mosaics in a variety of hues, and a grand piano in one corner. Entering that salon, we saw a man leaning against the latticework railing of a French window looking out at the square.

Tato, Yolanda said to him, meet my new friend.

As the man turned reluctantly to us, he let out a loud fart, a prolonged, echoing noise, a meteoric sound.

I stopped breathing.

Then he cleared his throat and a thick wad of saliva sprayed from between his lips, landing on the gleaming parquet.

He turned back to look out at the world, which hadn't stopped. The chandeliers hadn't fallen, the frescoes hadn't faded.

We were in a people's democracy, and in the name of equality, Yolanda, her *tato,* and the rest of her family had been moved from their remote village and dumped into Prince Rinek's palace in the noble city of Krakow, capital of the kings of ancient Poland.

Just like I was thrown out of my village and dumped into the hiding place in the home of Juzak and Juzakowa.

The excitement of the great holiday, the cooking, the guests, the heat of the stove, and the aromas of food had confused the good Mrs. Kowal, apparently dulling that most subtle sense that allowed her to know, the way many Ukrainians and Poles knew, who was a Jew. It was a very well-known talent. The Germans needed scientists to measure, test, consider, and decide who was a Jew, a Jew that had to be quickly exterminated. Not the Ukrainians and the Poles, who needed only one look. The blondest hair, the bluest eyes, the pinkest skin, and the most upturned nose couldn't fool them. After all, there were many such Jews who had the right look, my mother, for instance. How I hated that phrase: the right look.

The look of a non-Jew.

Jew, dirty Jew.

You didn't need such subtle discerning skills to recognize a Jew like my father or me. It was enough to look into our eyes. If the good Mrs. Kowal had seen my father's face, if he hadn't been sitting with his back to the door, if he hadn't covered his face with his hands, if he hadn't run off, she would have seen it immediately, even though she was tired and drunk: a Jew!

Not a cousin. What cousin?! A Jew!

My father looked very Jewish.

A little like Kafka, and I resembled him.

Huge eyes that hunger had made even larger, such a wise forehead, high and broad, fair skin, prominent ears, maybe a bit too prominent. I inherited my father's ears, and I thought they looked terrible, protruding and ugly, so I always tried to hide them.

Good, clever, spiritual, industrious hands, skilled hands.

And once again, we were saved by a strange miracle.

Our death continued to live with us.

I sensed the heavy, viscous fear of death that had invaded the room with the entrance of the neighbor, Mrs. Kowal. Like the rolled-up sleeves of the scratchy jacket that have always weighed down my wrists, like the crying from the orphanage built of red bricks, the crying that has become submerged forever in the catacomb of my heart—so a flash of that fear is trapped inside me, alive and well.

My mother and I got up from the fairy-tale table after my father slipped away, and went back to our hiding place too.

It took a few days for my mother and father to realize that we would keep on living. Our life went back to its routine—the regular, constant fear of death.

And I saw and was invisible.

THE HIDING PLACE WAS SMALL. MOST OF THE TIME, WE LAY there, my father, my mother, and I, and several million lice on a make-shift bed in the right-hand corner: mattresses, pillows, covers, and rags. Bedding and pieces of cloth. Threadbare down quilts covered in mauve satin. Wonderful white feathers sprouted from the seams, and I pulled them out, tossed them up, blew on them, spun them around in the air, and watched them fall silently. I stroked my eyelashes, my forehead, my lips with them.

It was lovely, almost like making soap bubbles with the colors of the rainbow sailing around in them, and they drift off, float, fly away, and burst, and the drop, as tiny as a wretched tear, falls to the floor.

And there were blankets made of knitted squares of many colors. They would keep unraveling at a new place each time, and my mother kept trying, in an endless Sisyphean effort, to keep the pieces together and stop them from unraveling.

There was one squashed pillow without a pillowcase. The pink cloth was stained with a variety of shades that formed wonderful shapes. Those shapes held the most amazing creatures: a horned dragon, a king riding a swan, a fat man with four chins and a hat.

The dragon could turn into a fish, and the fat man into the imprisoned princess's tower. And the king riding the swan into a girl and a kettle. And the wonders never ceased. When you looked at it quickly or moved your head only slightly, the background between the dragon and the fat man turned into a boat and the background between the king and the swan into a pear with a stem and two leaves. A whole world resided in my ugly, stained pillow, like the clouds that floated by in the village, like on the toilet walls, like in the new furniture in Krakow, the lacquered furniture that forever smelled of pungent, pleasant varnish.

There were also pillows in red-and-white checked pillowcases. They weren't interesting.

We spent all our days, all our nights, all our time there, in that makeshift bed. We couldn't speak out loud. We only whispered.

Sometime Edjo, the Juzaks' son, would come to play with me. I loved that pleasant, quiet, polite, and handsome Edjo very much.

I loved the games we played together on the makeshift bed among all the pillows, blankets, and rags. They were spectacular settings for our amazing adventures—mountains, canyons, hills, and valleys. We climbed, slid, crossed, dug, attacked, rebuffed, won victories, conquered. We had wonderful times in our ragtag landscapes.

And all of it, of course, very, very quiet, very, very silent.

We were as quiet as my wonderful trained gray mice, Mysia and Tysia.

I used to draw on that makeshift bed too, on the blank pages of the book of menus my mother dictated to my father, and I used to look at books—the cookbook my father bought my mother when they moved into their new house in Bochnia, and the books that survived from the Jewish gynecologist's library. They are all in my possession now: the bilingual Hebrew-English Bible, a very large book with red edges from which my father took his stories of the children of light; *Mein Kampf*, with the photograph of Hitler on the cover, his eyes punctured, probably by me; the four-volume *Encyclopedia of Sexual Knowledge*; and *The Power and Secret of the Jesuits*, by René Fülöp-Miller.

That was the book I loved browsing in the most. A gold symbol was imprinted on the black cover, and it had a great many illustrations, marvelous prints, all of them etched in my brain.

I could find almost all the important things in the world in the books we had in our hiding place: food and sex, politics and religion.

WE DIDN'T EAT A LOT. I REMEMBER MAINLY BREAD, AND SOMEtimes a potato that Juzakowa brought or my mother managed to grab out of the pot boiling on the stove. Juzakowa, my mother said, was trying to get rid of us any way she could. Mostly she tried to starve us, so we'd die or be so afraid of starving that we'd go out to the Aryan side, the side of life, but for us the side of death. Certain death.

Her husband, Juzef Juzak, was the one who forced her to take in and hide my mother and father, without the girl, of course, without me.

Hiding Jews was a terrible risk, the risk of death. If they found us, the Germans would murder us immediately, and they would murder Juzak, Juzakowa, and their sweet little boy, Edjo, as punishment, as an example to others.

Juzakowa told my mother that the city was full of placards in three languages—Ukrainian, Polish, and German—that listed the punishments anyone hiding Jews could expect. Death was the lightest of them.

That's how it was.

Can we judge her?

Can we judge a mother who wants to save her only child?

Sixteen-year-old Ania died of tuberculosis in my mother's arms. My mother caught it from her. If the Red Army had been late in liberating us, she probably would have died too. Even so, her recovery was a miracle, and it was all because of the hunger during the war.

Hunger saved my mother.

When she was starved, the Koch bacillus was starved too. That theory became known years later, when the war was no longer in the world, but penicillin was in the world, a drug I found out about only after the war, along with the atomic bomb. What did penicillin and the atomic bomb have in common? The mushroom!

In her efforts to get rid of us by starving us, Juzakowa would take her husband and her son for long visits, mainly on holidays, to relatives who lived in a village. She would lock us in the apartment without leaving us food in the hope we'd die of starvation or go outside to look for food, and the Germans would kill us instead.

Once, when the Juzaks went to visit relatives without saying when they'd come back, without saying if they ever would, my mother, my father, and I stayed in the hiding place with only one slice of bread, and after that slice was eaten down to the last crumb, time passed—I don't know how much—until it was clear that we couldn't go on anymore, and my mother, the survival genius, took action.

My mother knew that in the entrance around the corner of the building we were hiding in lived a woman whose husband was imprisoned in a concentration camp. She also knew the name of that woman, Mrs. Tchernikowski, and she knew that her husband was the manager of a soda factory—all from Juzakowa's gossiping.

My mother decided to disguise herself as a Polish woman whose husband was also a prisoner in that camp, in the hope of getting us something to eat.

She concocted a brilliant plan. My father wrote a note on a piece of used paper.

Then he wrinkled and dirtied it, and tore the edges. My father, with his skilled hands, was the king of forgers.

My mother, who had the "good look"—blond hair, light-colored eyes, and fair skin—pinched her pale, sunken cheeks until they were rosy, bit and chewed her lips until they swelled and reddened, and put on the best remnants of her threadbare clothes.

My mother and father parted with a goodbye kiss, and my mother kissed me too, a rare kiss. They parted as if they were at their own funeral.

The locks were pushed aside, the chains removed, the hooks lifted, the key turned in the keyhole, and the door to the staircase opened, squeaking on its hinges. It was the first time that door had been opened since Hania Seremet dumped me into my parents' hiding place.

My mother, the forged, wrinkled note in her fist, slipped out.

Out, to the Aryan side, the side of life, the side of death.

My mother told me, told me, and told me.

THE MOMENT SHE STEPPED OUT THE DOOR OF THE BUILDING —it was a bright, glowing afternoon—her head began to spin. The world spun around in dizzying circles. She almost fainted, after all those months of darkness, of lying down, of hunger.

The enormous light blinded her, and while her pupils tried to contract, she leaned against the wall of the building, the building we were hiding in, and saw the geranium plant on one of the windowsills. Like a predator, my mother leaped forward and snatched the plant, held it in her arms, and hid her face behind the flamboyant leaves and red flowers. Who would suspect that a woman carrying a blooming geranium plant was a weary, hungry Jew who had come out of her hiding place to get food for her chicks? Since when did weary, hungry Jews walk around on the Aryan side carrying flowering plants?!

That was a long time after the final liquidation of the ghetto.

And then a child came along. Ukrainian and Polish children were famous for their remarkable ability to recognize and hunt down Jews. The boy began circling around her suspiciously, scrutinizing her thoroughly. My mother was sure that was the end of her, the end of all of us, that the boy would begin shouting: Jew! Jew! Jew! And the Germans would come and whatever happened would happen. Her only hope was that they would kill her at once and not torture her. But it didn't happen.

That plant apparently saved us all. It was so contrary to the accepted image of a persecuted Jew that the boy walked away, perhaps sad that he hadn't come upon a Jew he could turn in and get a reward for, possibly even something to eat.

Perhaps he had a mother suffering from tuberculosis and a little sister with whooping cough.

Or maybe he was just a nice, curious boy?

My mother was saved once again. And so were we. The boy went away, the street was deserted. Stumbling along, weak and hungry, my mother passed the corner of the building, hugging the plant in her arms, and went into the stairwell of the building where the Polish woman, Mrs. Tchernikowski, lived, the woman whose husband was imprisoned in a concentration camp. She hid the plant behind the door, went up the stairs, and rang the bell. The door opened.

My mother went in and told Mrs. Tchernikowski the brilliant story she'd made up: my mother's husband had managed to smuggle a letter to her, and in it, he wrote about becoming friends with the soda factory manager and lending him some money—550 zlotys—with the idea that the manager's wife could return the money to my mother, who needed it now more than he did.

Mrs. Tchernikowski, thrilled to hear that her husband was alive and had a friend, gave my mother a whole loaf of bread, seven cubes of sugar, a piece of chicory, and a small amount of money. That was what she had. She promised to get more food and money for the next time, which never came.

She also gave my mother a jacket, the scratchy wool jacket of indeterminate color that belonged to her husband, the soda factory manager. I wore that jacket for a very long time. It was long, down to the floor. They used to tie it around my waist with a thick, coarse rope and pull it up to make it shorter. There were knots at the ends of the rope to keep it from unraveling. They'd roll the sleeves up around my wrists till my fingers showed.

To this day, I feel two rolls of very thick, heavy cloth around my wrists. A kind of ghost memory described by people who still feel amputated limbs.

Even now, as I write, I feel them around my wrists: rolls of thick, scratchy wool of indeterminate color.

Burdensome, onerous, restraining.

Why didn't they shorten the jacket, why didn't they cut the sleeves? Questions without answers, forbidden questions. They didn't shorten anything.

My mother came back without the plant that saved her life, all our lives.

She had picked a bunch of blazing red geraniums from it and left it behind the entrance door.

My mother came back like the angel of plenty: with a whole loaf of bread, seven cubes of sugar, a piece of chicory, the soda factory manager's jacket, and a bunch of blazing red geraniums.

From the moment my mother left until she returned, my father stood tensely, his ear to the door, his hand on the lock, waiting. Perhaps it was in that position that my mother and father waited for Hania Seremet, who had threatened to throw me out of the village and take me to the hiding place, even though Juzak and Juzakowa absolutely did not want me, and had agreed to hide my mother and father only if they came without the girl.

My father opened the door a crack as soon as he sensed my mother coming.

Mother bird, he whispered. Mother bird, that's what my father called my mother. She said that about herself too: I'm a mother bird. If I weren't who I am, none of us would have remained alive. If I weren't who I am, we would all have been murdered. Your father had no initiative; I had to take care of everything. That's what she said.

Like a mother bird with her chicks, I fly away to bring you food. I save you. I saved us.

Like a mother bird, she stole into Juzakowa's kitchen again and again, reached into the pot and snatched a potato from the boiling water. With her burned hands, she broke off a piece of potato and put it in my mouth, broke off another piece and put it into my father's mouth, and only then did she break off a piece and put it into her own mouth. That's exactly what she did with the whole loaf of bread Mrs. Tchernikowski gave her. First she broke off a piece of bread and put it into my mouth, then she broke off another piece and put it into my father's mouth, and only then did she break off a piece and put it into her own mouth.

The sugar cubes were given the same treatment. With his amazing Swiss pocketknife, my father cut each cube into three unequal pieces. Mother bird put the largest piece into my open mouth. Only then did she put a small piece into my father's mouth, and finally a small piece into her own mouth.

While the sweetness of the largest third of the sugar cube dissolved in my mouth, I looked at the bunch of blazing red geraniums. I hadn't seen any flowers for a while, but I remembered very well how they looked. I pulled off three velvety petals, and in front of our triangular piece of mirror, I pasted them onto my lips with my saliva. How beautiful!

One petal on my lower lip, and two very close together on my upper lip.

I didn't have a doll, but I knew that dolls' lips looked like that.

It was incredibly beautiful. And I wasn't hungry.

The chicory was melted in hot water. I don't remember whether the hot water was from Juzakowa's kitchen or whether we could heat water in our hiding place.

When my mother and father put the glasses to their lips, smelled the aroma of the chicory, and took the first sip, a look of pleasure spread over their faces and they kissed. That time, it wasn't a goodbye kiss.

MY MOTHER, MY FATHER.

My father, Salomon Goldman, born in the town of Bochnia in the first year of the twentieth century, 1900, had two brothers: Henryk and David. My father was the oldest, and David, the youngest, was born "beyond the grave"—that's what they called children born after their father had died.

Nice, serious names. Especially Salomon. Not Shlomo, Salomon.

A soft, pleasant voice, a bright face darkened with the shadow of stubble in the evening. A broad, high forehead that invaded his dark, straight hair in two deep gulfs. Prominent ears, gaunt cheeks, a slightly protuberant lower lip, thick black eyebrows, and the eyes—brown. A very focused expression, wise and compassionate.

That's how he looked.

I look like my father.

What luck.

The three brothers were born very poor.

There was no father. Maybe he disappeared even before he died.

Their mother's name was Rachela—a hardworking woman who supported herself and her fatherless sons by sewing on an old machine she paid for in installments. She lived in fear that the sewing machine would be taken away from her if she missed a payment, like in the book Theodore Dreiser wrote about Sister Carrie.

My father didn't tell me very much.

He told me that his entire childhood was accompanied by the rattling of the sewing machine—days, nights, days.

He told me that his mother tied his baby brother David's cradle to the sewing machine lever with a rope so that days, nights, days, the cradle rocked with the rhythm of Rachela Goldman's hard labor. She was the grandmother I never knew, my father's mother. He also told me that he went to *cheder* with many other children, where he learned to read from any direction.

From the time he was a child, my father worked to support himself and his family. There was a bookbinding shop in their neighborhood, located in a basement. Lying on his stomach, my father would peer for hours through the grating into the sidewalk-level shop. That's how he learned the secrets of his first profession, bookbinding, and he earned money by binding prayer books for spoiled girls from wealthy families.

My father told me that only once in his life did his mother buy him something new. A pair of shoes. The soles were painted red, and he was so proud of them that he started walking a special way—lifting his foot high with every step and leaving it in the air so that the bright red of the soles would gleam and the whole world would admire his new shoes. He did that for the short time it took for the color to wear away.

My father told me that story when we were in the hiding place, during the war, and even though the Germans tried to murder us then, and it wasn't only shoes I didn't have—there was no bread either—the story made me very sad, and to this day, thinking about my father's harsh childhood saddens me.

My father told me little, and I never asked.

He told me how he learned accounting through a correspondence course. He always had to work. A sick mother, two little brothers.

He told me how he went to Vienna, or was it Berlin, passed the exam with high marks, and became a certified accountant, a profession that saved his life, and my mother's and mine, so many times.

He told me how naive and bewildered he was when he came for the first time to the capital of the large world—Vienna? Berlin?—and decided to have his hair cut and to shave so that he would look clean and neat for that important, fateful exam. And there, at the barber's, they shampooed and cut his hair, shaved him, massaged his face and scalp, gave him a manicure and a pedicure, cleaned him out of his money, and he, paralyzed with embarrassment, didn't protest.

His meager supply of money ran out. Luckily he had his return train ticket. There was no money left for food. A young man from a small provincial town, Bochnia.

After his mother took sick and the sewing machine stopped rattling all day, all night, all day, the creditors came and took it away. My father became a Communist. He read Marx, the entire *Manifesto*, studied ceaselessly, and worked endlessly to support his mother, his brother Henryk, his little brother David, and himself. Later, the brothers became Communists too. My father made sure that Henryk went to school and that little, sickly David would sometimes have a chicken leg or a bit of meat to eat.

Communism became their religion.

It was dangerous to be a Communist in Poland in those days. It was illegal. Henryk was caught at some underground activity, tried, and sent to a prison that had a very bad reputation: the Bereza Kartuska prison. Young David even considered going to Spain and joining the International Brigade that fought with the Republicans against the fascist, Franco. If he'd been killed there, I would have had an uncle who died a romantic death, like something in Lorca or Hemingway, like Gary Cooper and Ingrid Bergman.

There could have been some poetic justice in that for me, the daughter of a salon Communist.

The younger brother, David, who didn't live to grow old, disappeared in the war, maybe in Russia, maybe in Poland, and we don't know if he died and if so, where and how.

David, the youngest brother, was the one who buried the treasure in the house my father built for my mother in Bochnia, the house my mother called a golden cage.

In his will, my father left that house to Hania Seremet so she would agree to hide me as a Christian girl at her parents' house in the village of Marcinkowice. That house was supposed to provide the basis for my existence and education if my mother and father were murdered and I remained alive.

My father sent Hania Seremet to that house in Bochnia, armed with a map, a false map showing the location of the treasure buried there by his youngest brother. David had buried the treasure in the cellar, but the map showed it in the attic.

My father had many talents, and was also an idealist. He believed with all his heart in Communism, but he knew how to get rich from buying and selling building materials. That's how he built the beautiful modern house in Bochnia that my mother hated because it was in Bochnia, a provincial town, and my mother thought of herself as a citizen of the world who should live in a big city, like Krakow, for example.

After the war, the beautiful house in Bochnia was nationalized and divided into four apartments. David never came back, and when Henryk returned from Russia, where he was saved from the Germans, the two surviving brothers went to the house, bribed the tenant who lived in the cellar, dug up the treasure, and split it between them.

I didn't like Henryk. Like my father, he was a Communist, even before the war, and as soon as he came back from Russia, he was given a good job in the party apparatus.

Henryk was dumpy, had a big potbelly, and happily, didn't look anything like my father. His wife, stupid, ugly Malvina who married him after the war, also had a huge stomach, and the baby that came out of her was all wrinkled and green. The baby's name was Felix, maybe after Felix Dzerzhinsky. They used to wrap him in a kind of pillow they tied his limbs to with ribbons because he was born crooked and they hoped to straighten his bones. Henryk and Malvina lived nearby, and Malvina once asked me to watch Felix, her little baby. I was busy the whole time waving flies away from his smelly body, wrapped in a pillow.

It was terrible.

My joy was unbounded when, owing to his high-level job in the party apparatus, Henryk was given a villa in a far-off neighborhood and they moved there.

We stayed in Krakow, and later we immigrated to Palestine. Some anonymous people threatened my father's life, and once again we had to leave everything behind and flee.

There, in Palestine, which was the Land of Israel, my father died at the age of fifty-eight. He didn't have a single gray hair on his head when he died so young. Not a single filling or crown blemished the whiteness of his teeth, which had so rarely been exposed in a generous, sudden smile, a weary, sad, disappointed smile.

TWO BOOKS ALWAYS LAY NEAR THE HEAD OF HIS BED WHEN he had a bed and a roof over his head—a volume of Sholem Aleichem's letters and *The Good Soldier Schweik*.

On the nights he wasn't too tired from building the bright Communist future, he would read them, laughing sadly. Every now and then he would translate Sholem Aleichem's stories for my mother.

My mother always claimed she didn't know Yiddish. Maybe if you knew Yiddish, you were considered less respectable.

I remember the treasures my father had in his pockets when we were in the hiding place together: rubber bands; stoppers; bits of silver paper that he used to make the miniature, magical cups; cutouts of newspaper maps with the front lines marked in red; a crooked rusty nail; a shred of thin rope; a small cardboard spool with three threads wound around it—white, black, and brown—and a needle stuck in them in such a way that the point didn't prick his hand when it dove deep into the pocket, and next to the needle, seven pins and two very valuable and important safety pins; large and small buttons in various colors, all mixed with shreds of fragrant *machorka* tobacco. And there were, of course, the spring-up magnifying glass my father used to steal fire from the gods, and the greatest of all his treasures: the amazing pocketknife, the red pocketknife with dozens of pull-out blades that had some functions the world had never known.

Those were the treasures in my father's pockets when we were in the hiding place, but after Stalin and the Red Army saved us and we went back to Krakow, there was a revolution in the contents of my father's pockets. The number of treasures decreased greatly, replaced by a clean handkerchief, carefully ironed and folded. I ironed my father's handkerchiefs. I ironed all the laundry. A big girl, very big, though childish and not serious, my mother claimed.

There were fewer bits of fragrant tobacco in my father's pockets after the war, and added to his normal, pleasant smell was the faint aroma of shaving cream.

I loved watching my father shave. He used to dab a dollop of white cream on my nose. My father was already an important supervisor by then, and he had a luxurious office and a Skoda in a light celadon color, the color of my velvety reading robe, a car with a driver.

The driver had a broken nose and only one ear. Jacek broke his nose and Wacek ate his ear. That was before the war.

My father always made a living, fixed everything, did my arithmetic homework with me, and helped me paste together the hard pieces of the cardboard castles I used to build. He also took me to his office sometimes, and sometimes he bought me drawing materials—paper, paints, and once even a huge box of pastels.

I treasured those wonderful pastels so much that I used them so sparingly that they turned into thin powder, blended together into a sad gray color like the gray of the bottom of an extinguished stove.

Colors that crumbled before they had a chance to be used.

The store that sold colors, paints, paper, and brushes and always smelled pleasantly of turpentine was located on Florianska Street. There was a huge, yawning antique gate at the end of that street, and every time someone yawned without covering his mouth with his hand, people said to him, why are you yawning like the Florianska Gate?

We went there sometimes, after the rain.

After the rain, we went to a *photoplastikon* on that marvelous street, a small dark room with a circular stand in the center surrounded by a bench upholstered in velvet. Binoculars were affixed to the circular stand, and when you pressed your eyes up against them, you could see wonderful things, three-dimensional, illuminated, breathtaking pictures of far-off places. The pictures changed every few seconds, and every performance lasted about ten minutes, maybe less. There was a different performance every week; the order of the pictures was changed. There, at the *photoplastikon*, I saw the Seine, the Tiber, the Thames. Even the Mississippi.

My father took me there, paid for the ticket, and waited outside. When I came out, the lights streaming from the display windows glistened on the cobblestones. My father held my hand in his warm, dry hand.

I think he must have been glad that I drew so well, that I cut and pasted and sculpted. My father, with his skilled hands, admired clever hands.

My father never stroked me or hugged me with his skilled hands, so dry and pleasant to the touch, never too slippery and never too rough, but he knew how to make tiny cups from silver cigarette paper with them, teeny-tiny cups I could fill with water and even drink from.

I can make cups like that too. My father taught me.

What a pity that my father and I never became friends, never talked. I took no interest and never asked, and my father left me to the authority of my mother, whom he loved and admired very much. He was embarrassed in my presence, I don't know why, and after the war he was always so busy earning a living and creating his just, better world.

I missed out on my father.

MY MOTHER BELIEVED THAT SHE LOOKED LIKE MARLENE Dietrich. Several pictures of her as a young girl, which were saved along with other family photos because they had been sent to her younger sister, Salka, to Palestine, show my mother in a femme fatale pose. A femme fatale from Oswiencim, in Galicia—a provincial, ordinary city whose only advantage was its location, at a very central railroad intersection.

Trains would arrive there from all of Europe, with cattle cars crammed with live people. A short time later, they would all be dead.

The Germans would murder them, poison them with gas, burn them in crematoriums, and scatter their ashes in woods, fields, poplar groves, and the Sola River.

As a girl, my mother used to swim in that very same river, the Sola, and because she didn't have a proper bathing suit, she wore a nightgown that swelled with water so that she looked like a funny giant balloon.

Oswiencim, my mother's birthplace, became Auschwitz.

Gusta Gruber, my mother, was one of six brothers and sisters. More than six had been born to her parents, but some of them died in childhood, from diphtheria, whooping cough, tuberculosis. The rest grew up to be decent, talented, and very good-looking people.

Then the Germans came.

Of all my mother's siblings, only Salka, the youngest, prettiest child born to her parents when they were no longer young, the daughter who immigrated to Palestine, remained alive.

Maybe that was why, after so many years, I decided to write this history—these things, this story.

It's important to me.

I'VE OFTEN THOUGHT THAT I SHOULD TELL WHAT I KNOW. Sometimes I could see these things in my mind's eye, as clear as crystal, but they vanished quickly and I didn't know how or where to begin the story.

I don't like these stories. They make me feel a vague, unpleasant, inexplicable sense of guilt.

Maybe I've always felt that my mother was right and I don't fully appreciate her heroism. Maybe it aggrieved me to hear her say that unlike other mothers, she didn't give birth to me only once, but over and over again, time after time.

Or maybe I didn't want to be like those people who came to talk to my parents after the war, the ugly, shabby people who sometimes had numbers tattooed on the inside of their forearms, and sometimes spoke an ugly, unintelligible language, and when they spoke Polish, they spoke it incorrectly and with a ludicrous-sounding accent. I didn't want to be one of them, the ones who survived, even though I knew that I was one of them. I knew that I was a Jewish girl, and I knew that those people were Jews. It's terrible, I thought, it's horrible. Me too? Like them? A Jewish girl thinking about Jews the way anti-Semites thought about them?

The Jews must be murdered—that's what the Germans decided.

And so must I, a Jewish girl like me. So I am one of them.

And maybe no one's interested in these ancient stories.

In moments of doubt, I decide that I can always toss it all into the wastebasket.

Perhaps give a copy to the boys, Ari and Michael.

That thought, about my sons, allows me to go on. I've decided to tell the story, I promised myself I would tell it, and that's that. I'm trapped in this process that I don't enjoy for even a fraction of a second. I'll finish writing, copy it, hand it over for editing, and they'll correct my pathological spelling mistakes, which cry out for divine vengeance, as my mother used to say, and we'll see.

I don't like admitting it, but my murdered family never interested me.

Those people who are gone, the family.

When my mother told me about them, I always tried to escape from their lives and their deaths.

My mother told me, told me, and told me about her childhood, her youth, her parents, her brothers, her sisters, and their sons and daughters, the children. She told me, and it was exhausting, depressing, repellent, boring.

And it always made me feel guilty.

Maybe if there hadn't been a war in the world, and everyone had remained alive, I wouldn't want to be close to them, just as I always tried to avoid being close to my Uncle Henryk, my father's brother, who was saved in Siberia, to his stupid, ugly, bucktoothed wife Malvina, and to their greenish son, Felix. Maybe.

Neither life nor death gave me the opportunity to know them.

MY MOTHER'S FATHER, MY GRANDFATHER, SHLOMO GRUBER, was the last of his parents' children. He was born after Malka, Yettka, Rachel, Leah, another Leah—the first died in infancy—and Feige. He was the first boy after so many girls, the beloved son of Isser and Perl Gruber, the mythological Bubbeh Perl, whose name was given to so many girls in the family.

My mother told me how her father, when he was a baby, used to stand up in the gallery that surrounded the hall where all the girls in the family sat plucking and sorting down feathers, and urinate on them from above, to their cries of joy. Here was a man!

Shlomo was a scholar, and very spoiled. He married the beautiful Rivka, who, throughout their life together, until the Germans murdered them when they were already quite old, loved and pampered him. She took care of him, bore him sons and daughters, the ones who died in childhood and those who continued to live, raised them and ran the business—the import and retail distribution of beverages.

And these are the names of the sons and daughters, sons-in-law and daughters-in-law, grandsons and granddaughters of Grandma Rivka and Grandpa Shlomo Gruber, who were murdered by the Nazis: their oldest child, Moshe, married Bronke, who gave birth to Pnina, the Perelka my mother couldn't save. Their angelic daughter, Minka, the most wonderful of all, who was disfigured with a humpback, married Dov and had two daughters, Pnina and Rachel. Their daughter Feige married a man whose name I can't remember, and gave birth to their daughter and son—Pnina and Geniek. Their son Leibek never married and had no children.

All those people, the adults and the children, were murdered.

The Germans murdered them all.

My mother, Gusta, my father, Salomon, and I were saved.

Aunt Salka, the youngest daughter, was saved in Palestine along with her husband Moshe and their two children, Dan and Ruth.

My mother's father, Shlomo Gruber, was an extremely gifted man.

My mother told me all that, she told me, told me, and told me.

How beautifully he painted, what gorgeous decorations he hung in the sukkah, how many languages he knew, and how he secretly devoured the novels she stuffed herself with: Dostoyevsky and Tolstoy, Romain Rolland, Victor Hugo, and Dickens.

People from the whole area, Jews and goyim, would come to ask his advice, to have him translate letters for them and write letters to the authorities for them.

Just like my father.

I wonder whether he helped his beautiful wife Rivka with the housework, the business, raising the children. Rivka was renowned for her beauty far and wide. She had many suitors, even from other cities.

My grandfather, Shlomo Gruber, loved her very much.

In the evening, when she finally sat down to rest after a hard day's work, her small, weary feet soaking happily in a basin of hot soapy water perfumed with eau de cologne he used to bring her from Vienna, or was it Berlin, my grandfather would take off her head covering, and with a small pair of manicure scissors would cut her black curls, which grew so quickly under her head covering, very short, as he hummed arias from Viennese operettas written in the glorious days of the Austro-Hungarian Empire when it was ruled by the beloved Emperor Franz Joseph.

Then, so my mother told me, told me, and told me, my grandfather would sit on a low footstool at my grandmother's feet, take one foot out of the basin, wipe it gently with a soft white towel, and give her a pedicure. One foot, then the other foot. They both sat there in the circle of amber light spread by the oil lamp, and continued to sit there even after my grandfather had finished the haircut and the pedicure, inhaling the scent of Viennese, or was it Berlin, perfume, quietly discussing their wonderful children, their disabled daughter, their dead children, their livelihood.

Shlomo Gruber was a fair-skinned redhead. My mother looked like him, so said Salka, the youngest child, the only one of my mother's sisters to be saved. Salka herself looked like her mother, the beautiful Rivka.

They were well-to-do bourgeoisie and lived in a spacious private house, where they ran their business on the ground floor. They were honest merchants, generous people. They were kind and magnanimous to their clerks and servants, mainly Poles who reciprocated with loyalty, respect, and love. My mother remembered a young village girl, a servant, who strayed from the straight and narrow, married, and continued to visit them, to show off her baby.

A box containing money always stood in the same place—members of the family could take what they needed.

The house was spacious, but the toilets were in the yard, and only the parents had a separate bedroom. All the children were crowded into communal rooms, and sometimes they slept two in a bed. That's how it was.

My mother told me, told me, and told me.

Every morning, the man who drew water from the well brought some water, bent under the weight of the wooden pails hanging from either side of the yoke he carried on the back of his neck across his shoulders.

When my mother was a girl, they did not yet have electricity in the house.

Even though Shlomo was a religious man who always wore a black satin robe and a velvet yarmulke on his head, and had a full beard resting on his chest, and even though beautiful Rivka was also a religious woman who wore a head covering and a wig only on holidays, they allowed their children to decide their own futures, to go to gymnasiums and even to the university, even in Vienna, or was it Berlin, to read secular books and be Communists, even Zionists.

How many bitter herbs their children fed them. My mother, who was a Communist, albeit a salon Communist, even went to prison. Beautiful little Salka ran away to Palestine with the Hashomer Hatsair youth movement. Salka was a staunch idealist. She abandoned her safe, protected, bourgeois life in the home of her well-to-do parents, and like my mother, immigrated to Israel to become a pioneer.

Jackals, sun, sand, camels, grit. She paved roads, established kibbutzim, became a master floor-layer, and married the nice-looking, generous, and elegant Moshe Sandel.

Salka Sandel, née Gruber, and Moshe Sandel had two children, Dan and Ruth. They're sabras. Children born in Palestine.

After the Red Army defeated the Germans and saved our lives, my mother and father wrote to Aunt Salka, to Palestine, to Tel Aviv, to Ben Yehuda Street. They were living in the same place they'd lived before the war. There were some people whose lives were almost unaffected by the war, who didn't even have to move from their homes! In Palestine, for instance, that far-off place where God was born and the sea was dead.

Those relatives in Palestine sent pictures that showed good-looking, smiling people who weren't the least bit worried. Salka, Moshe, and the children, Dan and Ruth, exotic names from books—from the thick black volume with the red edges and strange letters you read backward, from right to left, and from the literature of the children of light.

Children of light, that's what my father called the Jews when he told me stories from the Bible in the hiding place, during the war. How lucky for us that we weren't really lit up, because then they would have found us in a minute.

My mother and father made very sure that I didn't hear or know the word "Jew"—the word of death, *Zyd*.

Dan and Ruth, Ruth and Dan, lovely names, names redolent of oranges. Were they Jews too? Later I learned that the sabra children in Palestine didn't think they were Jews like me.

They believed they were more successful, more beautiful, more heroic. They believed that the Germans would not have been able to murder them. They believed they would have fought the Germans, would even have defeated them!

They didn't understand very much, and to tell the truth, they didn't even try to understand. Maybe it didn't really interest them, those sabra children from Palestine.

Aunt Salka and Uncle Moshe once sent us oranges. A crate of oranges, a gift from Palestine, oranges that were still innocent then, that didn't threaten me with their "sabraness." Oranges that appeared when the world around us was white and Grandpa Frost had painted magical flowers on the windowpanes. When we opened the crate and removed the silky, rustling paper, each orange glowed like a little sun, and they

1. My maternal grandparents: Rivka Gruber, née Bernstein, and Shlomo Gruber.

2. My father's mother, Rachel Goldman, with her two younger brothers, Henryk (*left*) and David (*right*).

3. My mother (*right*) and a friend in Hashomer Hatsair uniforms.

4

5

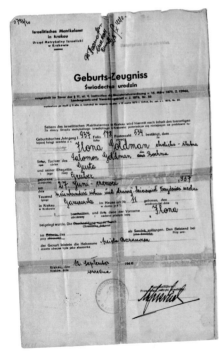

6

7

4. My father.

5. My mother.

6. My birth certificate.

7. My mother and father, in their
beautiful new villa in Bochnia.

8

8. My father, my
mother, and me at
the entrance to their
Bochnia villa. I was
about two months old.

9. With my wooden
horse toy—a common
Polish toy—on my
mother's lap. This was
before the war; I was
a year to eighteen
months old.

9

10

10. Me on the famous rooftop terrace.

11. Me and my nanny from the convent. She turned out to have syphilis.

11

12

POLSKIE KOLEJE PAŃSTWOWE

Seria **A**

Zaświadczenie № 130320

do

biletów odcinkowych tygodniowych

Ważne do dnia 31 grudnia 193*9* r.

P. *Salomon Goldman*

(imię i nazwisko)

zamieszkały w *Bochni*

Plac Gazaris № 9

(dokładny adres)

Sprzed. P. K. P. Serja H. Nr 9a   DRUKARNIA PAŃSTWOWA.

13

12. Me on the rooftop terrace. The dress was probably made of red velvet.

13. My father's Polish State Railways pass, probably the last one he had before leaving Bochnia.

14a

14b

14a and 14b. *Above,* A "Registration Card for Jews"
issued by the Germans to my father in the ghetto.
The stamp in the upper left confirms "ARMBAND provided."
Below, The inside flaps of my father's registration card.

15a

15b

16

15a and 15b. Passes from the ghetto. One of them was possibly forged by my father.

16. An embroidered armband, which Jewish workers were required to wear.

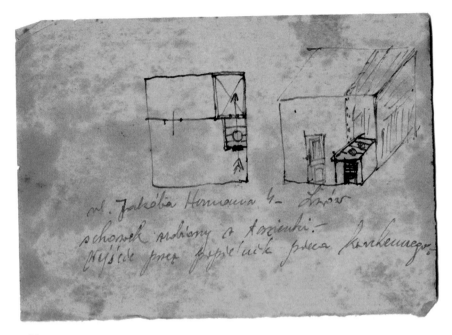

17

17. A diagram drawn by my father (after the war, when giving testimony to the Jewish Committee) of the hiding place he had designed and built in the ghetto. One crawled into it through the kitchen stove's ash-removal opening.

18. The carved wooden box entrusted to my mother for safekeeping. In it were jewelry, diamonds, precious stones, pearls, and watches.

18

19

19. One of the pictures that Hania Seremet instructed me to draw when I was in the village, as proof that I was alive, so that she would be allowed to continue collecting money from my parents. The shepherdess is me, with imaginary braids. P.K.P. stands for Polskie Koleje Panstwowe (Polish National Railways). It is like a snapshot, with half a cow, a glimpse of another cabin. Overall, an optimistic drawing.

20. Another one of my drawings proving that I was alive.
There is even a puss in boots.

21

21. Hania Seremet and
me at the photo studio.
Hania is wearing a sweater
embroidered by my mother;
I am in a satin dress sewn by
my mother. Immediately after
the photographs were taken,
Hania took the dress away
from me.

22. Me at the photo studio,
briefly wearing the satin dress
that my mother made me.

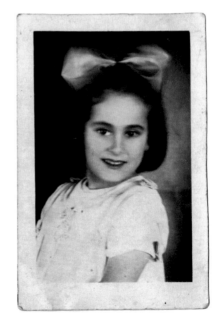

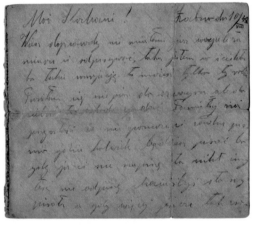

23a

23a and 23b. Once in a while, Hania Seremet wrote to my parents in hiding; she addressed the letters to my mother's fake name. These letters also served as evidence of my existence. For some reason, I am called "mama" in them, Polish for "mother." There must be additional phrases and code words that I cannot decipher.

24. The last, surreal telegram sent by Seremet to my parents in hiding: "Send immediately for Irke. Hanka."—meaning, in effect, "Come at once and take your child!"

23b

24

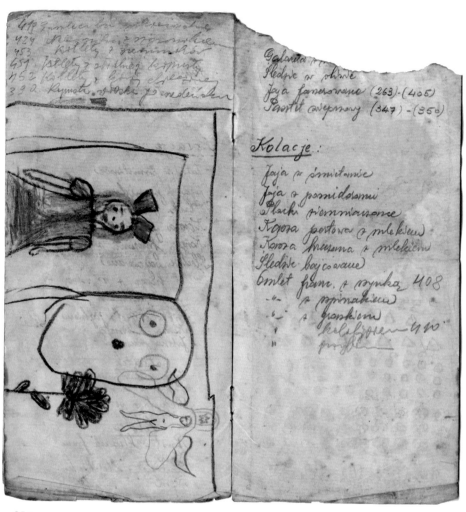

25a

25a and 25b. Pages from the recipe notebook that my
mother dictated to my father. In it were menus for each and
every day of the year. No menu appears more than once.
In the blank spaces, I added drawings. It should be noted
that food was scarce, sometimes nonexistent.

Niedziela

Zupa ze śliwek z kartoflami (85)
Pieczeń cielęca
Sałata z czerw. kapusty - Knedle -
Budyń z bułki

Poniedziałek

Zupa grzybowa
Kiszka postradzone
Legumina krakowska

Wtorek

Zupa kalafiorowa
Zrazy natorne
Kartofle - Buraczki
Doktór przydzień

Środa

Rosół z uszkami
Paluszki z serem pomidor.
Kompot

Czwartek

Zupa fasolowa
Bifsztyk cielęce z jajkiem
Kasza - Marcja
Jabłka pieczone

Piątek

Zupa pomidorowa
Pierogi z pluskami
Budyń z serem

Sobota

Rosół - Klineski frau.
Kura
Kartofle - Marchewka
Krem

26a to 26e. Some of the books that survived the war with us, found in the doctor's office where we hid. I have them to this day.

26a. *Mein Kampf.* I believe it was my hand that mutilated the portrait.

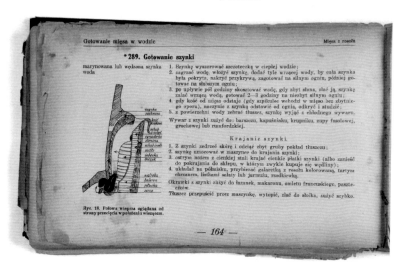

26b. A modern and glossy cookbook that my father gave my mother on the occasion of their move into the new house in Bochnia.

26c. *The Power and Secret of the Jesuits*, embossed in gold. This book included beautiful etchings.

26d. *The Encyclopedia of Sexual Knowledge*, in four volumes.

26e. A bilingual Hebrew-English Old Testament Bible, printed in England.

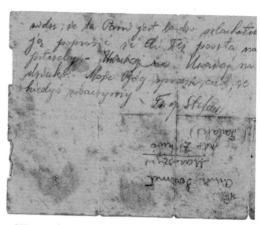

27a

27a and 27b. The note written by my father, pretending to be a gentile concentration camp prisoner who was owed some money by a gentile Pole. My mother carried the note from the hiding place over to the Aryan side, seeking bread, and the plot worked: she returned to the hiding place with bread.

To Mrs. Anna Seremet,

Macoszyn, near Zolkwi (the mill)

My dearest of all Annu!

I have been in a concentration camp for the longest time. God willing, someday we shall see each other again. I am healthy, though much weakened. My heart is with you and with my Irena, and I worry about your fate. I may get permission to receive a food package. It is very good that I had that money, which you know of. It has helped me a lot. I lent 550 zlotys of it to the Lvov soda factory manager, with whom I've become friendly. He asks that you seek reimbursement of this money from Mrs. Tcherniakowski, Lvov, 11a Panienska Street, first floor. So get this money back from that lady, because now, as I am away, you will very much need it. From the manager's stories, it seems that this lady is very noble and that you can also ask her to help you in hard times. Take care of yourself and of the child. Perhaps God will allow a miracle and we shall meet again.

Yours, Stefan

27b

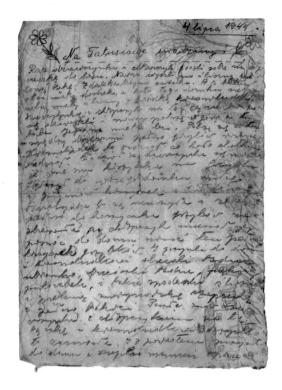

28a

28b

28a and 28b. A fairy tale that I dictated to my mother in honor of my father's birthday, when I had already been in hiding eight months. On its reverse side (not to scale), the story's illustration: a girl, a boy, a dwarf, mushrooms, a house with a smoking chimney. Everyone is smoking. Cigarettes were desired and rare in hiding.

4.6.1944

For my father's birthday.

Once upon a time, a girl and a boy went walking in the woods. Suddenly they reached a wonderful grass clearing. From afar a deer ran. On the corner there stood a tiny house. Next to that house sat a small Krasnoludek [dwarf], cute and bearded. The girl and the boy enjoyed this grass clearing very much. Till suddenly they looked upward, and there was a Baba Yaga flying a broom. They looked down and saw that between the trees, around and around, many mushrooms grew. The Krasnoludek sitting next to his house knew this. He saw that the girl had no basket to collect the mushrooms. The Krasnoludek entered his house, brought out a basket, and gave it to the girl. The girl was very happy and began collecting many mushrooms in the basket. Finally the basket grew so heavy that the boy needed to help her carry it home. They returned home and made Krasnoludek beautiful clothes, beautiful shoes, a beautiful sweater, and gorgeous pants, a great jacket and a hat and many sweet and tasty things. The girl and the boy returned to that grass clearing in the forest and gave everything to Krasnoludek. And when they got back home they told their mommy everything.

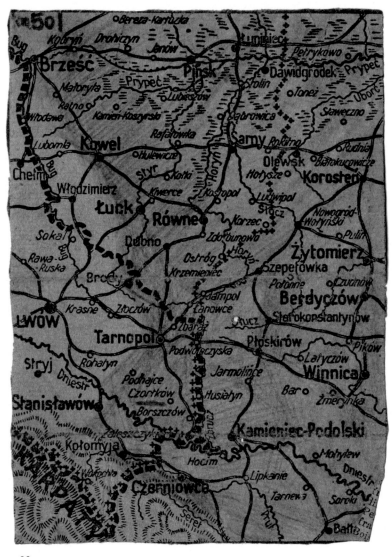

29a

29a and 29b. Newspaper map clippings on which my father would mark the front lines.

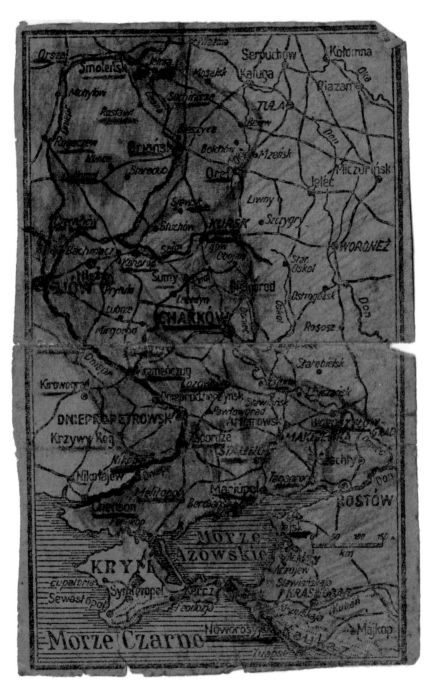

29b

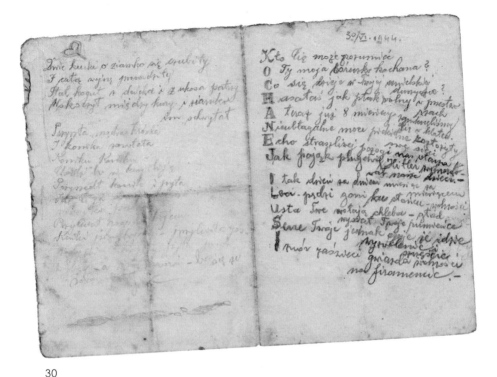

30

30. An acrostic composed by my father. An acrostic is a series of lines or verses in which the first letters of all the lines, read top to bottom, together spell out a word or phrase. In the original Polish poem, the acrostic was created from "Beloved Ilona" (Kochanej Ilusi).

30.06.1944

Who is it that can understand you, oh, my beloved goddess

What moves within your angelic soul, hopping like a free bird in the sky

And now—eight months captured in a cage

Uncompromising forces of darkness have spread their nets

The sound of a fiery blaze surrounds

Like a despised spider Hitler weaves his webs

And thus, day after day, month after month, our heart sprints, runs, gallops to freedom

Your mouth calls for bread, hunger sucked the blush from your cheeks

But through it all your heart feels, liberation nears

Happiness and the star of liberty will shine again in the skies.

31a to 31h. Some of the family members murdered by the Germans. All prewar family photographs survived at Aunt Salka's in Palestine.

31a. Uncle Dov, husband of my mother's elder sister, Minka. He was a brilliant chemist and scientist and avid photographer. Most of his family photos were taken by him.

31b. My paternal grandmother, Rachel Goldman.

31c. Aunt Minka with her and Uncle Dov's daughters, Pnina (*left*) and Rachel (*right*).

31d. My uncle Leibek Gruber, a dentist. This is a photograph from before the war that was taken in Vienna, Berlin, or Warsaw; I am not sure which.

31e. Winter, before the war: Aunt Minka with Pnina.

31f. Pnina.

31g. Aunt Faiga, one of my mother's three sisters.

31h. Little Rachel with the German navy cap.

32

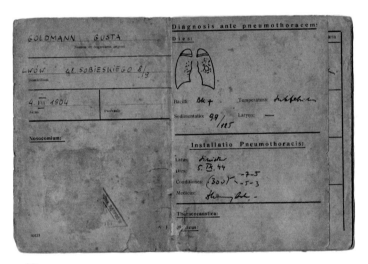

33

32. My mother, very ill, my father, and me. This is the first photograph of my mother after her release from the sanatorium. She is wearing a sweater that she embroidered in hiding, like the one that she embroidered for Hania Seremet and many other decorated sweaters that Rozalia Juzakowa sold at market.

33. My mother's tuberculosis treatment records booklet.

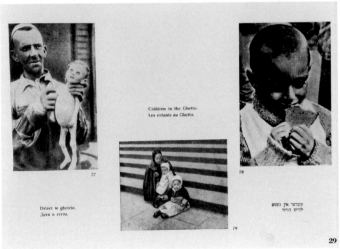

34

34. The cover and interior images from a black book that my father brought home—in it I first saw the horror. This was a bilingual Polish-English album printed in January 1945.

35

35. My father, my mother, and me during a summer vacation at the southern Poland mountain resort town of Zakopane. This was after the war, probably 1947.

36

36. My pastel portrait by painter Jadwiga Madziarska, Jonasz Stern's lover. To this day, I regret not seeing the tiny black dots from the original dress material.

37

37. A letter I wrote my father, who was traveling to Warsaw on business, while I was again at some camp:

> In Warsaw, beloved Papa!!!
> In Londek, your disobedient Ilusia.

38

38. One of the notes my classmates wrote in my diary before we traveled to Palestine:

Remember!
Be a good Pole,
always and everywhere,
and every Pole
will love you.
A souvenir for Ilonka from her school days.
Wrote herself,
Franas Jadwiga
Krakow, 10/X. 1949.
T.P.D. school.

39

40

39. A greeting card for my mother's birthday. The Jews already had a homeland in Palestine. My father drew the symbol for me and I colored it.

40. Ruti and Dan Sandel, my cousins in Palestine, Salka and Moshe's children. Between them is tacked a small postcard with the familiar Herzl profile. This was where we were heading.

had a wonderful fragrance. A source of sheer delight: the beauty, the fragrance, the taste.

I still hadn't developed the urge to kick those oranges the way I kicked the orange on the deck, slippery with vomit and tears, of the immigrant ship, *Galila*. While my stomach churned convulsively, and despite the fear that the ball of cotton that was absorbing the blood of my first menstruation would fall, heaven forbid, I kicked one of the oranges that Tzippi with the tanned, exposed sabra thighs and her sabra friends had thrown from the command bridge down to the crowd of new immigrants standing weary, worried, and anonymous on the slippery deck, watching the silhouette of the mountain emerge from the fog shrouding it on a very cold day—December 31, 1949.

The orange sank into the depths of the ancient sea.

The next day, it snowed in Tel Aviv.

WE ARRIVED IN PALESTINE, THE LAND OF ISRAEL, THE STATE of Israel, Zion, the Holy Land, the promised land, the land of milk and honey, terra sancta, *ziemia obiecana*.

A country that lay along the coast, and inside it, two more seas—that's what they call those lakes: God walked on the water of one of them, the live sea, and the other was a dead sea, a sea of death. And trapped between lands that have been lush and endlessly fertile since the dawn of time, the Mediterranean Sea, gods and goddesses, demigods and nymphs, muses and monsters, and also architects, sculptors, painters, poets, and sometimes even a few special gods possessive of their solitude, gods with the powerful need to prove their absolute superiority to the rest of the creatures, mortal and immortal. The God that was, is, and will be till the end of time, and with him, the Messiah, not only the one who walked on water, but also the one that had yet to appear.

Even before we left Poland to become immigrants, I knew so many things about Palestine, things redolent of oranges, the beautiful pictures, and the sad, frightening stories of war: the Haganah, the Arabs, the fallen soldiers—stories that worried my mother and father greatly.

For one of their birthdays, I drew a picture that symbolized for me the Land of Israel, Palestine—a domed building, a palm tree, and a camel, the camel that Jonasz Stern, the sunken-cheeked knight of melancholy beauty, my mother's girlhood friend, didn't know how to draw, so I drew it myself.

The son of my mother's friend from the Hashomer Hatsair, Mania, fell in that war the Jews in Palestine called the War of Independence. He was a soldier. The Germans didn't murder him, the Arabs did, in battle. But he was dead in any case, Mania's only son. He'd been a boy. Gidi was his name.

I remember my mother and father sitting together in the evening, worried, talking, and I, curled up in the armchair that turned into a bed at night, tried not to listen, not to understand. More terrible stories. I summon all the wonderful, familiar monsters in the varnished grain of the wood of the new, modern furniture that smells pleasantly of varnish. I wet my thumb with saliva, press it hard against my eye, close the other eye, and abandon myself to the endless flow of forms taking shape between my lashes in all the marvelous colors of the rainbow, like in soap bubbles, but I still hear: Palestine. The Haganah. Arabs. War. Danger. State. Worry. What's going to happen?

I know so much about that far-off place, so tiny, on the bottom right side of the map. I've known for a long time, forever, from books, and even before the lice taught me to read, from the stories my father told me in the hiding place, during the war, when the Germans wanted to murder us.

Stories from the black book with the red edges, printed in strange, square letters you read backward.

Stories about laws engraved in stone and handed down in a storm, about brothers, murder, love, jealousy, springs, shepherds, sheep, loves, and sorrow, under skies brimming with stars as numerous as the grains of sand on the beach, as numerous as the grains of sand in the desert. And the stories the nice priest told during religion classes. Cities where God lived and was murdered—Bethlehem, Jerusalem, where the head of the Judenrat handed God over to the Romans to be crucified, to die in suffering, all close to the walls of the Temple, one of which survived. I saw it on a postcard: blocking a dark, narrow alley, tiny figures wrapped in white-striped shawls crowding together at its foot. Jews, like at Uncle Isser Laufer's wedding. They're so small and blurry, you can't see that all of them are crying, but the postcard says, the Wailing Wall. The Wall of Tears.

How different the Jews in Feuchtwanger's book were from the Jews I knew, the Jews who used to come tired, white, thin, and worried to see my mother and father and tell them stories I didn't want to hear.

There was a different kind of Jew, Jews with pretty names like Dan, Ruth, and Uri. Is that what the Jews were like in Palestine?

My mother also told me about her youth, her unrequited loves. One of her loves took her very far away, to Palestine. His name was Avreim'ele. They were in the same youth movement, the Hashomer Hatsair. And he, a young pioneer, immigrated to Palestine. She was so in love that she followed him there. White-skinned, redheaded, pampered, not at all a hard worker. A salon Communist who filled herself with uplifting novels and dreams of a great love. She went to fulfill that love.

Pioneers, Kibbutz Mishmar Haemek, Kibbutz Beit Alfa, paving roads. I don't know what happened to her love, but her health collapsed—teeth loosened, malaria attacked her, the rapacious sun ate away at her white, jiggling flesh, and she had to return, to sail back to her native land, to Poland, to her parents' house, to Oswiencim, which was still a quiet, innocuous provincial town.

She took a small turtle from the Holy Land as a memento. It got lost on the way, on the ship, and never reached Oswiencim.

It took a long time for her to regain her strength.

Before her pioneer love, my mother had another love, and it too was tragic. His name was Zimek. She continued to dream of him all her life, even though she loved my father. That's what she told me. I didn't like hearing and knowing that. Those stories repulsed me.

He was from Czechoslovakia, an engineer, a friend of Dov—the giant, gentle, beloved husband of Minka, my mother's older sister. Smart, funny, idealistic, handsome, and tall. My mother told me, told me, and told me, but she got carried away in her description of him.

They were all Communists, young, fervent, and idealistic, from good, provincial, bourgeois, well-to-do homes. They chose to live in the big city, Krakow. Penniless. Maybe they didn't want help from their parents. The legend has it that they were hungry. They met at Jonasz Stern's studio. His lover then was a senior operating room nurse, and she used to steal food for them from the hospital kitchen.

They were believers, believers in the religion of Communism.

Free love was part of their ideology. People lived together in unusual relationships, threesomes or foursomes. Sharing Zimek's heart—and perhaps his body—with my mother was a girl named Hani, also Czech. Another aspect of their ideology was modesty, a kind of asceticism. No makeup or adornments. The fanciest outfit was a white blouse and a navy blue gabardine skirt. No jewelry, no high heels, and of course no silk stockings. A short, boyish haircut. Down with the bourgeoisie!

The petite Hani was not like that. Though she was as good a Communist as my mother, she used to wear lipstick and rouge. Her brunette hair flowed to her shoulders and bangs darkened her forehead. Her necklines were low and lacy, and she wore silk stockings on her graceful legs. My mother had a complex all her life: she thought she had thick ankles.

Zimek, my mother's love, preferred my mother and proposed to her. That was in the spring, on Planty Boulevard, where years later I strolled with my father. The chestnut trees glittered with tall white candlestick flowers and the lilac bushes already had the fragrance of damp tears. My mother, with her characteristic arrogance, told Zimek that getting married was a bourgeois act unsuitable for young revolutionaries like them.

Even though she loved my father, she was tormented her whole life by what she said that day.

Zimek married the fancy-dressed coquette, Hani, and they went to Moscow to be close to the sacred activities. They were never heard from again.

They never came back. No one knows what happened to them.

My mother was quite an adventuress. Her activities in the underground Communist cell led to her imprisonment. Someone informed on the members, someone broke down under questioning. Police detectives came at night, found Communist propaganda materials, brochures, leaflets, placards, grabbed her and put her and some other comrades in jail. They put the political women in a cell with whores and female criminals. Even though that was rather interesting for all those bourgeois, spoiled Jewish girls, they declared a hunger strike, demanding that they, the political prisoners, be held separately. My mother told me, told me, and told me.

Those whores and female criminals were nice, and even though it made the political women's jail stay less interesting, the principle of separation was right and just. That's what my mother said.

Her mother and father went to visit her in jail. Oh, the shame of it. A girl from such a good family. Shlomo Gruber, the distinguished, handsome Jew with his long, blond beard, wearing a black kapote and a velvet hat, and the beautiful Rivka, his wife, wearing her most elegant holiday wig to hide her black curls, trimmed by her husband with a pair of manicure scissors, came to visit their rebellious daughter in jail, bringing her a package. Such aggravation.

They still didn't know what other aggravation was being prepared for them by that redheaded daughter who thought she looked like Marlene Dietrich and posed dramatically for pictures like a Hollywood star, her head crammed full of novels, uplifting ideas, and political slogans that blinded her, just as they had blinded an entire generation of good, smart people all over the world.

When my mother was released from prison a short time later, she went looking for and found work as a kindergarten teacher. She had no formal professional training. She just went to the most prestigious, progressive kindergarten she could find—how could she not; after all, she was my mother—a kindergarten run according to the methods of the educator Fröbel, and presented herself as a kindergarten teacher. Of course, she was hired immediately, even though dozens of candidates with diplomas and letters of recommendation were competing for the job. That's what my mother told me, told me, and told me. And naturally, she succeeded at the job. She charmed the children and they loved her, constantly stroking her yellow hair and her pink cheeks. She was radiant and beautiful.

My mother's sharp intelligence and courage, the power of her love, her pride, her ingenuity, her monumental ability to survive—all those saved me, my father, and her.

Mother bird, my father called her.

That's how she was.

MY MOTHER MET MY FATHER WHEN SHE CAME BACK FROM Palestine, after she'd recovered from the blows delivered by fever, sun, pioneering, and love. She told me how, at first, she didn't really like him; it wasn't love at first sight. She considered him a provincial merchant. He was, after all, from Bochnia. My mother considered herself a native of Krakow, the capital of high culture, although she too came from a small town that had no advantages over Bochnia: Oswiencim.

My mother, not yet anybody's mother, believed that my father, not yet anybody's father, wore clothes that were too bourgeois and old-fashioned, not like her bohemian friends, those Communist revolutionaries, poets, writers, philosophers, and painters.

He wore provincial shoes and—how awful!—a coat with a fur collar! Though he was a Communist, he looked like a small-town Jewish merchant.

And then my father smiled.

My mother told me, told me, and told me.

That smile, that good, beautiful, warm smile captured her heart.

They had a modest wedding. My father was already a widower and my mother wasn't a young virgin. The marriage took place in 1936. My father was thirty-six, my mother thirty-two. I was born a year later, in 1937, on June 27.

My mother left the excitement of Krakow and her wonderful bohemian life for Bochnia and the new house my father built for her.

It was a house out of a modern fairy tale. They hadn't scrimped on materials. After all, my father was an importer and retailer of construction materials. It was the most stylish, lavish house in the entire district. When the Germans came, it was chosen to be the headquarters and home of the district commander, the *gauleiter*, because it had all the most modern and luxurious innovations: sunken tubs you had to walk down three marble steps to get into, like in Hollywood movies; Italian ceramic tiles; faucets from Berlin; expensive parquet; French windows; central heating; the most modern kitchen fixtures; everything. The outside of the house glittered—mica crystals had been mixed with the plaster that covered the modern Bauhaus structure.

That house required a great deal of work. My mother, mistress of the house, complained. She was forced to hire a maid, a cleaning woman, a gardener, and a cook, and after I was born, also a nanny for me. That nanny, Kasia, my first nanny—a poor girl, her gaze modestly cast down, who wore a long-sleeved gray dress with a hundred buttons all crowded together, adorned only with a white baby collar—had been brought up in a convent.

One day, out of the blue, a peasant woman we didn't know showed up at our door: Kasia's older sister. Carrying on and screaming with fury, she grabbed Kasia by the ear, hit her, almost pulled her ear off, and told my mother that the pious girl, her younger sister, had already managed to give syphilis to several young men from her village, including her husband, who had passed it on to her.

Panic ensued. My mother and father didn't calm down until after Dr. Fishler, our family doctor and friend, did some tests and pronounced me healthy.

My poor mother. She wasn't used to such great responsibility, the responsibility of a mother, after long years of life as an unmarried revolutionary, a pioneer, and a bohemian. It was too much work for her. Luckily, she had books.

She'd never wanted that huge house. She didn't like it. So many windows to clean, hundreds of handles and kilometers of parquet to polish, flowers to take care of on the famous terrace—my mother never stopped reminiscing about it—and on top of everything, the baby. Me. It was a good thing I was quiet and never cried, and when I did cry once, when I was a year old, they immediately summoned the good Dr. Fishler, who said I had a terrible abscess on my leg.

And the cook. We had to eat, after all. Every day.

The cook was a very haughty woman who threw my mother out of her kitchen. Only rarely did she agree to give away any of her cooking secrets.

A golden cage, my mother said.

A golden cage it was, but a short time later, just as the old gypsy woman had predicted, all was lost, though we remained alive.

THAT'S MY MOTHER. THAT'S MY FATHER. I KNOW SO LITTLE about their past, their childhood and youth. What a pity it is that I never asked. What a pity it is that I hated those stories. What a pity it is that, for some reason, they always made me feel guilty, I don't know about what.

Father, what a pity it is that you never stroked my head till I fell asleep.

If I'd been the daughter of my father and his first wife, who died so young, whom he'd married even though Dr. Fishler told him that her days were numbered—if I'd been his daughter with his first wife, maybe he might have been less embarrassed by my existence?

Maybe he would have held me tightly in his arms, and maybe I might even have cried, and the tears would have been absorbed by his neck, always scented with the warm fragrance of shaving cream, fresh, cool eau de cologne, and tobacco.

If my mother's first love, Zimek, had refused to accept my mother's stupid objection that spring, on that boulevard where, to this day, lilacs bloom with the scent of tears of mourning, and had taken her by storm, and I had been their daughter?

The tears should begin.

Gusta Goldman, née Gruber, Mother,

Salomon Goldman, Father,

Did you love me?

The tears should begin.

And maybe not.

I will die with half my tears uncried.

I WAS ASHAMED OF MY MOTHER WHEN I WAS A GIRL. OF HER endless complaints, her criticism of everything, her need to talk ceaselessly about the war, the Germans, her illness, her "good appearance," and always in order to gain something—a discount, a small favor, special treatment.

I remember two family vacations in Zakopane, the same mountainous vacation town where the Poles shot at me in Leah Kichler's camp for Jewish children. Only the two of us, my mother and I, went on the first of those vacations, and we stayed in an isolated cabin. It rained constantly, and my mother, who always had initiative—after all, it was because of her that we were saved from the Germans and stayed alive—showed initiative that time too. For the tidy sum she paid him, a farmer agreed to drive her into town in his wagon. My mother went and came back with a treasure: books she bought and books from the library!

One of them was *The Jungle Book*.

That vacation was magical. My mother, unlike herself, didn't complain.

The second vacation was the only time the three of us—my mother, my father, and I—traveled together.

That time, the wonderful vacation turned out to be a trap. My mother constantly embarrassed us. Nothing suited her, nothing satisfied her.

The carriage driver drove too quickly, it was dangerous, we'd turn over, she'd saved us from the Germans for nothing. The train was too crowded, she didn't have air—after all, apart from the hole in her lung, my mother had suffered from claustrophobia since the war, when we had to squeeze together in the bunker behind the stove in the Lvov Ghetto, when there was an *aktion*, my father was at work, I was already in the village, and she had no work papers!

I never believed her, I admit it. That claustrophobia seemed to me like an act, the pampered bossiness of weakness. I was angry, but silent. I never said a single critical word to my mother.

What a pity.

It wasn't only burning shame that I felt, but also strange pangs of conscience, because after all, I was to blame for everything, the Germans, the war, the illness.

In a restaurant, I saw my mother take the pats of butter left on plates, wrap them in a napkin, and put them in her handbag. What a disgrace. How shameful. But I saw and was invisible. How lucky!

We traveled in the mountains, the forests, the spacious pastures, the wonderful "Eye of the Sea" Lake, a deep black lake encircled by mountains, the lake of ancient tales. No one knows how deep it is. Maybe it's an enormous estuary. Maybe its black water trickled into it from the other side of the planet, from Australia, for example. I didn't want to be there with my mother and father. I kept asking myself how else she was planning to mortify me. I wanted to trickle down to Australia.

My father embarrassed me once too, the only time he took me to the pool. It was a Sunday. We rode the red tram. It was so pleasant to feel his dry, warm hand holding mine, to inhale his smell. The pool was already crowded with people gleaming in their blond nakedness.

We separated at the entrance to the changing rooms.

The nauseating odor of moldy soap scraps, the decrepit bodies of the women also reflected in the dirty, cracked mirrors. I came out first, wearing an ugly, scratchy, striped wool bathing suit that was already too small on me. When it was wet, it clung to my body, and there was a kind of balloon of water between my legs that I somehow had to wring out without anyone noticing. I so yearned for a red bathing suit, the same model Ewunia had, except that hers was gold colored.

You'll look like a clumsy circus girl in that bathing suit, my mother had said. It suits Ewunia, she's thin and lithe. Not you!

Some people have taste, others don't.

How could I compare myself to Ewunia.

Then I saw him, my father, come out of the changing room wearing a shapeless black wool bathing suit, his body above and below it naked.

My father was black.

Curly black fur grew on his skin. Even his back had dark fuzz that seemed to mark where his lungs were. He stood out in the surroundings like a visitor from another planet pretending to be like everyone else.

A Jew.

A black mistake.

I was ashamed to go over to him. To belong to him.

I jumped into the shallow end of the pool.

I didn't know how to swim.

My father sat down at the edge, read a newspaper, smoked a cigarette.

I couldn't move for a long while.

I didn't get out of the pool until it was time to go home. People looked at him.

I could feel how everyone mocked him, laughing at how strange and ugly he looked.

I was so ashamed.

Or maybe no one even gave him a second glance.

Chill shame sank very deep, down to the level of my tears.

I HADN'T ALWAYS THOUGHT OF MY FATHER THAT WAY. WHEN the war was in the world and the Russians started bombing Lvov, and we were in our hiding place in the home of Juzak, the carpenter and alcoholic, my father was different.

The heavy bombing always began at exactly the same time every night.

First we heard the sirens. They wailed and everyone ran to the shelters. We didn't.

We were Jews, we were hiding, no one could know we existed. That would definitely be the end of us, certain death. They would inform on us to the Gestapo and they would murder us. The bombing was better.

First, the sirens sounded and enormous lights hung in the sky, turning night into day, illuminating the blacked-out city.

Then, when the sirens died down, in the hollow silence, there was a moment when you could hear a deep, boiling murmur that began very, very far away and grew stronger, becoming thick and viscous, enveloping the body and seeping into every crevice, until it turned into the thunder of the bomber engines.

The thunder was punctuated by dry, regular barrages of antiaircraft cannons. There was a cannon like that on the corner of the street we were hiding on, Panienska Street. My father wasn't happy about that. He said that it wasn't good for us because a position like that was a target for the bombers—our dear bombers, pilots of our Red Army, of our Stalin, the Stalin who promised, "We shall celebrate in our streets too."

Meanwhile, it was an inferno.

Wave after wave of bombing squadrons swooped down over Lvov and the bombs started falling on the city from the lit-up skies above it. The air turned into a solid mass, shuddering as it was ripped open, torn apart.

The walls shook.

The windows had been smashed in the first wave of bombing, and Juzak had immediately boarded them up. The tattered rags they called curtains didn't go back up.

The antiaircraft cannon on the corner fired salvos, sometimes choking and jamming. My father said that wasn't like the Germans.

When the bombing squadrons came, my father would keep us standing all night in a corner of our hiding place, a different corner each time —a corner he called the "safe corner."

My father based his safe-corner theory on a thorough observation of aerial photos of bombed cities. He'd noticed that every house still partially standing always had one angle, one corner, left totally intact up to the roof. That was the safe corner.

And that's the one my father chose for us each night.

He identified the safe corner by calculating the direction from which the bombers were coming, wind direction and speed, and the construction of the foundation and walls of the building. We stood in a different corner each and every night. There were four corners. If there'd been seven, we would have stood in seven. I don't know where we would have stood if the room had been round. In the middle?

I felt very safe in my safe corner, only sorry that I wasn't allowed to look at the lights, the flames, and the path of the salvos coming from the bucking, coughing antiaircraft cannon. The residents of the city had written a very useful song in honor of those bombings that Juzakowa sang to us:

> Wajnka is laying waste the land from above the clouds,
> Lighting up the sky with flares.
> Flying and laying waste and singing,
> Dropping his bombs slowly, slowly.

The bombings were extremely thorough and slow.

Several buildings on Panienska Street, where we were hiding, were hit and several people died, including some who were in the shelters.

We remained alive.

Only the sweet mice, my gray trained mice, Mysia and Tysia, disappeared.

Lost forever in the first bombing.

After a few nights of bombing, we began hearing new sounds—a kind of quick rustling that split the air, and a short time later, the sound of an explosion, a hit!

The *katyushas* have started speaking! my mother and father cheered. Our dear *katyushas* have started speaking, they've started singing!!

My mother told me that only then did she begin hoping again that we wouldn't die.

We didn't die, and I was seven. We were saved and went back to Krakow.

WE WERE ALIVE. WE WON THE WAR. WE WENT BACK TO KRAKOW, and after Jonasz Stern, the famous painter who didn't know how to draw a camel, pulled some strings, we got a room in the luxurious city apartment of the dispossessed, aristocratic Pani Jaroslawa Morawska, whose apartment had been expropriated by order of the new regime and divided among six subtenants. They'd stuck her with a family of Jews. Jews!

After the liberation, my father joined the Polish Communist Party. The number on his membership card was less than one hundred. Up until he received letters threatening his, my mother's, and my life, and was forced to emigrate from his homeland, to immigrate to Palestine, my father had always been proud of his Communist Party membership card. He was in such a hurry to improve the world, to rebuild it, to wipe out injustice. And that world filled up with placards, photographs, paintings, statues, oratorios, poems, songs, plays, speeches—all about Stalin, the *batiushka*, the liberator, the hero, the *generalisimus*. Everything was Stalin, the sun of the nations.

My father was given a high position: he was the state comptroller of all the breweries in Poland, and he had an elegant office with a huge oil painting of a defeated Napoleon retreating through the snowy steppes, fleeing from Moscow, and a celadon-colored Skoda, like the color of my velvet reading robe, like the color of the varnish on our new furniture, and a driver with a broken nose and a chewed-off ear.

And then my mother and father remembered that little girls my age usually go to school. They registered me in the neighborhood school, I don't recall what grade. I was eight.

My mother and I went to the school. From a distance, I could already hear the clamor of the children. When we reached the school, it turned out that all the children were girls. They were gathered around the entrance to the building, all dressed in blue chemises, like the blue chemise Panna Zofia Duda, my mother's Parisian dressmaker, had made, with starched, stiff white collars.

The larger the girls were, the lighter the blue of the chemise was.

Inside was a long corridor lined with doors. The building reminded me of the orphanage in Lvov.

On the first floor, on the way to the classroom, we passed a large cabinet. Through the dark glass doors I could see the glittering eyes of stuffed animals surrounded by fur, jars with twisted reptiles in a yellowish fluid, birds' nests, and the bleached skeleton of a small animal. A blind bird of prey was taking off from the top shelf, its wings spread, and next to it, on a real branch, a wise owl blinked its single yellow glass eye. And there was a little rabbit too, listening attentively as it stood on its hind legs, ears perked—just like the little rabbit my mother told me about, told me, told me and told me, the little rabbit I'd received as a gift, the one whose paw ended up dangling from the white cat's mouth.

All those animals were completely dead. The dead rat, my beloved pet, would have fit in perfectly.

My mother left and I went into the classroom. The teacher arrived, and all the girls stood up. She told me to sit near a girl with red braids.

The surfaces of our desks were wonderful. Names, dates, words, sentences, drawings, and shapes I couldn't understand were carved on them. I immediately read everything that could be read, and went on trying to decipher the inscrutable.

On the top edge of the desk were two holes for inkwells. The girl with the red braids had already put her inkwell in one of them. I put mine in the empty hole and carefully arranged my pencil and my pen, with its shiny new nib, in the groove next to it. I put my notebook right in the middle of the desk, on the spot where the words "red ass" were carved in large, beautiful letters. The teacher called out names from the register, including mine, which sounded unusual, then took a book out of her bag and read from it.

I knew the book. I loved it. It was about a redheaded girl who lived on a green hill.

How wonderful, I thought. Here's a book I love, and sitting next to me is a girl with red braids!

The teacher asked some of the girls to read aloud passages from the book. She asked me to read too. I read well, the way I liked to—with emphasis and facial expressions, putting on a whole show. This isn't so bad, I thought—they have books here, in school too! But then she told us to open our notebooks and copy something from the blackboard, maybe the homework assignment, and it turned out—how tremendously embarrassing it was—that I didn't know how to write.

What a surprise! A girl who reads so fluently doesn't know how to write!

I was always bent over a book or a piece of paper, but all I did on the blank paper was draw the stories. I felt no need to write them.

My mother was summoned to a meeting with the teacher, and they decided I had to have private lessons.

My first teacher was a young woman named Ola, Ola from the top floor. I liked going up to her place on the top floor. We lived on the first floor. The roof was made of glass, and the higher the floor, the more light there was.

Ola from the top, brightly lit floor wrote row after row of beautiful, neat cursive letters. They surprised me very much. Until then, I'd only seen printed letters from books and newspapers, the letters that lay unmoving between the scurrying lice. Ola left empty lines between the ones she filled with letters, and I had to copy them in my own handwriting. On the bottom three lines of each page, Ola drew a row of rabbits seen from behind. It was a kind of decoration, and Ola had a system: first she drew the round tail, then the body, and finally the head and the ears.

The meetings with Ola were terribly boring. I didn't learn how to write, but I did accumulate a collection of notebooks of Ola's nice cursive letters and my wretched squiggles, and at the bottom of every page, a row of stupid rabbits.

They decided to change my teacher.

The second writing teacher was much older than Ola and looked like a witch out of books. She lived on the adjacent street, Batorego Street, next to the medical clinic whose waiting rooms were hung with horrifying posters of the children of alcoholics and people with syphilis. Her tiny apartment was overflowing, and I thought that if she only opened a small window—one was never opened when I was there—all the contents of the apartment, all the furniture, wardrobes, pictures on the wall, porcelain figurines, crystal pieces, sets of dishes, napkins, carpets, pillows, all that overflow would stream out, down to the street, onto the heads of the alcoholics spitting on the sidewalk on their way to the clinic, where they would spit into the spittoons, which were also overflowing.

The teacher's name was Panna Hortensia Zagarek. My mother told me that she'd never married. She'd been a schoolteacher all her life, and now that she was retired, she gave private lessons.

I tried very hard not to look around me when I was there, mainly not at her face. I had no choice but to look at her hands. They were white, with thin fingers, swollen knuckles, and flat white nails cut close to the skin. Her palms were etched with deep parallel grooves, puckered, like a plissé skirt, as if they'd been left in water for hours.

Laundered hands.

A sort of reddish fringe circled her eyes, and her lids were thin and transparent. They rustled with every blink, almost like the waxed paper my mother wrapped the rolls in that she spread with yellow, fragrant butter and packed with ham for me to take to school, the rolls I used to trade for Yolanda's two thick slices of pitch-black bread spread with a layer of moist brown sugar.

Anything not to meet the prickly, stabbing glance of Panna Hortensia Zagarek.

She was very curious. She hadn't seen Jews for years. Maybe she thought they were all dead, that the Germans had managed to murder them all. Maybe that made her sad. Maybe when she was a teacher, she'd had Jewish pupils she liked. And there I was, a Jewish girl who survived, what a strange phenomenon!

She asked me a great many very embarrassing questions. Were we rich, where did we live before the war, where were we during the war, and how did we stay alive at all? I had the feeling that she was angry.

Was it impolite to have remained alive after everything that happened?

I was a girl from a good family. I had to answer the questions adults asked me. I stammered out answers, wishing the time would pass, that the endless hour with her would be over.

Maybe I learned to write just so I no longer had to see Panna Hortensia Zagarek and her laundered, plissé hands, or hear her nosy questions.

ANOTHER UNEXPECTED TRAP LAY IN WAIT FOR ME AT SCHOOL: arithmetic. That was more than I could handle. I didn't understand a thing. My brain retreated, closed off, turned into stone. Books saved me. Again books. I read everything written, understood it instantly, and remembered it forever. I learned my favorite texts by heart and recited kilometers of poetry. It was quite impressive and earned me success with the adults, who were sometimes even willing to forgive me for my total failure in arithmetic and penmanship. I was outstanding in literature, history, geography, nature, and especially religion. There were only girls in that neighborhood school, my first school, and a tall, young priest with a pleasant voice taught us religion.

I already knew many of the stories. My father had whispered them to me in the hiding place, during the war, when he avoided saying the forbidden word, "Jew."

I was an outstanding pupil in Father Tomasz's religion class.

The class was preparing for the confirmation ceremonies. It never entered my mind that I couldn't take part in all those beautiful, colorful ceremonies, or wear a white dress, white stockings, white shoes, and a crown of flowers on my head, looking righteous and modest, my eyelids lowered, my heart beating, my hands pressed together in prayer, my mouth opened slightly, the tip of my cool, pink tongue emerging to receive the flesh of sweet Jezusik, which would melt in my mouth in the light of the hundred candles illuminating the dark that was permeated with the scent of incense, while on the altar, in a golden goblet, the blood of the son of God seethed before the eyes of the painted saints and the statues.

It didn't happen. What a pity, it didn't happen.

My mother didn't show much interest in what I did at school, and my father obviously didn't take an interest, even though he did my arithmetic homework every evening—he was so very busy building Communism and improving the world. Yet they somehow found out about the preparations for confirmation. My mother lost no time making an appointment with the principal of that venerable old girls' school. The principal saw us in his large, well-lit office. A giant bookcase covered an entire wall—the gates of paradise. The glow of the letters embossed in gold on the spines enthralled me through the glass doors.

In our honor, the principal got up from his armchair behind his massive desk, which resembled the one my mother hid under when the Gestapo searched our hiding place. On the wall behind him hung two crossed swords with the symbol of Poland—a splendid eagle, its white wings spread against a vivid red background—between them. The red above the eagle was slightly redder, covering something that had once been there. Prominent on the walls, covered with faded wallpaper, were unfaded squares, each with a nail sticking out of it.

The principal, Pan Direktor Mieczyslaw Sokolowski, expressed deep sorrow about my great weakness in the sciences and praised my abilities in the humanistic subjects, particularly religion. He went on to explain that I was his only Jewish pupil, the first in many years. He'd realized right away that I was Jewish—my beautiful eyes told him that—but he had assumed that I was a Jewish girl who had converted to Christianity, a mistaken assumption, as it turned out, and of course I was under no obligation to participate in the confirmation ceremony and was excused from attending religion lessons.

What a pity! Dear Father Tomasz. How much I loved the stories!

At every religion lesson from then on, Father Tomasz would say hello to me and ask how I was before I left the classroom to sit on the bench in the hallway, jealous of the girls who remained inside. Finally there was a subject made up completely of beautiful stories—stories I'd been told, not ones I read to myself, but stories like the ones my father told me when we lay together on our makeshift bed in the hiding place—finally there was a subject like that in school, a subject that was all stories, and I was sent out of class. What a pity!

I WAS LEFT WITH BOOKS, MY LIFESAVERS. LIFESAVERS MADE of rather impermanent material that melted in water and tears, made of paper. I devoured them in a single breath, sometimes in the light of a pocket flashlight under the covers. Every night, my mother would tell me over and over again, Ilusia, that's enough, it's late, you have school tomorrow, instead of doing homework, you devour books, you didn't memorize the multiplication table, you don't know how much seven times eight is—and I don't care, I said to myself—you write with disgraceful spelling mistakes that cry out for divine vengeance, and you're ruining your weak eyes, oh, my child of sorrow, what will become of you? And I pleaded, Mamusiu, just a little more, another drop, this is the most suspenseful, the saddest, the funniest part. Just to the end of the page, just one more chapter, a little bit more, please please please!

And the rest in the light of the flashlight, under the covers. Another page, another chapter, just one more chapter, and the most wonderful book of all would be finished.

Oh the sorrow!

Only the next book had the power to comfort such sorrow. Or I could start the book again a second time, a third, a fourth, and cry and laugh and worry at the same places over and over and over again.

I never thought about the fact that those books had been written by live people. That didn't interest me. Nor did I notice that they'd been translated from various languages. Their presence was like the sky and the earth, trees and water, cats and flowers. They were food for my soul, nectar and ambrosia for my heart. I did know the names of the books, but only from my journeys through the wonderful library catalogues.

Oh, those marvelous catalogues, yellowing, crumbling pages, alchemical formulas for distilling pure joy, those wondrous, fading handwritten lists.

Promises that were kept.

The name of the author, starting with the last name. Sometimes they were strange. Maupassant, Guy de, for example.

The handwriting of those sublime formulas changed every now and then. Maybe the librarian died, and the listing continued in a new, different handwriting, smaller, maybe feminine? Pleasant cursive letters, not like my abysmal, appalling, shocking handwriting, not to mention my disgraceful spelling mistakes that cried out for divine vengeance! Copying the names of writers and books from the marvelous faded catalogues with their intoxicating fragrance, I recognized the only advantage of knowing how to write. After all, I'd been reading for such a long time before it became clear that I didn't know how to write. I made my own catalogue. In my appalling handwriting, but with no spelling mistakes, because I tried very hard not to make any when copying the names of the writers and the books.

When I went to one of my libraries, which I did almost every day, my eyes swept across the packed floor-to-ceiling shelves collapsing under the heavy weight of paper and faded bindings, overflowing with books, suffused with life, suffering, tears, laughter, and longing. Oh, then the marvelous sense of possession would rise in me, the supreme confidence that I would read them all. All! Sometimes I was terribly, horribly afraid that the books would end before I died, but there were always new books printed on fragile, brittle paper, dissolving my fears. And they too, those new books, were wonderful. They kept coming, coming, and coming, more and more books, all the time. How marvelous.

It was a national mission. That was the hope of the leaders of the new regime, the Communists, my father among them, the hope that they would bring the light of culture to the people, the farmers, the workers, the ignorant, filthy masses.

Everyone was so poor, the war had ended not long before, and they still hadn't stopped translating, writing, and printing books on whatever paper they could find, just as long as they were there, they were cheap and available to everybody. To me too. So that they never cost more than a movie ticket.

I was reassured and continued to maintain my endless catalogue.

I loved the books from the library even more than the new books my mother and father bought. I loved the smell of the old ones. The new ones had the unpleasant smell of a kind of strange glue, a smell that never evaporated, like the smell of the pigskin suitcase or the lacquer of the new furniture. I loved the corners where the paper had worn thin, and sometimes even crumbled from having been thumbed so much. I loved the yellowing pages and even the stains, but most of all, I loved the notes written in the margins in many strange and different hands, and all the marks, underlinings, and scribbling next to them. Those old books were alive, and the proof was the marks left on them by those who had read them before me. And maybe some of those marks were left by people who had since died? You could feel in them the time that had passed, the time that was passing. And now it was my turn.

Reading was considered an occupation that stole time from my schoolwork and ruined my eyes, but luckily my mother also loved books and read all the time, had always read. She was the first to tell me about Romain Rolland's *Annette and Sylvia*, the magical spirit.

Thank you, Mamusiu, thank you.

You're dead now, but still, thank you.

I don't forget the books I read when I was a child. They are burned in my brain, and each has its own scent, its own rhythm and beat, which have been with me my whole life. I remember when and where I read them, their shape, the thickness of the paper, the picture on the cover, if there was one. I even remember the pages that had been torn out and the ones pasted in by the concerned, diligent librarian, the healer and surgeon of tattered books.

I was most proud of the Polish authors I read. But I also read many books by French, English, American, Russian, and Czech writers. There was a Spanish one, Cervantes, and there were writers from Scandinavian countries. One book was about hunger, not an unfamiliar subject for me. Someone said that Knut Hamsun liked Nazis. What a shame! And I even loved some German writers. My mother and father knew the language of the Germans, and they read their books in the original. I, on the other hand, read only Polish, and books that weren't written in Polish I read in translation. I didn't attribute any importance to that. I don't recall any translation that I thought wasn't good. Only later in my life did I begin to understand that all those books were written by people, human beings. That happened when I discovered biographies. More than once, I was sorry to find out all sorts of things about the people who wrote those wonderful books.

I preferred them to be good, beneficial forces of nature that existed in their own right.

I could read anywhere and in any position. Hiding, under the desk, riding on a tram, sitting down, standing up, walking, through noise and commotion, in terribly crowded conditions, while eating.

The subject of reading while I ate led to an endless cosmic conflict with my mother. I never understood why I had to waste valuable time and stop reading while I was eating.

And, of course, reading in the light of a small pocket flashlight, under the covers.

But there was one place for reading that I liked more than any other. That was in my armchair, the armchair that metamorphosed into a bed at night.

And there were clothes that I liked to wear when I was reading—a velvet robe that had come in one of the wonderful packages from America. It was light green, a kind of celadon, a color that hadn't yet begun to repulse me, not to mention that I had nothing else. I always wore what I received, what I was given. It never occurred to me that I was entitled to express a wish about my clothing, let alone refuse or protest. Even when times were better and clothes were tailor-made for me in Panna Zofia Duda's salon, it was my mother who chose the material and the pattern because she understood those things better than anyone. Some people have taste and some don't, my mother used to say. And she had taste.

I used to curl up in my armchair, my left hand clenched in a fist like a little ball and buried in the soft, warm, furry collar, my right hand hidden deep inside the neckline, and the open book resting on my pressed-together knees.

I wasn't there. I was bewitched. I had disappeared into the book's plot.

The world around me faded, moved away, vanished.

When I had to turn a page, I whipped out my right hand, did the job, and returned it quickly to its warm hiding place.

That is a position for winter reading. When you're sitting and reading like that, Grandpa Frost should be drawing tropical ice flowers on the windowpanes.

All my life, I've found myself returning unconsciously to my winter reading position, a position that must have come from within my body.

My father also brought books home from work, books you didn't buy, books you received, given to you as a gift. Those were thick, gray volumes—*The Communist Manifesto, The History of the Bolshevik Party, A History of the October Revolution, Protocols of the Reichstag Fire Trial During Which Dimitrov Defended Himself, The Biography of Lenin, The Biography of Stalin.*

I loved Stalin.

Most of the books my father brought from work were about Stalin, Batiushka Stalin, the *generalisimus,* our savior. One especially huge and splendid book had smooth, shiny colored pages. Embossed on the light leather cover was a medal showing the one and only profile against a background of the red flag waving jauntily in the wind. The letters stood out in gleaming gold. I had never held such a large, heavy, splendid book before. I didn't read it; it was in Russian. I looked at the pictures and photographs, all of them showing the good, mustached *batiushka* I loved so much. There were also pictures of mountains, cities, rivers, and fields, fruit ripening on tree branches, tractors, many tractors, and women dancers with lots of braids. There was one photo of a large river and a mighty dam. The fruit was also amazingly large, and one farmer was holding a beet the size of a wagon wheel.

I loved Stalin. He and my mother saved us from the Germans, and books saved me from life.

AFTER I LEARNED TO WRITE, AND AFTER I WAS EXILED FROM Father Tomasz's religion lessons, my mother and father decided to transfer me to a different school—a new, highly progressive, modern school. I didn't learn religion there, and both boys and girls attended.

It was a palace, a small, luxurious palace, stunningly beautiful. The party had confiscated it from its owners and turned it into a new school for the children of atheistic, well-connected Communist Party members. Children of farmers from remote villages, like Yolanda, were added, along with the children of especially ignorant poor workers. The good, just future had already begun. Here it was.

My mother and I went to the principal's office. Another principal. None of the details of his ordinary appearance hinted at the fact that he was a sadist. There were no crossed swords in his office, and the red above the proud white eagle's head wasn't darker to cover the prewar gold crown. On the other hand, all the right, predictable pictures were hung there: Marx, Engels, and Lenin in profile, Tovarish Stalin smiling against the background of the red flag waving jauntily in the First of May wind, and pictures of our Polish leaders.

The classroom was in a large, brightly lit room, almost a hall. That was a school in slippers. In that school, located in a palace with exceptionally beautiful parquet floors, the children took off their shoes in the first-floor wardrobe room when they arrived and put on slippers with soft felt soles. Before she left, my mother whispered to me that in the afternoon, we would buy slippers. Meanwhile they gave me a kind of felt covering to slip over my shoes. I trudged to my classroom.

And school days began in my new school. Days of boredom, thick, viscous, stretched-out days that never ended.

THE BEST THING ABOUT MY NEW SCHOOL WAS THE BOYS.

I always liked boys.

Very much.

I remembered Daniel, the sweet, beautiful boy who was murdered, and I remembered Edjo, the son of Juzef Juzak, the carpenter and alcoholic, and his wife, the Ukrainian, devout Russian Orthodox Rozalia Juzakowa, and I remembered the violent, frightening boys in the orphanage who never touched me, and I remembered the boys from the square cobblestone courtyard, the cellar and attic children, who asked me to play embarrassing games with them. Street children, my mother said.

And now the boys in my class. Two of them told me they loved me.

Zbigniew Zielinski and Edward Herek.

Zbigniew was large, strong, and serious. He'd read all the books I'd read. Edward was more delicate, read fewer books, but wrote poetry. But it was Zbigniew Zielinski who wrote me this poem:

> My dear Ilka
> You are fixed in my memory
> My dear Ilka
> I dream of you every night
> My dear Ilka
> You don't love me
> My dear Ilka
> Your heart of gold belongs to Edward Herek.

I already knew what love was.

I'd read the books.

I made up my mind that when I grew up, I would die of love.

There were other good things at school. I discovered that people listened to me. Every time I asked a question, said something, read out loud, they listened to me. Until then, I hadn't known that was possible. After all, I saw and was invisible.

I realized that I was heard, and maybe even seen.

I also discovered the pleasure of being naughty. I was always laughing. It was contagious, and everyone around me laughed too. What was so funny? All my report cards said my conduct was "unsatisfactory," except for one, where my grade for conduct was left out.

I spent many lessons outside the classroom. That happened mainly during the lessons given by Pan Zagurski, the arithmetic teacher, known as "Aforementioned" because the word "aforementioned" appeared in every other sentence he spoke. While I was outside, I made faces through the glass door, making the whole class laugh, and was sent to the office of the principal, Pan Direktor Arkadisz Podgorski, the sadist.

Pan Direktor Arkadisz Podgorski, the sadist, suggested to my mother that every morning, before taking me to school, she take me to the fields that surrounded the city so I could take out my excess energy there, empty out those reservoirs of laughter.

Not a bad idea.

Children from other schools less modern and progressive, and apparently a lot less Communist, sometimes came to study in the ground-floor physics and chemistry labs. They used to leave behind notes with strange drawings of naked people and vulgar curses carved onto the bathroom walls, sometimes curses directed against us, the children who believed in the "cat religion"—that's what they called atheists, the sons and daughters of party members. They also left behind pictures of the saints, especially of Mary, Jesus's mother, the queen of Poland. I collected those pictures and added them to my other treasures—the dolls I drew, colored, and cut out that were mine until they were stolen from me, and reproductions by famous painters that appeared on the last page of the women's weekly, *Girlfriend*. I recognized some of those paintings from the books of reproductions scattered around the room of Jonasz Stern's bleached-blond lover, Jadwiga Madziarska.

In one corner of the lab stood a human skeleton, its teeth clenched, looking at us through dark eye sockets. It didn't scare me or repulse me. Just the opposite, I used to sneak over to it, and when nobody was looking, I'd play with its arms, arranging them in strange positions, and once I even tied a ribbon around its polished skull. All those pranks came to an end when they found a letter between the skeleton's grinning jaws. It was an invitation from hell to Aforementioned, a letter written in an appalling handwriting. That was the first time I realized that you could identify people from their handwriting. What a fiasco, and I'd been reading the Sherlock Holmes books since I was very young. There was no end to my embarrassment and astonishment. I recalled Pani Mleko and the cookies my mother baked and asked me to take to her.

I was ordered to go to the principal's office.

The principal sat me down across from him, the letter from hell in his hand, written in my ugly handwriting, full of spelling mistakes that cried out for divine vengeance. The principal put a pen and inkwell in front of me and ordered me to sign the letter with my first and last names. If I didn't, he would call for my parents to come, and who knows what might happen.

I didn't know what to do. A solid ball formed in my throat, like when the nice laryngologist, who removed my third tonsil, injected me with anesthesia. The corners of my mouth turned down, as if heavy weights had been hung on them.

And so I sat there, helpless, humiliated, paralyzed, and I didn't do anything.

The recess bell rang, an hour passed.

School was over.

All the children went home.

And the principal?

He sat across from me.

Never dropping his gaze from me.

I don't remember whether I finally signed. Maybe I refused and my mother had to come. I only remember the prolonged torture, the piercing look of the principal, who sat opposite me and stared, stared, and stared.

My anger at that stupidity was added to all the anger I already had, to the accumulated shocks, to my anger at the evil Mrs. Hela Fishman, who didn't give me the clown doll, to my anger about the insoles, the painful glasses, the horrific pom-pom hat, the anger at my mother, who gave my dolls away to those twin girls I didn't know. To all the other angers.

I USED TO COME HOME FROM SCHOOL, THE HOUSE KEY DANGLING from a string hanging around my neck. On the way, I ate my lunch in an elegant restaurant. My mother opened an account for me there so she wouldn't have to be home when I arrived. I rode to school every morning, summer and winter, in a crowded tram—a little girl carrying a large, smelly pigskin bag, hanging on to a cluster of people, one leg on the bottom step of the entrance to the tram, the other dangling in the air, hands clutching the copper pole. In winter, if I didn't have time to put my gloves on before I boarded the tram, the pole would scorch my palms, leaving severe cold burns on them.

On the way home from school, the tram was less crowded and much more pleasant and interesting. Naturally, I tried to stand in the first car, in front of the large panoramic window. Through it, the world drew near and moved past, and not far from me, the driver played on the tram's operating system, on all the levers, handles, spouts, wires, and wheels. Everything gleamed in polished gold copper like a kind of complicated musical instrument, maybe an organ, and the driver was like an organist, a maestro, a magician. I always waited expectantly for the lovely ding-dong of the warning bell.

Everything on the tram was beautiful and fascinating—the smell, the movement, the sounds, the blue lightning flashing on the gleaming steel tracks, the shower of sparks from the electricity on the cables breaking apart like a display of fireworks.

I knew most of the drivers, and was glad when they remembered me. I liked the driver Pan Jan best of all. He saved the tiny fish and the water flea my nature teacher gave me as a gift. On my way home one day, I was standing in my favorite place next to the driver, my smelly yellow pigskin bag in one hand, and in the other, a jam jar in which the tiny, snakelike fish was swimming around happily. Suddenly it jumped out of the jar, landed on the floor of the driver's compartment, and slid into the tangle of wires, handles, spouts, and levers.

Disaster!

The driver, Pan Jan, applied the brakes, and the tram came to an abrupt, lurching stop. The passengers flew forward and immediately began a thorough search for the tiny, snakelike, silver fish.

The fish was found, and Pan Jan, all the passengers, and I breathed a sigh of relief.

At home, the fish moved to its permanent new home—a huge, round crystal goblet designed to hold an aristocratic drink called cognac. The goblet stood on one leg on the massive desk, which was part of the new, elegant set of furniture that smelled eternally of lacquer. The fish contin-ued to show suicidal tendencies. More than once, the good-natured, wiz-ened old Wyzgowa would find it in a corner, dry and half-dead, covered with a dustball, but it would always revive in its splendid crystal goblet.

That tiny fish of mine had many wet lives, and it lived for months inside and outside the cognac goblet until it disappeared once and was never found again.

I called it Alexander, after my nature teacher—he was the only teacher who didn't get mad at me, but laughed when he saw the skeleton wearing the ribbon, or holding its hands together in entreaty.

DURING THOSE YEARS IN KRAKOW, I DEVELOPED SEVERAL RULES and habits that I stuck to scrupulously. Naturally, I could never step on the cracks on the sidewalk. I always tried to take two or three steps at a time when walking upstairs, and if possible, to slide down the banister. I had to look everywhere for secret passages, torn fences, gates that joined two streets, and I had to open every gate and close every open one, drag my fingers over the fence posts and feel the rhythmic banging. I had to save bugs from drowning in puddles and destroy ants' nests. I had to draw glasses or mustaches on all the newspaper pictures of important people, except, of course, on Stalin: his vision was as sharp as a falcon's, and he already had a mustache anyway. The color green always had to be within reach. If someone asked, "Green?" and I didn't have it close by so I could pull it out and show it the way you show a laissez-passer or an important document, I was a goner, disqualified. I had to leave a deposit called a *fant*, and to get it back, I had to complete whatever job I was given.

And I had another habit: spitting, or more precisely, accumulating saliva in my mouth and playing with it—an offensive habit, but more fascinating than any other, one requiring enormous skill that improved with time. I used to collect a large amount of saliva, keep it in my mouth until it got gluey, then slowly spit it out in a single glob, with the intention of sucking it back in before it fell. If the Olympics had included such a category, I would have won a gold medal.

Another one of my habits, probably my favorite one, starting from when my mother and father remembered that girls my age go to school: being sick. I'd wake up on winter mornings with a sharp pain in my throat. My mother would immediately rub a piece of alcohol-soaked cotton over the thermometer—the same one she'd used during the war and, until the hole in her lung hardened and scarred, the one that had always shown the low-grade fever tuberculosis patients had, causing their cheeks to blaze with a beautiful, suspicious redness.

The thermometer was placed in my open mouth. Under your tongue, my mother would say, and be careful. The mercury is poisonous; don't break the glass!

Five minutes, and the thermometer was removed. Hooray!

What joy. I have fever, angina, I'm sick! Sick!! Sick!!! I'm staying home.

I remember the compresses that absorbed my fever. I had to drink hot tea, a lot of hot tea—strong, sweet, steaming amber-colored tea in a glass with a silver handle.

The tea was important, but it wasn't enough. I had to drink a goggle-moggle. My mother beat two egg yolks with a few teaspoons of hot milk and a teaspoon of honey in a porcelain bowl decorated with pictures of sheep wearing pink ribbons and shepherdesses wearing crinolines, one wearing a powdered wig and playing the flute for them.

But before anything, I had to gargle. Gargling was very important. A few purple gentian violet crystals were poured into a glass of water, and they spread as they dissolved slowly, creating wonderful twirling shapes—flowers, spirals, snails, fireworks, miraculous shapes, until the water turned light purple. I had to gargle with that water every hour.

I wasn't allowed to swallow it. That purple water had a metallic taste that reminded me of the taste of the metal banister in the ghetto and the taste of the frozen copper pole in the tram.

I'm sick! I'm sick!!

I'm sick!!!

Oh, the feeling of exoneration.

After all, I'm sick, I have an excuse for everything I neglect—the book I didn't return to the library on time; the arithmetic homework I didn't do; the multiplication table I didn't learn—oh, that terrible arithmetic homework, the dentist of the brain!

Today I won't see Pan Zagurski, the arithmetic teacher who always said, when he came into class, Goldman, out! And only then did he start the lesson. Pan Zagurski loved arithmetic and hated me.

And the pampering: my mother would bring me hot semolina cereal in bed. A lump of fragrant yellow butter slowly dissolved in the center, and the edges were sprinkled with brown-red cinnamon that gave off the exotic aroma of books about far-off countries.

I'm in bed!

Oh my bed, my wonderful bed.

Covered with a light, fluffy down quilt lined with gold brocade. A pyramid of pillows under my head and behind my back. The quilt and the pillows are covered with fine white linen flowing with lace ruffles, and each one is monogrammed with my mother's initials, G. G., Gusta Goldman. The letters are surrounded with a pattern of leaves, flowers, butterflies, all in white-on-white embroidery. When you fall asleep on embroidery like that, the pattern is imprinted on your skin.

My father didn't like those decorations. Seeing them made him think of the poor women who labored for whole days and long nights, for a pittance, embroidering those decorations for all the salon Communists and petite bourgeoisie. Before he went to sleep, my father would turn over the pillows so that the hard labor of all those indigent women wouldn't stab his eyes or be imprinted on the skin of his face.

Oh my wonderful bed, an entire world, a perfect world.

What a pleasure it was to dive between the crisp, cool sheets. How wonderful it was to put the gold-colored blanket into the white blanket cover. To force it open, almost tearing the fabric that had been tightly pressed together in the linen press, to inhale the aroma of starch and the fresh, gleaming white cloth.

No more makeshift rag bed teeming with lice.

I never thought about that makeshift bed now.

Those days, when the war was in the world, didn't occupy my mind. I didn't talk about it with other children who were saved like me. It wasn't interesting. My constant attempts to escape from the grown-ups' conversations were enough for me.

A princess's bed, without a pea. It was especially nice to lie in bed when Grandfather Frost painted wonderful pictures on the windowpanes and the stove was burning.

PANI WYZGOWA LIT THE STOVE EVERY MORNING.

Pani Wyzgowa lived in a shabby, moldy, damp little room off the kitchen, a kind of alcove. She was a remarkably tall woman, thin and strong. When she walked, her bones knocked together and creaked.

It was out of a lofty ideal that the government permitted Pani Wyzgowa to live in an alcove off our kitchen: the new regime believed that if people from remote, primitive villages, who had been downtrodden for generations, came to the city, they would rejoice and join in building the splendid glass house of Communism, as Julian Tuwim wrote.

Meanwhile, until she rejoiced, Wyzgowa was a servant.

She worked for us too. My mother called her a maid, not a servant, because after all, my mother hadn't stopped being a Communist, albeit a salon Communist.

She would come every morning, even on those mornings when I was lucky enough to be sick and carefree, carrying a galvanized metal pail full of coal she'd brought up from our supply in the cellar, and light the stove with them, the wonderful stove that stood in the corner. It was a tall stove that almost reached the ceiling, and it was covered with thick, embossed ceramic tiles the color of caramel candy.

Pani Wyzgowa would kneel at the opening of the stove as if she were prostrating herself, and remove the previous day's ashes, which had such a familiar smell. She removed them slowly and carefully, so they wouldn't scatter on the parquet or the carpet, the beautiful carpet that the Polish Culture Ministry didn't allow us to take when we were deported to Palestine, claiming that it was a work of art and therefore belonged to the Polish people.

After removing the previous day's ashes, Pani Wyzgowa would fill the gaping black opening with new coal from the pail, fine coal, large, hard, deep black lumps that flashed blue light—coal millions of years old that burned slowly, spreading its heat.

Finally, after kindling the coal with a skill that bordered on sorcery, Pani Wyzgowa would close the heavy iron door of the stove opening.

Slowly, the marvelous heat would spread through the room.

I'm in bed. I don't owe anyone anything. Today I'm a princess.

MY FREQUENT SORE THROATS AND ANGINAS WORRIED MY mother and the laryngologist, Dr. Jan Janowski very much. We saw the doctor in his office in the government clinic on Batorego Street, after a long wait in the large room whose walls were covered with posters warning of syphilis and alcoholism, showing horrible pictures of adult syphilis patients and children born to alcoholics. I'd seen illustrations of syphilis patients before, in the four-volume *Encyclopedia of Sexual Knowledge* rescued from the Jewish gynecologist's library.

Some of the people sitting on the benches in the waiting room looked like the people on the posters. They had the nauseating smell of drunkards, the smell of alcohol sweat I remembered so well from Juzef Juzak, the carpenter and alcoholic, who saved our lives. There were spittoons made of peeling white enamel in every corner of the waiting room. They were full. The foul, eye-burning stench of urine, alcoholics' urine, came from the toilet at one end of the waiting room.

Dr. Jan Janowski was a very handsome man, and he treated me with extraordinary politeness, like a knight serving his lady. He always addressed me in the third person: would the lovely young lady be so good as to sit down, might the young lady open her mouth so we can have a look. . . . Open wide, perhaps a bit wider? Aaaa.

Dr. Jan Janowski stuck a cold spatula smelling sharply of antiseptic so deep into my throat that it made me nauseous, then brushed iodine on my swollen, pus-filled tonsils.

Then he turned to my mother—the permanent, familiar *sorgenkind* expression on her face—and said there was no choice, the tonsils had to come out. Actually, only the third tonsil. I had three. Three tonsils.

Why should I have three?

I didn't know what the news meant, but it didn't sound good. And my mother's face darkened. Although they both were quick to promise me mountains of ice cream, I was very worried.

Dr. Jan Janowski operated on me in his private clinic. The injections of anesthesia were very painful. My throat turned into stone, it tasted numb, and I had the scary feeling that I was suffocating. The chair was very much like Dr. Tadeusz Olshewki's, the dentist's Inquisition chair. And the strong light he shined into my throat was like the dentist's too.

Then, moving like an elegant magician, as he recited a poem—a La Fontaine fable about a fox that stole into a garden—Dr. Jan Janowski removed my third tonsil.

The fox that caught the goose.

He gave me some ice, I spit out some blood, the paralysis passed, and again I had a few pleasant days of vacation from school without any conscience pangs.

The operation helped. The era of my lovely anginas was over.

THE HOUSE WE LIVED IN ON SOBIESKIEGO STREET IN KRAKOW had a concierge, or maybe she was called a janitor. Jozefowa.

Her husband spent his days lying on a low stool in the stairwell, in an alcohol stupor, tears dripping from his bleary, inflamed eyes. He was the depressive kind of alcoholic. The melancholy, morose stench of drunkards rose from his corner. He never worked.

Jozefowa toiled for a measly few pennies. Communism still hadn't found the time to improve her situation. She was gaunt and strong. It was her job to clean the staircases and the courtyards, a job she did with excessive thoroughness. I think that all the dirt she cleaned stuck to her, her husband, and their children. There were two, a daughter and a son.

The daughter's name was Dorotka. She had a huge head. My mother said she had water on the brain. Her head, resting on a thin, stemlike neck, took up half of the upper part of her body. Faded hair as light-colored as straw grew on that monstrous head, hair so painfully sparse that it didn't cover her giant skull, but exposed naked pink skin that was as shiny as the ribbons her mother wove lovingly into two pathetic braids that were even skinnier than the tails of my adorable trained mice, Mysia and Tysia. Her ears, red, tiny, and as transparent as slices of tropical fruit, were stuck to her head behind her braids. They looked like they'd been taken from another head.

Sometimes reproductions by famous painters were printed on the back pages of magazines we subscribed to. That's where I saw a painting of Dorotka in a group of princesses. Her hair, clothes, and posture were different, but it was Dorotka. Velasquez had painted her in the company of *infantas*.

Or did I see that reproduction in one of Panna Jadwiga's books?

The son of the concierge, Jozefowa, was named Marek. My mother said that he was retarded, an idiot. He always smiled with his mouth wide open, ground his rotten, green teeth, and made strange snorting and grunting sounds. Thick, smelly drool dripped from his mouth onto a bib that Jozefowa had tied carefully and lovingly under his chin. Marek was a good, quiet boy, and it was my permanent job to pass by him quickly, without breathing, to get away from him. It wasn't easy. He was always happy to see me coming, and he would welcome me with enthusiastic gestures and excited barks.

The Communist regime was always trying to do right by Jozefowa, who toiled with staunch courage to support her beloved children and her depressive alcoholic husband, who guzzled pure alcohol, her money, and her lifeblood. Not only did she toil cleaning the staircases and courtyards, but she also carried rolled-up rugs from rich people's apartments and beat them with twigs on the stand in the courtyard.

A round belly had begun to grow under Jozefowa's apron, which you could see was checked, despite the layers of dirt stuck to it.

A son was born.

An exquisite baby.

Jozefowa sold that beautiful, healthy baby.

She sold him so she could support her daughter, Dorotka, with all the water in her brain; her drooling son, Marek; and her melancholy, good-for-nothing alcoholic husband.

A nice couple that lived on the other side of Rinek Square, the city's central square, bought Jozefowa's wonderful baby. The husband was an engineer who helped plan the steel city of Nova Huta, a new city to be built near Krakow. The wife left her teaching job to devote herself to raising her beautiful new baby. She used to stroll down Planty Boulevard with him. Concealed in his elegant carriage, his head of golden curls resting on a muslin pillow, his body covered with a lace blanket, the baby looked like a small dauphin. In her few moments of spare time, Jozefowa would hurry to the avenue, hide behind the statue of the writer Artur Grottger, beneath whose pedestal a pair of embracing lovers were sliding into hell, and lie in wait to steal a glance, to enjoy the shining face of her perfect baby, then return to her labors, to the alcove under the steps, a kind of cellar, poverty dripping from its walls and from a small barred window that looked out on the feet of the passersby.

One day, Jozefowa stopped lying in wait to look at her wonderful baby.

And once again I saw the belly swelling under her apron.

A boy was born.

He was born in the seventh month, a baby the size of a hand, premature. His cleft lip exposed pink gums up to the nostrils of his tiny nose.

A harelip, my mother said.

Born a month and a half before my mother, my father, and I left Poland, that premature baby died.

The baby died despite Jozefowa's desperate efforts to convince him to go on living. She sat in the dark, stinking stairwell on her alcoholic husband's stool, on the threshold of her cellar, and tried to breastfeed the miniature baby with its scrunched-up dwarf face and cleft lip.

In spite of myself, I saw her breast, a wrinkled brown sack, drooping and empty.

The baby died a few days before we left Krakow for Palestine.

I saw the coffin that Jozefowa's good-for-nothing alcoholic husband brought, a coffin the size of a box of chocolates.

My mother told me that Jozefowa dressed up her dead baby, put him in the box of chocolates, and before she buried him, took the box to the photographer's studio to have his picture taken as a memento. The photographer took a half-profile picture of the baby so that the cleft lip wouldn't be prominent.

On the day we left for Palestine, Jozefowa stopped us, standing with her arms and legs spread, her blouse rumpled, her hair disheveled, and, crying bitterly from the depths of her soul, tears about death, life, vile poverty, and the blows fate had dealt her, she asked us not to leave. I remember her trying to kiss my mother's feet. My mother must have been one of the few people who treated her decently and respectfully, who listened to her stories, stories without a single glimmer of hope.

It was very sad, and also embarrassing. We left. I was twelve and a half.

WAITING FOR US AGAIN AT THE TRAIN STATION WAS JONASZ Stern, the famous painter who didn't know how to draw a camel, beloved Jonasz, my parents' good, loyal friend. Tears flowed from his eyes and curses from his mouth.

He didn't understand how we could do such a crazy thing, betray the mission, abandon the struggle to build a better, more just, more beautiful world and go away. And to where?

To that remote place, Palestine! To a place where adventuresome Jews lived! With that little, egomaniacal tyrant, Ben-Gurion!

A pocket-sized, imperialistic state sitting like a Lilliputian slave in the pocket of those capitalist, imperialist Americans, kissing their ass! That's what he said—"ass." In our house in Krakow, we never used vulgar words. He was very angry.

Jonasz refused to understand, even though he saw the pornographic postcards we received that threatened my father's life.

My father, Salomon Goldman, the veteran Communist, the Communist with pure intentions, the important, incorruptible supervisor who didn't change his name to a Polish name, had to take his family and run for his life, not for the first time, and emigrate from his homeland.

Jonasz Stern, who hadn't changed his name either, became one of the last Jews in Krakow.

Jonasz Stern, who became the rector of the Krakow Art Institute, who won international prizes and broke endless hearts. He used to make gefilte fish, his Jewish specialty, for his admiring students. He'd create a tableau, wonderful abstract scenes and death scenes, and he gave his black cat the fish bladder, a bubble that didn't burst like soap bubbles did.

At the end of his long life, he painted gravestones.

Jewish gravestones: Here lies Jonasz Stern.

Jonasz Stern was buried more than once. A mass grave was his first burial place.

A herd of Jews, Jonasz Stern among them, was caught in the *aktion* of the final liquidation of the Lvov Ghetto, and the Germans, with bayoneted rifles and trained dogs, forced them to run to an idyllic birch forest near the city.

There, they were ordered to dig.

To dig their own grave, to undress and stand at the edge of that gaping grave.

Group after group of people stood on the edge of the grave. Jonasz was in the first group of murdered people. He stood on the edge of the grave, naked and tall, and so very thin. He must have tried to cover his genitals with his beautiful, slender hands, the praying hands of Albrecht Dührer. The dogs barked. The Germans aimed their weapons. The volley of shots toppled the naked people into the grave, dead. Jonasz Stern was one of them.

And so, group after group was added to the pile of murdered people on top of Jonasz, who was alive.

When the murdering was done, the Germans left with their weapons and their dogs.

All was silent.

Night came.

Covered in the blood of the murdered people, Jonasz crawled out and ran until he collapsed in the bushes on the border of a village.

It was morning.

A little girl saw him and called her mother.

The young, compassionate woman tossed him a slice of bread and some clothes.

And so the painter, Jonasz Stern, died, was buried, and was resurrected. That's how it was.

That was one of the stories Jonasz Stern told us on his way to spend the night in the corner room of Panna Jadwiga Madziarska. He used to come into our room and talk about what had happened to him after he parted from my parents, who escaped from the ghetto to the hiding place, after they gave me the name of a Christian girl and sent me to the village with Hania Seremet.

He talked about the escape, the hiding places, the sneaking over borders, and about death, his constant companion on the journey.

Jonasz's war ended on the Romanian-Hungarian border, on the first train he managed to board back to his homeland, to Poland, to Krakow. To Communist Poland, where, from now on, everything would be beautiful, true, and good.

But a new struggle awaited him, and the invincible Jonasz continued to paint the pictures he wanted to paint, against all party dictates preaching social realism, and he led a group of gifted artists. Wajda and Kantor were his students. He won that war too.

Before we left Poland, before they stole our citizenship in the country where we were born and where our ancestors were born, and became immigrants, Jonasz wanted to give us a parting gift.

The smell of turpentine and oil paint—the dense smell of his studio —has been my favorite smell since then.

My mother didn't like any of the abstract paintings leaning haphazardly against the walls. Jonasz pulled two old landscapes out from under his bed. Those my mother liked, and so did my father. My mother didn't attribute much importance to my father's opinion. She was convinced that her taste was immeasurably better than that of the rest of humanity. Some people have taste and some don't, she would repeat, usually when she didn't like something. And she had taste.

We also received a series of woodprints Jonasz had made right after the war—scenes from the ghetto, the Lvov Ghetto, scenes my mother remembered and recognized—along with his entreaties not to go,

Communism would conquer anti-Semitism in the end, and we should continue fighting resolutely for a bright future.

Jonasz Stern wouldn't stop trying to convince us to stay. He begged, he cried, he spouted long sermons. It was a steady stream of slogans that, even then, in 1949, sounded like embarrassing, banal, cliché-ridden, schoolboy recitations—although to my ear they sounded lofty, genuine, and good.

The modern, rebellious, free artist believed in those slogans until the day he died at a ripe old age. Maybe he had no choice but to believe.

WHEN JONASZ CAME INTO OUR ROOM ON HIS WAY TO PANNA Jadwiga Madziarska's corner room, he would sit with my mother and father at the round table that could be extended—an option they had never taken advantage of. The other people who came to visit my mother and father, the ugly, lonely people who told stories I didn't want to hear, sat around that round table.

The table was part of a set my mother and father ordered from a car- penter-artist, based on a magazine picture. Times were better, and my father had already become an important supervisor. That set of furniture was elegant and luxurious, made of solid, heavy wood, coated with the most expensive and splendid imported lacquer—walnut brown. The edgings were coated with darker lacquer in a chocolate color, while the rest of the furniture was painted with a special lacquer, an extravagant whim, in an unusual pale green color, a stunningly beautiful celadon, like the color of my velvet reading robe, like the color of my father's Skoda.

The new set of furniture wasn't as splendid as the one we'd left behind in Bochnia, but it was still luxurious. The pieces looked like a kind of ar- chitectural stage set—the height of Hollywood living-room fashion. I also loved the way they smelled, the pungent smell of lacquer that never evaporated.

Magic tricks and miracles hid in the lacquered designs that covered the colossal structure of the wardrobe.

It contained landscapes, wonderful wild horses, menacing monsters and flying witches, tropical plants and fire-breathing dragons—fully populated whole worlds that came into being, changed, and vanished as I wished.

My gaze traveled there, in the lacquer landscapes, when I tried to fall asleep and not hear the stories of our guests, the stories with words that lashed out, that blamed over and over again: ghetto, liquidation, *aktion*, transport, cattle car, concentration camp, ramp, spotlights, selection, Gestapo, dogs, electrified barbed-wire fences, hard labor, lice, typhus, hunger, cold, kapo, execution, gas chambers, crematoriums, death march, a loved one murdered, a baby's head smashed against a wall, a pregnant woman raped, grandmother, grandfather, mother, father, brother, little sister.

I traveled through the lacquer world of the wardrobe, among the horses and monsters, the witches and dragons, and when the words insisted on seeping into me, I would wet the tip of my left thumb with saliva, rub it over the lashes of my eye, almost completely closed, except for a very thin slit, press down a little, and focus on the desk lamp. The light filtering through my lashes created shapes that moved in a flowing spiral dance in all the colors of the rainbow.

I wanted so much for those people to leave and not to come back; I wanted everything they talked about not to be, not to have ever been.

I wanted not to hear.

I wanted to sleep.

Oh, Poland, so many murdered people buried in your lush land!

BEFORE WE LEFT AND BECAME IMMIGRANTS, EVERYTHING in our room was packed. The set of furniture was packed too: the wardrobe was packed, with all the worlds that lived in the grain of its wood, covered with fragrant, walnut-colored lacquer, and the round table that could be extended, an option never taken advantage of—the table whose underside was covered with the drawings I'd made and no one ever saw. They're probably still there now. I loved to crawl under it, draw pictures, and look out. When you look at the world from such a low place, under the table, everything looks different: the furniture legs look like people's legs in brown stockings, and chairs' legs look like children's legs. Maybe the hiding place under the table reminded me of the pigpen where the pigs gave me shelter and friendship when I lived in the village.

The armchair was packed too, the one that turned into a bed at night and was the wonderful place I curled up in to read during the day. And my parents' two enormous couches, six chairs, and all the rest of the ornate, cumbersome pieces of furniture were also packed. Blankets and pillows, pots and pans, and the fine china were packed. The pictures and books were packed. Everything was packed and sent by ship to a far-off country—a country where camels roamed, the camels that even Jonasz Stern, the painter, didn't know how to draw.

We lived for about a month in the empty room that had become so very strange.

I covered the naked walls with photographs and pictures I cut out of newspapers and magazines. In the middle, I hung the reproduction of the *infantas*, with Dorotka in the center, Dorotka, whose tiny, premature brother with the harelip had just died.

Everything was packed. The piano too. My mother and father were not allowed to take their money out of Poland, and in order to save what they could of it, they were forced to buy a piano. To receive permission to take a piano out of Poland, one of the family members had to know how to play, or at least had to be learning how to play. My mother took me to Madame Halina Czerny-Stefanska, winner of the Chopin Competition prize.

Madame Halina Czerny-Stefanska, in her long purple dress that threatened to split open over her breasts and her large rear end, ordered me to sit next to her on the stool upholstered in red velvet that stood in front of the gaping jaws of the piano. She told me to repeat several sounds she made with her fingers—amazingly thin compared to how fat she was—fingers that ended in nails with very shiny red polish on them, like varnish. Her fingers dashed over the keys in alarm, as if they were on fire. Despairing but determined, I did what she said. After a few seconds, Madame Czerny-Stefanska declared categorically that the girl, meaning me, would never know how to play the piano, and it was doubtful that she would ever know anything at all, but for a considerable sum, she agreed to give me a letter confirming that I was a student, and that letter enabled us to buy a piano, pack it, and take it with us to Palestine, where it would be sold for money we could use to pay for an apartment and for our living expenses.

And they bought a bicycle for the purpose of selling it in Palestine. It was a good thing there was no bicycle-riding test. I never learned how to ride one.

We were allowed to take things for personal use, but that too was according to a limited list, and every item suspected of having artistic value had to be authorized by a special office, based on a photograph. We were prohibited from taking a number of things, including a gorgeous wardrobe and an antique carpet in quiet pastel colors that my mother bought from people who had broken into the apartment of her acquaintances murdered at the beginning of the war. All the contents of that apartment had been stolen by neighbors, an educated, well-off family that broke down the door between the two apartments and took over an entire floor. The father of the family was a professor of philology, an important functionary in the party. They didn't even have subtenants in their apartment, which they enlarged through thievery.

The carpet and the wardrobe went back to the apartment of the murdered acquaintances, and when my mother asked the new tenants for pictures from the photo albums of those acquaintances, murdered by the Germans, their apartment plundered by Poles, everything was denied and she didn't get what she asked for.

How humiliated my mother and father felt, how sad were their last days in Poland when they had to deal with the many bureaucratic obstacles the regime placed in their path and in the path of the other Jews who had to leave Poland, their homeland. Tormented, exhausted people, bereaved, beaten people in mourning who had been saved from the Germans by a miracle, like me, and also the repatriates back from their "summer camps" in the Soviet Union—from Siberia and Central Asia.

Parting from my classmates made me very sad. I said goodbye to my two loves—the serious Zbigniew, and Edward, whose every sorrow generated a poem—and from my two good friends, Bassya and Clara.

Bassya, who was always laughing, had two thin braids and her brown stockings were always rolling down her long, thin legs. She had a mother who looked exactly like her, only taller, with braids that crowned her head like a *krakowiak* dancer, and taut stockings that didn't roll down her legs. Bassya and her mother used to talk to each other. I never talked with my mother. My mother used to tell me something—usually an order or a criticism—and I only responded, as sparingly as possible. Bassya's mother was a teacher, but not in our school. What a pity.

I parted from Clara too, but maybe not for too long. Her parents had also decided to emigrate from Poland. Clara, who was smart and even knew arithmetic, had two thick black braids just like the kind I wanted. Sadly, my hair was thin and ugly.

Smart Clara's father was a judge. They had been in Russia during the war. He changed his surname from Nussbaum to Kwiatowski. My father didn't change his name. We were always Goldman.

Salomon Goldman.

Goldman is a lovely, distinguished name. You don't change such a distinguished name. Nussbaum is also a distinguished name, but Clara's father changed it to a Polish name anyway. There were other Jews, and not a few, who changed their names. They did it because of anti-Semitism. The Polish anti-Semites.

How strange, I thought then. Not only were the Germans anti-Semites, but the Poles were too. What's it like to be an anti-Semite? And if a Jew changes his name, does he stop being a Jew?

Before saying goodbye, before my voyage to Palestine, my classmates wrote their farewells in my autograph book. One of them hoped I would remain a loyal Pole my entire life, and all Poles would be proud of me and respect me.

We had to leave, there was no choice. I was a young girl, my parents decided for me. We didn't want to leave, but the danger of anti-Semitism was lying in wait for us once again.

Had the Germans won after all? Would there be no Jews left in Poland?

I WAS ALWAYS HIDING. MY MOTHER SAID I ALWAYS LOVED to play hide-and-seek when I was little, but then it wasn't me hiding, it was the world. Maybe that was when I started to believe that I saw but was invisible? I'd close my eyes, cover my face with my hands, and the world stopped existing. Then, with joyful cries of *ku-ku*, I rediscovered it.

That's what my mother told me. And she told me that when she had to go out with me for a walk in the park when the nanny had a day off—perhaps it was when they found out that my convent-educated country nanny had syphilis—she would leave me in the carriage and sit on a nearby bench to read a book in the hope that I'd fall asleep and not need attention. That was because I was an ugly baby with an elongated head covered in black fuzz, and she'd rather that people didn't connect us in any way.

That's what my mother told me.

Then the Germans invaded.

A few weeks before the invasion, with very bad timing, my father filled his warehouses with tons of merchandise, building materials. How could he have made a mistake like that? After all, my father knew the Germans, spoke their language well, had passed his accountancy tests in Germany, had read *Mein Kampf* in German, read all the German newspapers, and listened to German radio.

But when that radio announced the invasion, my father was surprised. Surprised!

So surprised that he froze in front of the radio from the shock, as if mesmerized by the green eye.

That's what my mother told me, told me, and told me.

All his knowledge, education, and brilliant intellect, all that Lenin, all that Trotsky, all that revolution and that Stalin! My father was surprised, stunned: how could it be? My father had no initiative, my mother said. He was in shock. He was passive.

We had to get away immediately, escape from the Germans, to the east, the east, the east! The front was racing toward us!

Everyone was getting ready.

My father didn't move from the radio. That's what my mother told me, told me, and told me.

There was no cash. My father was the kind of merchant who pays on receipt of merchandise. The warehouses were bursting, and we had scarcely a penny! And no valuables. No jewelry, no silver, no diamonds.

My mother, a graduate of the Hashomer Hatsair, a pioneer, a Communist, albeit a salon Communist, did not approve of adornments, ornaments, or jewelry. She scorned all those bourgeois manifestations.

When she was young, her fanciest outfit was a navy blue, pleated gabardine skirt and a white blouse.

When she became Mrs. Goldman, the wife of the rich merchant, the dressmaker in Krakow made her clothes that were elegant but modest, tasteful, not nouveau riche, heaven forbid! Proper clothes for a salon Communist.

That's why there was no jewelry, no gold, and no diamonds.

It was then that my mother showed her organizational skills—her genius for survival, which saved our lives. As my father sat there, hypnotized by the radio, paralyzed by the news, and devoid of initiative, my mother arranged for a wagon, a driver, and a workhorse. The main thing was to get away, and as quickly as possible.

From the Germans, the front, the bombing, the war.

The wagon was full of straw. It was used to carry harvested wheat from the field to the hayloft. The wagon was harnessed to a workhorse that had huge, white-spotted hindquarters. And there was a driver, a man grateful to my father for some help he'd given him.

Many people liked and respected my father during his lifetime. And after his death too.

My mother packed some bedding and crammed clothes and coats into a few suitcases. There was no time, and winter was coming. With a mighty effort, my father pulled himself away from the radio and the three of us, my mother, my father, and I, a little two-year-old girl, climbed onto the wagon.

Dr. Fishler, my parents' friend, the gynecologist who performed so many abortions on so many of my mother's friends, Communists and even pioneers who came back from Palestine pregnant, climbed onto the wagon with us.

Dr. Fishler performed an abortion on my mother too, a few months before the German invasion. She had been carrying twins.

What luck. How much I hated those stories about my mother.

My mother, the intellectual, the salon Communist, the former pioneer, did not believe in uncontrolled reproduction. In her eyes, one child was the maximum a good family could allow itself.

We weren't barbarians, after all.

What luck. If the babies had been born, we wouldn't have survived for even one day.

That's what my mother told me, told me, and told me.

We fled eastward.

The German army was behind us. The motorcycles, the tanks, the infantry. Above us, the bombers.

We ran away and left behind everything we had—warehouses full of merchandise, the luxurious new house my father built for my mother from the best materials, the most elegant, most modern house in Bochnia, the villa my mother called a golden cage and didn't like, even though the tile was from Italy, the mirrors from Venice, the fine china figurines from Limoges, and the crystal only Moser.

And of course—the famous terrace.

The terrace on the villa roof, with its no-less-famous planters filled with brightly colored petunias. Those planters were my mother's—the salon Communist's—pride and joy.

For seven days, seven workers carried sacks of soil to that terrace, to those seven large planters.

My mother told me that when the villa was finished, she and my father stood at the door to their new home—it was on a drowsy small-town afternoon—and an old gypsy woman who was passing by went up to them and said, Tell your fortune, Madam? Your fortune?

My mother recoiled from her at first, but it was a lovely day, and although she was an atheist and a Communist, albeit a salon Communist, she gave in to the entreaties of the old gypsy woman, the witch. The gypsy woman spread her cards on an upside-down barrel left there by the builders, and with a sweeping, circular movement of her hand that encompassed the entire house, she said, Madam, you will lose all of this very quickly. You will all live.

I was in my mother's belly then. My mother and father chuckled tolerantly. They probably gave her a large tip; after all, they were generous people. Then they went into the house to eat the lunch prepared by their excellent cook, who didn't easily give away her cooking secrets.

When the German invaders arrived, the district commander, the *gauleiter*, set up his headquarters in that house. He slept in my parents' bed, covered himself with blankets that had my mother's monogram on them, tread on the rare rugs, bathed in the sunken tub tiled in Italian ceramics, and listened to the radio with the green eye that had mesmerized my father on the day the Germans invaded Poland, September 1, 1939, when I was two years old.

I wonder what he took from my parents' villa when he fled westward, away from our Red Army.

AFTER THEY DIDN'T SUCCEED IN MURDERING US, AND THE Red Army saved us, after the best had totally defeated the worst, after Berlin fell, after evil had been destroyed—my mother and father went back to Bochnia to see their home, their home before the war. I didn't go with them.

My mother told me, told me, and told me.

The house was standing on its foundations, just as it had when we fled eastward, the seven famous planters on the famous terrace on the roof were still there, and the petunias, the flowers my mother liked so much, were still blooming in them.

And so we ran, leaving behind us warehouses filled with merchandise, and the terrace, fleeing eastward on a wagon filled with straw, harnessed to a workhorse with large hindquarters. We rode at night and hid in groves, stables, and barns during the day.

The bombing was heavy and exact.

They bombed the roads on which people were running for their lives.

Many people and many horses were lying dead in the ditches on the sides of the roads.

We, for the time being, were alive.

My mother told me, told me, and told me.

What an amazing little girl I was. Two years old, and so quiet and happy. I never cried. During the long nights, I hid in the straw, and when they asked me, "Ilusiu, what are you doing?" I would reply, "Ika pee," meaning, "Ika's sleeping," one of those sweet children's mispronunciations that adults love so much.

What a good girl!

Since then, I've apparently developed the amazing ability to sleep under any conditions, anywhere and in any position. A kind of break from life, a miniature death, an escape. I can fall asleep under any conditions, anywhere and in any position, like soldiers, like mothers.

That way, I experienced death in small doses, as if it were a homeo-pathic medicine.

Later, they hid me in the Lvov Ghetto whenever there was a children's *aktion*. They hid me in a bunker that had been dug behind the kitchen stove. My mother told me, told me, and told me.

The smell of soot, the smell of coal, the smell of burned wood. The bunker a dark, narrow, suffocating alcove.

I wasn't home when they heard about that *aktion*, the children's *aktion*, and my father was afraid to go and get me. It was my mother who finally went out, even though she didn't have good papers, like my father. Maybe that's why he was always embarrassed around me, because he didn't go to get me, like my mother said.

Later, they hid me with a new name, a Christian name, turned me into a Christian girl, Irena Seremet, and hid me in the village with Grandpa and Grandma Seremet. I had forged papers that cost a great deal of money.

In the village, I slept in a kind of straw-lined box that looked like a coffin. It stood next to a divider made of wooden boards that separated the hallway from the cowshed. There were very interesting shapes on that divider—stripes, spirals, and circles in various shades of yellow and brown. In the middle of one of the round shapes was a hole. Later I learned the secret of that hole. I learned that wood grows around itself, circle after circle, and the smallest circle, the one in the center, is the old-est. That's the core of the tree. The core of the tree had fallen out.

That hole in the wooden divider that separated me from the cow was so wonderful! I could stick my finger through it or look through it and see the cow standing there swishing its tail.

Grandma Seremet told me that once, when there was a baby in the house, maybe Hania Seremet when she was a baby, they used to thread a thin rope through that hole, and tie one end to the cow's tail and the other to the baby's cradle. That way, every time the cow swished its tail—and that was very often—it would rock the cradle, just like my grandmother's sewing machine rocked my father's brother's cradle when he was a baby.

And maybe I grew circle after circle around the girl I was then, and she is my core.

My core didn't fall out. There is no hole inside me.

When my mother and father had no more money left to pay Hania Seremet and she threatened to bring me to their hiding place, which meant certain death for all of us—after all, Juzakowa had not agreed to hide the girl, me—my father had no choice, and he told Hania Seremet about the treasure buried in their house in Bochnia, buried in the attic, an enormous treasure. My father told her that if he and my mother didn't manage to survive and I remained alive after the war, she could go and take that treasure, and it would be enough to support her for the rest of her life, and would provide for me too, even cover the expense of my education, if I remained alive, of course.

My father gave Hania Seremet the diagram showing where the treasure was hidden. That diagram was a lie.

It was David, my father's youngest brother, who had buried the treasure. He'd happened to come to Bochnia after we'd run away, with a few bundles and a suitcase, on the wagon harnessed to a workhorse. David was a Communist too, and he almost went to Spain to join the International Brigade that fought Franco. If he'd gone, he might have died a heroic death, the proud death of a fighter against fascism, and not the miserable death of a persecuted Jew. We didn't know how David died. He simply wasn't there after the war.

When David came to Bochnia after we'd run away, he had a large number of gold coins threaded into a belt—a treasure. He hid that treasure in the cellar of my parents' house. He dug into a wall, took out a brick, put the stuffed belt into the hole, closed the opening, spread plaster over it, and camouflaged the new plaster with scratches and dirt. The art of forgery must have passed through generation after generation of my father's family, so my mother told me, told me, and told me.

My father learned of the buried treasure when Poland had already been invaded, when we were already in Lvov and he was working in the slaughterhouse and tanning factory, before Operation Barbarossa. David, his youngest brother, passed through Lvov, maybe on his way to Russia, and left my father the map showing where the treasure was hidden.

My father, who knew who the new tenant in his luxurious house in Bochnia was, never thought that Hania Seremet would dare to search it for the treasure. He assumed that, for the time being, she would be satisfied with the promise that it existed.

When the war was no longer in the world, when my mother and father went to see their house in Bochnia—which wasn't theirs anymore, because it had been nationalized by the new regime—they went up to the attic and found that the cement floor had been cut open. It must have been Hania Seremet who, through her connection with her Gestapo lover, had succeeded somehow in getting into the residence of the *gauleiter,* the German district commander, to look for the treasure with the aid of the false map my father had drawn for her. But despite all her efforts, the treasure was saved, because David had buried it in the cellar, not in the attic.

David never came back, and when Henryk returned from Russia, where he was saved from the Germans, he and my father, the two surviving brothers, went to the house, bribed the person who lived in the cellar, took the treasure out of its hiding place, and divided it up.

I always found it hard to understand that story about the treasure.

Why didn't my father give Hania Seremet the real treasure map? After all, he gave her his will bequeathing her the villa. Why didn't he want to give up the treasure? It's true that the treasure was David's, not ours, but my life was at stake.

Hania Seremet was not a patient person. She was brave and resourceful. She decided to look for the treasure immediately and not wait for the end of the war, but she didn't find anything there.

What a mystery! We'll never know how she managed to sneak into the attic of the district commander's residence and cut open the reinforced concrete floor.

AND SO, AFTER REALIZING THAT MY FATHER'S PROMISES WERE false, Hania Seremet decided to dump me at the hiding place on Panienska Street.

That was almost certain death.

But still, she didn't throw me into the street.

She didn't leave me at the gates to the ghetto the way she left Daniel with the transparent hands.

After the war, my mother and father considered reporting Hania Seremet to the special court that had been established to try Poles who collaborated with the Germans, to tell the court about her and the terrible crimes she committed, about the people she promised to rescue, to take out of the ghetto, and how she took all their money and in the end left them stripped of everything, left them to certain death at the hands of the Germans.

After much indecision, my mother and father decided not to tell about Hania Seremet's crimes against humanity. They decided not to turn her in, because I remained alive. I was alive. And so few children had been saved from the Germans.

When Hania Seremet realized that it was all gone, the money, the gold from my mother's mouth, even the promises, she sent an absurd telegram to Juzakowa's address, telling my parents to come and get me, and when she didn't receive an answer, she dumped me at my parents' hiding place, even though they had begged her not to. It meant almost certain death for everyone, because Juzakowa had agreed to hide my mother and my father, on one condition: that they come without the girl.

And so began a new chapter in my life—the chapter of the hiding place within the hiding place.

I had to hide from Juzakowa.

Every time my mother sensed that Juzakowa was approaching, I and all my lice had to quickly bury ourselves under the rags, the blankets, and the pillows on our makeshift bed, and I wasn't allowed to move or breathe. It went on that way for I don't know how long, until my mother decided to tell Juzakowa about my existence. That was quite a spectacle.

It happened like this.

We heard Juzakowa's footsteps and, as usual, with the instincts of a hunted animal, I quickly buried myself under the rags, the blankets, and the pillows on our makeshift bed. Juzakowa came in, and then, with a dramatic sweep of her arm—my mother had that sense of the dramatic, after all, she always believed that she looked like Marlene Dietrich—my mother whipped the rags off me, revealing my presence to the stunned Juzakowa.

Then my mother ordered me: On your knees now! Pray!

And so, kneeling in front of Juzakowa, my hands together in front of my face, I recited the Lord's Prayer.

Our Father who art in heaven,
Hallowed be Thy name;
Thy kingdom come,
Thy will be done,
on earth as it is in heaven.
Give us this day our daily bread,
and forgive us our trespasses,
as we forgive those who trespass against us;
and lead us not into temptation,
but deliver us from evil.

Then I mumbled all the other prayers I knew so well by heart, especially the Ave Maria.

My mother kneeled next to me in front of Juzakowa, and while I was reciting, she cried, she begged, she pleaded, she groveled: Look, Pani Juzakowa, look at this girl. She's Christian, a Christian girl. Listen, Pani Juzakowa, listen to her. This Christian girl is praying, sweet Jezusik is listening to her prayer, Mary, Mother of God, is crying for her now. In heaven, they're crying, crying, and crying, for their little Christian girl.

You're a mother, Pani Juzakowa, you're a mother too. You have your sweet Edjo, and your daughter, Ania, died in my arms, poor thing. Your Ania is crying in heaven now too for my little Christian girl. Ania is crying, and all the angels around her are crying. Don't let this girl die too. And she will die if you don't let her stay here, in the hiding place, with us.

Pani Juzakowa, Pani Juzakowa, please have pity, please save her. God will reward you!

And I kept praying.

My mother didn't stop talking, begging, sobbing. She even crawled over and kissed Juzakowa's feet, until Juzakowa also burst into tears and agreed to hide me too. From then on, I and all my lice didn't have to hide from Pani Juzakowa anymore. From then on, I hid with my mother and father from the Germans and only the Germans. I believed that's how it was in the world.

It was a considerable improvement. A very great relief.

AND THEN A GERMAN WAS MURDERED IN THE NEIGHBORHOOD, right on the street where our hiding place was, Panienska Street.

And again we had to find a hiding place within a hiding place. The German was murdered in a brawl, shot with a pistol.

At dawn the next day, Juzak came into the hiding place in an unusual state—completely sober—and in his phlegmatic way, the way he spoke on the rare occasions when he wasn't drunk, told us that on his way to work, he'd been ordered to go back, and all the streets in the neighborhood had been closed off by the Gestapo and a horde of soldiers.

Total curfew had been imposed, and the Germans were going to carry out a thorough search for weapons, from house to house, from apartment to apartment.

Weapons searches were known to be especially methodical. Every door was opened, every lock broken, every blanket unraveled, every mattress cut open, every wardrobe shifted, every drawer opened, every armchair moved.

They tapped on every wall like doctors to see whether there were any hollow spaces where something or someone could be concealed—maybe weapons, or Jews.

That was it, everything was over now, we'd be found and murdered.

The end.

It had all been for nothing.

What would happen to us now? What kind of death would we have? How would we die?

The hiding place was disguised as Juzak's workshop, and my mother, the genius of survival, thought up a brilliant plan, thought it up and carried it out. She told Juzak to put on clean, pressed overalls immediately, go to his carpenter's bench, and plane some boards that were always there as part of the disguise. An industrious, orderly man, busy with his respectable work, wearing clean, pressed overalls, would impress the Germans when they broke in to search, because everyone knew that the Germans were orderly, pedantic, industrious, and clean.

And that's what Juzak did. Just as my mother told him to.

My father and I squeezed into our hiding place within a hiding place, prepared earlier, a two-door closet with one door made to look like drawers—another of my mother's ideas. One side of the closet was a regular door with remnants of clothes hanging inside it. On the other door, Juzak the carpenter had pasted the outer part of drawers, with metal fixtures and handles—fake drawers—and my father and I squeezed together behind that masked door.

My mother's hiding place within a hiding place was under the massive desk left from the Jewish gynecologist's office.

She crouched there, under the desk, holding a large board that concealed her and made the desk look as if its center opening was covered. There were desks like that.

Juzak had made the board to match the size and color of the desk. The inner side had a handle my mother held as she crouched under the desk. In her other hand, she held a cyanide capsule, the most precious of all our treasures.

I believed that's how it was in the world.

My mother told me, told me, and told me.

It wasn't until the very last minute that she sensed the silent approach of the Germans, who wore rubber-soled shoes for their searches, and then she immediately inserted the board and hid the opening.

My father and I were already squeezed into the closet, which had the pleasant smell of varnished wood in the half of it that was disguised as drawers. My father didn't have a cyanide capsule. His dry, cold hand held mine. Apparently, despite everything, I breathed and my heart beat, and continues to beat even now.

That was the first time that I felt my father clutching at his heart. Even though the space was as narrow as a coffin, and even though there was a girl there.

What a pity that we never became friends, my father and I. Maybe it happened then, in that closet. Something in my father's heart was so frightened—he wasn't a brave person—and went so wrong then that his heart stopped and abandoned him when he was fifty-eight.

That is something else I still haven't mourned.

My mourning is in that closet, that hiding place within a hiding place, with Gestapo soldiers outside using every means to find me and murder me.

My mourning is in the closet.

And the Germans came inside. The Germans were in the room.

Juzak, for a change, was sober, and when he was sober, he was very phlegmatic. He stood at his carpenter's table in his clean, pressed overalls, planing a board with stoic calm. Curled, fragrant splinters of wood fell around him, and one of the soldiers asked in German, What are you doing?

I'm planing a board, Juzak replied through a mouth half-closed because the butt of a *machorka* cigarette rolled in newspaper was stuck to the corner of his bottom lip.

Why didn't you go to work, the second German asked. Juzak, laconically: There's a curfew.

Okay, okay, go back to work, the first German said.

And the way they had come in—they went out. . .

And the way they had come in—they went out. . .

And the way they had come in—they went out. . .

My mother repeated that sentence over and over again, repeated, repeated, and repeated, always with surprise, with great astonishment, with suffocating shock. Shock reverberated in her voice until the day she died, until she stopped being at the age of ninety and a half.

And the way they had come in—they went out.

That was the day Juzak didn't get drunk, and again, we weren't murdered, we lived.

According to the plan, if we were found, my mother would break open the cyanide capsule that had cost so much money. My mother hoped that the poison wasn't fake. It was well known that in the ghetto, they sold fake poison too. She would drink the cyanide, and, of course, die on the spot.

My father, according to the plan, was supposed to hold me in his arms and take off running. I was still small, almost seven, and because I didn't eat a lot during those days, I was also thin, so my mother said. He had to take me and run, run, run, as he shouted slogans: Long Live Stalin! Long Live the Red Army! Long Live the Communist International! And then, of course, they would shoot me and my father and kill us right then and there, saving us a great deal of suffering.

I thought that's how it was in the world.

Long Live the Communist International? An awfully clumsy slogan.

There was only one cyanide capsule. My father was stronger than my mother, so it was more natural for him to take me in his arms, run, and shout lofty slogans that already then were trite, while my mother had the prized cyanide. Besides, my mother had always been spoiled and egotistical. With her insomnia, her vertigo, her claustrophobia, her tuberculosis.

But none of that happened. We were saved. Once again, we hadn't been found. We lived.

I didn't cry then; I never cried. Everything seemed natural to me.

That's how it was, and maybe it was then that I started to dream of myself being the color of asphalt, or the color of crumbled bricks—the color of clotted blood.

Later, Juzakowa told us how everything had happened outside, on the Aryan side, the side of life, where death ruled. How the neighborhood had been sealed off, how a curfew had been imposed, no one went and no one came.

At dawn, Gestapo soldiers surrounded the neighborhood and spread out to all the doors on our street, Panienska Street. All was silent. Windows closed, doors slammed, people hid in their houses, worried. The terror of death shrouded everything.

The horror of death.

And they weren't even Jews.

They were Christians—Poles, Ukrainians. And that was the Aryan side, the side of life.

Then the Germans split into squads, silently and with exemplary orderliness. A thundering order clearly heard in the expectant silence sent the soldiers jogging to the closed doors of the buildings on Panienska Street, their bayoneted rifles ready for use. They were looking for the pistol that had murdered the German.

The search for the pistol—the most thorough, meticulous house-to-house search imaginable—began.

Juzakowa told us that the Germans broke into all the apartments. All the apartments one after the other, all the attics, all the cellars. Noiselessly, wearing rubber-soled shoes, with their well-known, supreme German calm, they went into the apartments and burned, ripped up, broke into, took apart, split open, destroyed, smashed, shattered, broke. Everything.

Only in our hiding place, nothing had been broken or smashed.

And the way they had come in—they went out.

My mother told me, told me, and told me, she told me until the end of her long life.

The next morning, a naked girl with a long, thin blue neck was found strangled in the trash can in the backyard of the house next to the one we were hiding in.

The Germans didn't find the Jewish girl in their search. The good people who were hiding her realized that they didn't have the strength to withstand such terror a second time, so they murdered her. That's what Juzakowa told us. She also told us that the girl was a redhead.

Juzakowa told us that she had freckles.

A little Jewish girl with red hair and freckles, my age.

The gun wasn't found.

And my mother told me, told me, and told me, told me so much, all kinds of stories, including the story about the mother goat and her seven kids. The smallest kid hid inside a clock, and the big, bad, hungry wolf didn't find it and devour it.

A STORY ABOUT A MOTHER GOAT AND HER SEVEN KIDS

At the edge of the forest was a small house.
Mother Goat lived in the house.
Mother Goat had seven kids.
The kids were hungry, and Mother Goat said,
"I'll go to the market and bring you good things to eat.
You'll eat them and you won't be hungry anymore.
But please, my children, be careful.
A big, bad, hungry wolf lives in the forest.
If he knocks on the door, don't let him in,
even if he says he's me, Mother Goat, your mother.
He has a gravelly voice and black feet.
Only open the door for me,
when you hear my lovely soft voice,
when you see my lovely white foot."
The kids promised Mother Goat they would be very careful.
And Mother Goat left.
The whole time, the big, bad, hungry wolf
was lying in wait behind a tree.
When the big bad wolf saw Mother Goat leave,
he waited for a while, then knocked on the door:
Knock-knock-knock!
"Who is it?"

asked the seven kids all together.
"It's me, your mother, Mother Goat,"
said the wolf in his gravelly voice.
"Please open the door."
"No you're not!
You're not our mother!
Our mother has a lovely soft voice,"
said the seven kids,
and they didn't open the door.
The angry wolf went away,
he went away and ate one hundred soft-boiled eggs.
Now his voice became soft.
The wolf went back to the house where Mother Goat
and her seven kids lived.
He knocked on the door:
Knock-knock-knock!
"Who is it?" asked the seven kids all together.
"It's me, your mother, Mother Goat,"
said the wolf in his soft voice.
"Show us your foot, please,"
said the seven kids.
The wolf stuck his black foot through
the crack of the door.
"No you're not!
You're not our mother!
Our mother has lovely white feet,"
said the seven kids.
And they didn't open the door.
The angry wolf went away,
he went and dipped his foot in a sack of flour
until it was white.
The wolf went back to the house
where Mother Goat and her seven kids lived.
He knocked on the door:
Knock-knock-knock!
"Who is it?" asked the seven kids all together.
"It's me, your mother, Mother Goat,"
said the big bad wolf in his soft voice.
"Show us your foot, please,"
said the seven kids all together.
The wolf stuck his foot through the crack of the door
and it was white.
"It's you!
How wonderful!
You're Mother Goat, our mother,"

cried the seven kids,
and they opened the door wide.
The big, bad, hungry wolf burst inside
to catch and devour the kids,
and the terrified kids ran willy-nilly through the house and hid.
The first hid in the closet.
The second hid in the laundry basket.
The third hid under the bed.
The fourth hid in the stove.
The fifth hid under the desk.
The sixth hid behind the door.
And the seventh,
the smallest kid,
hid in the clock.
The big, bad, hungry wolf found the first six kids
and devoured them.
But the wolf didn't find the seventh kid,
the smallest kid,
who hid in the clock,
and he fell asleep on the floor.
And then...
Mother Goat came back,
carrying a basket full of good things
to feed her kids.
"Kids! Kids! Kids!!"
Mother Goat called in her soft voice.
No one answered.
Only the wolf, very fat now,
lay sprawled and snoring on the floor.
Oh dear! What happened?!
And then...
the smallest kid jumped
out of his hiding place in the clock
and told Mother Goat all that had happened.
Mother Goat took a pair of scissors
and opened the stomach of the big, bad, sleeping wolf.
All the kids jumped out joyfully.
Mother Goat and her seven kids
collected a lot of stones
and filled the big bad wolf's stomach with them.
Mother Goat sewed up the big bad wolf's stomach
and they all hauled him into the forest.
When the wolf woke up, he was very thirsty.
He dragged himself to the river
and drank.

He drank... and drank... and drank.
He drank the whole river
and... exploded!
Mother Goat and all her seven kids
went back to their little house at the edge of the forest.
Mother Goat cooked a delicious meal.
They all ate till they were full, satisfied, and happy.
Especially the smallest kid,
who hid in the clock,
the kid that the big, bad, hungry wolf
didn't find and didn't devour.
From that day on,
sweet-smelling smoke is always rising from the chimney
of the little house at the edge of the forest,
and a delicious meal
made by Mother Goat
is always waiting for the seven kids.

I THINK OF MYSELF AS THE SEVENTH KID, THE SMALLEST ONE.
Many years later, I had other, completely different hiding places.

The war was no longer in the world, and I wasn't such a little girl anymore. Many of those hiding places were sweet. I hoped I would be found. Those were the games of hide-and-go-seek with boys.

Aware of every breath.

Anticipation rising from the bottom of my stomach.

Anticipation that made my heart pound in my throat.

Anticipation that made my knees weak.

It was new, it was surprising. A surprise that was scary and sweet at the same time.

Maybe I'd manage to die of love when I grew up.

But it was the hiding place in my mother's bed, under the blanket, in the small sick bay on the immigrant ship *Galila*, that is the last of all my hiding places in this book and in this story, which ends in the port of Haifa.

THE SHIP, THE *GALILA*, BROUGHT ME, MY MOTHER, MY FATHER, and a great many other people from the port city of Bari in southern Italy to the port of Haifa in Palestine, whose name was already the State of Israel. My mother, my father, and I, and all the other passengers on the ship, were called immigrants, new immigrants.

There, they said that before Palestine became the State of Israel, people like us were called *ma'apilim*, illegal immigrants.

We boarded that ship after a long wait of several weeks.

We were immigrating alone, not as part of a group. Everything was done at my parents' own initiative, of their own free will—and that's how they changed from people into new immigrants. No one asked me, but I also became a new immigrant.

When my mother, my father, and I left Poland, no one was allowed to take money out of the country. They could only take things, personal belongings, and only on the condition that they weren't national art treasures. Every object was photographed, and you could only take them across the border if you had a special permit. You could also take a piano if someone in the family played or was learning to play, and a bicycle. My father bought tickets for the trip and gave all the money that was left to the Juzaks.

Our tickets were for the second car of the train. We boarded the train in Warsaw and got off in Bari, the port city. That railroad car was a kind of luxurious salon—with gold-fringed red velvet curtains and plush crimson upholstery. There was a shiny sink, gold-plated faucets, and even the tiny bathroom gleamed with fragrant cleanliness. At night, the armchairs turned into soft, comfortable beds.

The journey had begun.

We passed through cities and countries. There were stops and waits. At the Venice station, my father bought my mother a necklace of glass beads in all different colors. At the Rome station, my father bought a black beverage in tiny cups. It was amazing how thick and bitter that beverage, called coffee, was. We just touched it with our lips, and it disappeared.

Of all the countries, landscapes, skies, and stations we passed on that train, the only thing I remember are the stories I read in the new book of myths I got as a going-away gift from Bassya, my girlfriend from school, the one who laughed and talked with her mother.

The year was 1949.

During the time we had to wait, the port city of Bari shocked me. The extremes astonished me. On the one hand, the kind of sublime wealth and plenty I had never imagined, and on the other, filth and abject poverty.

There was one main street, the street of wealth and light. Shops filled with incredible things, decorations, fabrics, sweets, clothes, hats, jewelry, all so beautiful, so shiny, glittering, glowing, and flashing. For the first time in my life, I saw colored wrapping paper, flashing signs, and most amazing of all, the movie theater posters and the front pages of the weeklies—drawings of women with long lashes, flowing hair, open, blazing lips, stiletto heels, breasts bursting from deep necklines, and all of them in strange, totally illogical poses.

It was intriguing, embarrassing, and even frightening. In Krakow, Poland, we didn't have women like these, not even in drawings.

And there, in Bari, women like that even walked around in the streets! They had stockings with black seams in the back that were always crooked, and slits in their skirts that went all the way up to the place were their legs were joined together. Most of them wore gold-colored bracelets that had all sorts of glittering, lovely miniature charms hanging from them: cats, puppies, hearts, keys, chairs, and even a tiny phonograph and miniscule typewriter. How beautiful they were, how appealing.

I also wanted charms like the ones those ample women with the shiny black or bright red plastic belts tied tightly around their middles had. Belts like that sometimes came in the wonderful packages from America, but no one wore them in Krakow, Poland.

Those women had curly or wavy hair, sometimes bleached bright yellow, sometimes dyed red. Some had black hair. Their faces were also painted with all kinds of colors. Blue and green around their eyes, pink on their cheeks, and the reddest red, geranium red, on their lips. They had small, shiny plastic purses that they spun around on one finger like circus jugglers, and they wobbled as they walked on those impossibly high heels that were usually crooked. Sometimes they stood leaning on the doorjambs at the entrances to dark stairwells, their waists jutting forward.

They gave off a thick, insinuating smell, an embarrassing smell.

The flashing, glittering main street of the port city of Bari had a beginning and an end, with terrifying, overflowing slums bubbling at both ends and along its sides: Italy after the war.

Ruined buildings teeming with countless people, dark stairwells with a stench that made your eyes tear, ripped-out banisters, rickety stairs, and sometimes, as if by magic, a piece of stained glass that had somehow been saved, the light filtering through it projecting a brightly colored vision on the filthy floor. If you put your hand into the stream of filtered light beams, it too was flooded with the red, blue, and yellow colors, like in the church I loved to go to so much in Krakow.

And you could suddenly see a gorgeous piece of latticework, and sometimes, between the exposed bricks and vestiges of plaster, you could see the remains of a fresco, bits of people, trees, clouds, the pink, plump rear end of an angel or a cupid with turquoise wings.

Enormous women with breasts even larger than my mother's, wearing filthy aprons, would prepare huge trays of pasta and put them out in front of their houses, on the sidewalk, and street urchins would pee on them and play in the puddles and the sewage that flowed along the edges of the sidewalks. The children, half-naked even though it was so cold, would sail little boats made of newspaper down the channels of sewage and run the length of the stream to see which boat didn't dissolve, who the winner was, the one whose little boat was the most durable and traveled the farthest. Many of the children had sores at the corners of their mouths and on their legs.

Strange beggars who exposed the stumps of their amputated limbs, eaten away by gangrene, dragged themselves along the street, their blood- and pus-stained bandages trailing behind them. One, whose arms and legs had been amputated, sat on a piece of wood, a kind of board with four small wheels attached to it, and two cubes of wood strapped onto his elbows with belts. With the help of the wheels and the wooden cubes, the beggar moved with amazing speed, deliberately crashing into groups of playing children, into people and the painted women, running over trays of drying pasta, and they would all fight and shout, but mainly laugh. One beggar woman, an almost bald yellow midget with a huge baby, never laughed, she just cried, cried, and cried in an endless, monotonous whimper that no one paid any attention to. She reached out to me with her hand and her two bare, swollen legs. Instead of a big toe, she had a fresh, glittering red wound. On second glance, I realized that it was a stump covered with red nail polish disguised as a wounded foot. It was exactly the same nail polish worn by the women strolling down the street or leaning against the doorjambs.

There were women like that on the side streets too, women with red lips, but they didn't have any shiny gold-colored bracelets and there were many more holes in their stockings. Sometimes they didn't even wear stockings, they just had black stripes drawn down the backs of their legs, a kind of deception, to make it look as if they were wearing stockings. The stench that came from those women on the side streets was especially thick and tangible, and they leaned against the doorjambs of half-demolished buildings, laughing, chatting, and joking with the half-naked children who ran around and peed on the pasta trays, and smoking endlessly. When they laughed, their open mouths were empty, like my mother's was in the hiding place. They had no teeth.

And there were women who sold single cigarettes—one, two, or three cigarettes, not packs. American cigarettes that my mother and father loved so much. What a luxury, compared to the *machorka* butts, wet with drunken Juzak's saliva, that rolled around on the filthy floor of the toilet.

In the doorway of one of the buildings, sitting on a low stool, was a very old woman, bent in two, her lowered head between her knees. She seemed to have folded up years before, like my father's amazing Swiss pocketknife, the one he used to pull out my mother's gold teeth to buy me a few more days on the Aryan side, the side of life. That was when the war was in the world, and the Italians, like the ones who lived in that port city—the fat women, the owners of expensive shops, the beggars—were on the side of the Germans. They had Il Duce, Mussolini, and they were Hitler's friends. The Italians who weren't on the side of the Germans weren't liberated by the Red Army, but by the Americans, who waited so long, until Stalingrad, to open a second front. My father was angry at them. So very angry.

Once, the woman who was folded over like a pocketknife rose slightly from her low stool, picked up her faded skirt, and urinated. Her orange urine flowed under the trays of drying pasta on the edges of the sidewalk and made the children's paper boats sail faster.

And they all laughed good-naturedly.

We didn't have things like that in Krakow.

I once got lost in that port city, Bari. It happened on that glittering street, near the window of a shop that sold wondrous objects, miniatures like the ones that hung from the painted women's gold bracelets—

Lilliputian bottles, miniature tables, cars for midgets, even a table surrounded by teeny-tiny chairs.

Everything was so beautiful, so marvelous.

How I longed to have one of them.

Naturally, it never occurred to me to ask my parents to buy me something. I never asked them to buy me anything. The possibility never entered my mind.

I lingered at the shop window, I forgot the whole world, and I got lost. I found myself alone, without my mother and without my father. It wasn't pleasant, it was even frightening. But I never cried.

I stood there, and good people, seeing a different kind of girl, came over and spoke to me.

When we arrived in Bari, my mother taught me how to say in Italian that I didn't understand Italian: *No capisco Italiano.* And that's what I told those strangers. My parents found me a little while later. I was, in fact, a big girl already.

OUR SHIP ARRIVED FROM PALESTINE, NOW CALLED THE STATE of Israel, and anchored in the port of Bari. Its name was *Galila*, and it was disgusting.

My mother, my father, and I, along with a lot of other clumsy, short, drab people who all looked alike and smelled bad—from that moment, all of us new immigrants—crowded into the hold of the ship. The ship gave a few deep toots, a beautiful, serious sound filled with promise. Suddenly I felt it moving, sailing. The coast grew distant. We were on our way.

The ship's hold was a foul-smelling, damp, and slippery space, an enormous, very cold place fitted with long rows of three and even four tiers of narrow bunks.

My mother, who never stopped being a survival genius for even a minute, glanced inside, then immediately went and found the ship's doctor. The magic word, "tuberculosis," got her a real bed in the tiny clinic, a bed with a mattress, a sheet, a pillow, and a blanket, all of it starched and crisp, smelling white and fresh. She always carried her treatment records with her—pages with drawings of lungs and the hole gnawed by Dr. Koch's bacilli marked on one of them. Also written on them were the dates on which she had those terrible treatments when they injected special gas into her damaged lung to shrink it, allowing the hole to shrink and cicatrize. The hole had already cicatrized, but why shouldn't my mother save herself the suffering involved in staying in the ship's hold?

We were given bunks in the dark hold of the ship. My father took the lower bunk and I had the one above him. You had to climb a ladder to get to the upper bunks. The bunk above me was given to a man with an amputated leg, actually a nice man, but smelly. He had a whole pile of bundles wrapped in sackcloth stitched sloppily together with thin string. And those stitches had the tendency to unravel. Names and addresses had been written on them in indelible purple pencil, like on other bundles I remembered.

And he had a prosthesis.

He piled the bundles on his bunk, and hung the prosthesis on a rung of the upper ladder. He never once wore it. He preferred climbing down with crutches, which he did with embarrassing speed. Sprouting from under his armpits were wonderful, brightly colored silk ties with gorgeous designs. He'd wound them around the tops of the crutches as padding. He flew down the ladder.

In a voice filled with artificial concern, he'd ask anyone nearby, Aren't I just a little too quick?

When I was lying in my bunk, the prosthesis dangled over my nose. It moved more wildly when the sea was high and stormy, and a strange stench filled the air. But it wasn't until liquid started to drip from it, a kind of thick red soup that smelled like raspberry mixed with garlic, that the amputee admitted he was storing a few Polish kielbasas from Krakow in it, along with a jar of raspberry jam that his lover, Victoria, had made for him. Victoria's jar must have shattered and its contents seeped through the Polish kielbasas and dripped through the toes of the prosthesis.

The man didn't give up. He wrapped the foot of the prosthesis with the bandage the ship's doctor gave him, supposedly for his stumps. Very quickly, the bandage became saturated with the red liquid that smelled of garlic and raspberry. The towels he wrapped around it didn't last very long either.

The prosthesis dangled above my nose, dripping a kind of blood from something that looked like a hideous, sloppily bandaged wound. The raspberry jam was lost, but the nice, smelly amputee insisted on saving at least his Polish kielbasas.

He had no choice but to remove the soaked towels and bandages, pour the thick red liquid out of the prosthesis, wash the kielbasas and remove the bits of glass stuck in them, and rinse the prosthesis thoroughly, inside and out. A great deal of work.

And so, on its way to Palestine, to the Land of Israel, the prosthesis was taken up to the deck of the *Galila*, and in full view of several greenish new immigrants who still hadn't vomited all their guts out, the nice, smelly amputee cleaned his Polish kielbasas and washed the prosthesis with a powerful stream of water from a hose, rinsing away the remains of jam and glass.

At the end of the performance, after the feeble applause, some of the greenish people turned around and vomited the rest of their guts over the rail straight into the waters of the ancient sea where, I'd learned only two weeks earlier, mighty Neptune, holding his trident, and his beautiful wife, Amphitrite, lived along with the Tritons, the Sirens, and the Nymphs. The foaming waves were the manes of the horses harnessed to his chariot, and Aphrodite was born from the foam.

THE MEDITERRANEAN SEA WASN'T WINE DARK. IT WAS AS green and as gray as the people on the deck, the new immigrants, the people who looked so much alike, all of them almost the same height, quite short. It was hard to differentiate between the men and the women.

Though there were women with bleached, curled hair who were easy enough to pick out of the crowd, most of the women had dark hair and wore masculine suits with the trousers turned into skirts. They had enormous, very wide padded shoulders, and the skirts, stuffed with fat, jiggling bottoms, were short and tight-fitting, exposing thick knees that overflowed into stiff, low-heeled, black leather boots—the boots of German officers or Communist commissars. There were very few children.

Taking off those boots required the assistance of another person or a special device that the *Galila* did not have. The person removing the boots would grab hold of the heel of the boot that was stuck onto the fat ankle and calf of the wearer, and with both hands would pull as hard as he could, like sailors on the Volga—yo ho heave ho, yo ho heave ho. He pulled, pulled, and pulled until the foot came out, and the person pulling the boot lost his equilibrium and flew backward, waving the empty boot triumphantly.

Anyone watching that show without vomiting up his guts would give a faint laugh. Could it be that there too, on the new immigrant ship, *Galila*, a man and a woman fell in love because of those boots, like sweet Lyuba and dead Sergei?

Sometimes the women would take off their masculine suits, exposing their flesh encased in shiny pink satin corsets reinforced with whalebone and pink laces wound all around them.

One of them slept on a bunk across from me. She took off her suit, loosened the corset under her pink slip, and fell into her bunk without even bothering to remove her boots.

The nice, smelly amputee sat above me up there in the heights of his bunk, his washed prosthesis dangling on one side, no longer dripping jam that reeked of garlic, inhabited only by silently stinking Polish kielbasas, and on the other side dangled his real, hairy leg with a heel as black as the bottom of a shoe and nails as long as the talons of the stuffed birds in the school nature room. The dangling grew faster and more rhythmic. When I looked up, I saw the amputee staring fixedly at the breasts overflowing from the corset of the woman sleeping with her boots on in the opposite bunk.

Why was he in such a hurry? After all, he never got anywhere, and eventually, if we didn't sink, we'd reach Palestine.

Peeking out from his short pants, between his hairy leg and his stump, was a brown, grooved sack whose inner side looked like a chicken's stomach. Wyzgowa, my mother's gaunt maid, once brought a chicken from her village, a live chicken we could use to make "chicken soup worthy of being served to the emperor of China"—that's what my father used to say in praise of my mother's chicken soup. First they had to kill the chicken. And that was no easy matter. Wyzgowa, a village woman, volunteered to commit the murder. What a pity it was that I didn't have time to run out of the kitchen and had to see that amateurish slaughter and the chicken running around without a head. Finally, it died completely.

They plucked the feathers, opened the stomach, and took out everything that was inside. There were two tiny eggs that hadn't matured. Wyzgowa removed the stomach, cut it in half, pulled all kinds of brown granules out of it, and when she turned the stomach inside out, I saw grooves on it like the ones on the nice, smelly amputee's sack. I didn't eat that soup, and I didn't even taste the tiny eggs.

I fled to the deck, away from the rhythmic dangling and the stare directed at the overflowing breasts. It was cold, a sharp drizzle was falling, and the waves were flooding the deck that was slippery with the vomit of all those ugly, tired Jews, those new immigrants.

Most of them spoke an unpleasant language, the language of the people who came to see my mother and father after the war and told them terrible stories. In our house in Krakow, they said those people spoke *po zidovsku*, Jewish. They were *zidim*, Jews, and they spoke Jewish. Worst of all was when they tried to speak Polish. Oh, how they butchered it, raped it, murdered it.

That was not how we spoke Polish in our house, in Krakow.

CELINKA, MY GIRLFRIEND, WAS ALSO ON THAT SHIP. MY mother and father knew her mother and father.

They'd been in Russia during the war. That girl's father was a doctor, an old man, maybe even fifty, short, wrinkled, bald, with a very protruding bottom lip and yellow teeth. He spit when he talked, and he had bad breath. He was a pathologist. I was very sad when I learned what a pathologist was, and from that time on, I found it hard to look at him, especially at his hands, which were actually beautiful and spiritual. In Russia, during the war, Dr. Phillip Finkelstein was, for a change, a doctor for live people, soldiers in the Red Army.

People always said that his wife, Celinka's mother, was young. To me, she didn't look especially young, but she was a lot younger than her husband, Dr. Phillip Finkelstein. And they said that she was very beautiful, really beautiful, even when she wasn't standing next to her husband, whose ugliness would make even a less beautiful woman look gorgeous.

My girlfriend Celinka's mother had a lover, that's what people said. I'd read enough books to understand that however good that was, that's how bad it was.

Her name was Helena, Mrs. Helena Finkelstein, doctor's wife. She always wore lipstick that was as red as blood, as red as the geraniums my mother brought back with the bread and the soda factory manager's scratchy jacket when we were hungry, in the hiding place, in Lvov, when the war was in the world.

The nose of Mrs. Helena Finkelstein, doctor's wife, was covered with light matte powder, and her blazed cheeks with pink rouge. She used to encase her pale flesh in a pink, satin whalebone corset and tighten it in the front and in the back and all around with laces threaded through a hundred eyelets. I saw all that in the salon of the dressmaker, Panna Zofia Duda, who sewed for her and also for my mother.

Helena's body looked like an hourglass. It always had a special scent. It's French perfume, my girlfriend Celinka told me when she sneaked me into her mother's room, known as a boudoir.

Like in books.

She had a room all to herself.

Her own private room.

We tiptoed, even though no one was home. Celinka showed me the toilette—a table with a very large mirror. The top part was covered with pink marble, and the mirror, oval shaped, like an egg, moved on two hinges. The pink marble surface was covered with the most wondrous things. My soul yearned for everything that was there. Jars and boxes, vials and containers, brushes and combs, nail files, scissors and tweezers, and a kind of pom-pom that looked like a rabbit's tail that Mrs. Finkelstein, the doctor's wife, powdered her nose and her plump shoulders with.

And then Celinka showed me the most profound secret of all—the source of her mother's scent. The scent was captured in a pink crystal bottle that had a flexible tube in silk netting attached to its top. At the end of the tube was a flexible ball, also wrapped in a kind of gold netting, with a spectacular gold tassel at its tip. When Celinka squeezed the ball, a cloud of tiny drops sprayed from a small hole in the cover of the bottle, and each one of those drops carried the scent of Celinka's mother. A fragrant fog.

I had to pee, and Celinka opened a door for me that I hadn't noticed earlier because the mirror was fixed on it, and she took me into a bathroom off the boudoir next to the bedroom.

The bathroom was covered in black and white ceramic tiles, like a chessboard. It looked more or less like the bathroom my father had built for my mother in the Bochnia villa before the war was in the world. There were two toilets in it. I was confused. Could it be that one of them was for pee and the other for caca? And if I made a mistake, what then?

Finally I peed—I don't remember in which toilet.

And the air in the bathroom was also filled with the scent of Celinka's mother's perfume, as emphatic and stubborn as a stench. The scent that came from Paris, the city of *The Hunchback of Notre Dame*, the city of *The Three Musketeers* and of d'Artagnan, the city of Jean Valjean and Cosette, my spiritual sister, the city of Daniel and David from *The House of Thibault*, the city of Marie Antoinette and Napoleon, of Mado and Sergei from *The Storm*, of the guillotine and the Arch of Triumph.

In the living room of Dr. and Mrs. Phillip Finkelstein's home hung a photograph of a bearded, serious man, with his name written under it in nice, neat cursive letters: Dr. Theodor Herzl.

Celinka's father was a Zionist. That man in the picture, Herzl, was his Marx, Engels, Lenin, and Stalin. Dr. Finkelstein must have been very happy to emigrate to Palestine, the land of the Jews. His Dr. Herzl, Theodor Herzl, wanted there to be a state like that, a Jewish state in Palestine, and such a state was actually established, called the State of Israel.

Yet it was Stalin who saved our lives, his life, and the lives of his wife Helena and his daughter, my girlfriend Celinka.

Dr. Phillip Finkelstein had been a Zionist since he was a young man. He went to the gymnasiums where they learned Hebrew, the ancient language of the stories my father used to whisper to me in the hiding place. All those interesting stories were printed in very strange letters in the huge black book with the red edges. My father told me that the words written with those letters were read backward, from the end to the beginning, from right to left.

Dr. Phillip Finkelstein wrote and even spoke in that ancient language. My mother also knew some words in Hebrew, words that had survived from her heroic days in Palestine, that time of love, work, and malaria. My father knew some words in that language too, from when he went to *cheder*.

Celinka told me that her father's bookcase, behind glass doors shaded with green curtains, held a great many books written in Hebrew, in those strange, square letters that were read from right to left.

Dr. Phillip Finkelstein, the Zionist, used to travel to Zionist congresses. One month before the German invasion, he returned from one of those congresses, which he enjoyed very much, as usual.

My girlfriend Celinka knew the shapes of those Hebrew letters, knew what the dots that surrounded them meant, and knew how to read and understand words and even sentences in Hebrew, although they were quite short.

Her father, the Zionist, had taught her.

She was determined to learn that language, the language spoken in Palestine, as quickly as she could. She wanted to speak Hebrew and only Hebrew, and forget her native language, Polish. She learned everything with dizzying speed. She was a gifted girl, outstanding in all subjects, even arithmetic.

Celinka wanted to be a scientist when she grew up. I wanted to die of love when I grew up.

Meanwhile, Celinka decided that she wanted to be a sabra.

I didn't.

That ambition of hers turned into an obsession, and the obsession intensified during the voyage to Palestine.

After watching a group of young men from Palestine—one of whom was actually a girl—gather together, bark at each other, slap each other on the back, and distort beautiful Russian songs in their harsh, rough language, Celinka's face took on the expression of a self-effacing admirer and she tried as hard as she could to be near her new Olympian gods so she could pick up more expressions in their language, dredge up another word, which she diligently wrote down in the small pad she always carried with her.

After watching those sabras jumping around and dancing on the upper deck, she and many others from the tired, gloomy, surprised mass of people also began dancing clumsy, awkward, sad dances. Then the sabras scattered their sabra oranges as if they were manna from heaven.

Oranges rolled down from the command bridge onto the deck that was filthy with the new immigrants' vomit.

When Celinka found out that one of the sabras, the one who was a girl, was called Tzippi, she told me that from then on, her name wasn't Celinka, but Tzippi.

Tzippi!!!

Tzippi?

How ridiculous.

WE WERE ALL ON THE SAME SHIP: THE NEW TZIPPI, HER FATHER the pathologist, her mother, the beautiful Helena, and her mother's lover, who wore a kind of net on his shiny, sticky black hair every evening—all on their way to the promised land, Palestine, and I was there too, with my mother in the sick bay and my father in the bunk below me, and with us, all those other people, the new immigrants.

We were all together, and I vomited.

I vomited, vomited, and vomited.

I vomited from the minute I boarded that horrific ship's deck. I didn't eat, I didn't drink, I didn't sleep. I just vomited.

My father sent me to see my mother in the gleaming sick bay.

When she saw me, green and half-dead, she ordered me to get right into bed with her and hide under the blanket.

I didn't ask any questions. The situation was quite familiar to me, and understandable. Hiding was kind of second nature to me, especially in my mother's bed.

And so, until almost the last day of that terrible voyage, I hid quickly under my mother's blanket every time the nurse or the doctor came into the sick bay.

The sick bay was clean and white. I calmed down.

And then, on December 29, 1949, the doctor and the nurse came into the small, gleaming sick bay and I jumped immediately under the blanket and pulled it up over my head. When they left and I pulled down the blanket, I saw red stains on the sheet.

Blood on the sheet.

I was very frightened.

I thought my mother was hemorrhaging, like in *The Magic Mountain*, the way tuberculosis patients do, and like Grandpa Seremet in the village, who spit up blood and died, she would soon die too. But then I saw that the blood was coming from between my legs, that my underpants were soaked in blood, and I understood what my mother once told me, and I recalled what had happened to Celinka that summer, in camp. How miserable she was.

It was horrible, it was terrible, and it was happening to me.

That was my blood.

Suddenly, without being injured, you bleed. You can't control it, and there's no way of knowing how long it's going to continue. It's amazing, and it's terrible. Horrible.

And that feeling in the bottom of my stomach, unfamiliar pains, something tearing, something contracting. My mother had never mentioned that.

I'd gotten my period.

My mother was very proud of me. She gave me a large wad of cotton and told me to shove it between my legs.

How could I walk with it?

And what if it absorbed the blood, like the jam that was absorbed by the bandages and the towels wrapped around the prosthesis by the amputee who slept above me, and started to drip from between my legs?

How would I sit down?

And what if the blood stained my skirt and everyone saw it?

A nightmare.

And that's how it would be from then on?

Every single month, my mother said.

The doctor came in again, and again I hid under the blanket, despite the blood. The doctor told my mother that the voyage was over and we were approaching the coast of Palestine, the coast of the State of Israel.

My mother and I got dressed and went up to the deck. My father, tired and pale, running his hand over his high forehead, was waiting for us. Most of the people, the new immigrants, were already there, all of them green, exhausted, and excited.

A FEW YOUNG MEN WERE STANDING ON THE HIGH BRIDGE of the ship. They were different. Tall and sturdy, they were wearing very short pants rolled up so that the pockets were sticking out at the sides. They had on clumsy high shoes and woolen socks that came almost to their knees. Their tan, muscular legs were covered with blond hair.

Their heads were blond too, and they had a strange sort of haircut, a kind of high wave that fell over their foreheads, and even the dark-haired ones were blond.

They had blue eyes. Even the brown eyes and the black ones were blue.

One was wearing a sweater that zipped up from bottom to top and turned into a kind of thick roll at his throat. Another one also had a sweater like that, but it was tied around his waist. And there was another one who, despite the cold, was naked from the waist up and wore a large bandanna, in a pattern that reminded me of black-and-white checks, tied with elegant carelessness around his neck.

Standing with them was a girl, the one they called Tzippi. She also had blond hair on her legs.

They were different, beautiful, healthy, tan, and lively. They brought full crates of oranges. They spoke quickly to each other in a strange, mysterious language, laughing and gesturing with rough, impudent mischievousness. They slapped each other on the back, ran their fingers through their high hair to check whether the construction hadn't collapsed, and threw oranges from the crate on the bridge into the crowd of green, exhausted, excited people, the new immigrants.

And those people bent down and picked up the oranges from the filthy deck floor.

The sabras threw them, the people picked them up.

They told me, You see, they're sabras.

You hear? The language they're speaking is Hebrew.

They are a different kind of Jew, a new Jew.

They mock the meek Diaspora manners.

Poland, even Krakow, was the Diaspora.

What's a Diaspora?

They're resolute, they're brave.

They're heroes, they're free. A sabra is a kind of fruit with thorns on the outside, and an inside that's soft and sweet.

Well, we can't open up Tzippi to see how soft and sweet she is inside.

The glowing oranges rolled around on the deck, but I didn't bend down to pick up a single one.

I DIDN'T BEND DOWN. I WASN'T THE KIND OF GIRL WHO BENT down, not even to pick up an orange, a small sun.

My mother, my father, and I, and a great many other short, clumsy, green and gray people who looked so much alike, people called immigrants, new immigrants, stood crowded together, excited. It was so cold on the deck of the disgusting *Galila*, on the deck that reeked of vomit, Polish kielbasa, raspberry jam, sabra oranges, and sad, dirty, worried people.

We stood silently. It was very cold.

Mountains grew on the horizon, houses appeared, a golden dome— was it the one on their temple, the temple of the Jews in Palestine? Buildings, cranes on the wharf, strange trees, tall and as thin as brushes.

The port, Haifa, Palestine, the State of Israel.

And all I felt was fear that the ball of cotton between my legs wouldn't be able to hold all the blood dripping from me and it would drip down my legs onto the deck, onto the soil of Palestine, the State of Israel, the Holy Land.

And I was still a girl, although quite a big girl.

I see and am invisible.

I wouldn't hide anymore. From then on, I'd only hide inside myself.

The people, the new immigrants, whispered and jostled each other slightly. The amputee cried copiously. I felt my feet, imprisoned in my clumsy orthopedic shoes that had painful insoles inside them, step on something round and juicy. I looked down. It was one of the sabra oranges.

With a light kick, I sent it to the depths of the ancient sea, the Mediterranean.

We had arrived.

We had arrived, and a new story was beginning.

ALONA FRANKEL was born in Krakow, Poland, in June of 1937. After surviving World War II, she immigrated to Israel in 1949. Alona has written and illustrated over fifty children's books, including the international bestseller *Once upon a Potty*. Her books have won numerous prizes, including several Parents' Choice awards. For more information, please visit www.alonafrankel.com.